THE AMERICAN EXPLORATION AND TRAVEL SERIES

ADVENTURE AT ASTORIA, 1810–1814

ADVENTURE AT

ASTORIA, 1810-1814

By Gabriel Franchère
TRANSLATED AND EDITED BY HOYT C. FRANCHÈRE

UNIVERSITY OF OKLAHOMA PRESS : NORMAN

BY HOYT C. FRANCHÈRE

Harold Frederic (With Thomas F. O'Donnell) (New York, 1960)
Adventure at Astoria, 1810–1814 (Norman, 1967)

LIBRARY OF CONGRESS CATALOG CARD NUMBER: 67–15583

To the memory of my father, Frederick E. Franchère, M.D., F.A.C.S.

Editor's Acknowledgments

THE PREPARATION of this book has placed me in the debt of an excellent company of friends and acquaintances—an indebtedness that I am genuinely happy to record here. First among these is Mr. Edmond Gnoza, head of the Arts and Letters Division Library at Portland State College, whose aid and encouragement have been an inspiration, and whose own zest for inquiry, undiminished by sometimes fruitless results, has made him truly a partner to all my research activities. I am no less indebted to Professor Dorothy Johansen, of Reed College, whose patient scrutiny of my manuscript and whose knowledgeable suggestions have been invaluable. To Mr. Arthur S. Maynard, of the New York Genealogical and Biographical Society, I owe particular thanks; for he not only sought to supply me with bibliographical data about Gabriel Franchère, making a special search in New York City to this end, but also went far out of his way to search and have secured for me a copy of the probated will of my great-grandfather. Without him and the willing services of his friend, Mrs. Harriet Stryka-Rodda, of the New York Genealogical Research Society, I should have despaired of acquiring a copy of that important document.

I want to thank Mr. Thomas Vaughan, director, and Mr. Robert Fessenden, librarian, of the Oregon Historical Society, for their help in securing for me an excellent facsimile of the

Bibaud edition of Gabriel Franchère's narrative—not to speak of their many other helpful contributions. My thanks are due Mrs. Shirley Evilsizer, of the University Microfilm Company, Ann Arbor, Michigan, for her personal attention to the copying of the hundreds of Franchère letters and accounts in the American Fur Company Collection; and to Mr. Archie Motley, of the Chicago Historical Society, Mrs. Frances H. Stadler, of the Missouri Historical Society, and Mrs. Frances B. Macdonald, of the Indiana State Library, for their assistance in acquiring for me numerous facsimile reproductions and microfilm copies of other valuable papers and letters of Gabriel Franchère and of those with whom he carried on his business. I must make special mention also of Mrs. Barbara Churchill, of Neahkahnie, Oregon, for copies of many pictures that she secured for me from her own collection; and of Mr. Clark Spurlock, of the Portland Continuation Center, for his suggestions concerning a number of persons and places that Franchère mentions in his work.

Finally, I should like to express my gratitude to the many curators and directors of libraries and museums throughout the United States for their searches on my behalf, among these particularly Mr. Robert W. Hill and Mr. Gerald D. MacDonald of the New York Public Library, and Mr. Michael Brook, acting librarian at the Minnesota Historical Society.

HOYT C. FRANCHÈRE

Portland, Oregon
January 4, 1967

Editor's Introduction

I

JOHN JACOB ASTOR is not the hero of the narrative that is translated and set forth in the pages of this book. Had Astor not lived to become one of the greatest merchants in the United States, however, Gabriel Franchère might never have sailed from New York to the mouth of the Columbia River in search of furs. In fact, he might never have become a furrier of appreciable reputation in his own right.

Astor, born in July, 1763, was the son of a butcher in Waldorf, Germany, a small village eight miles south of Heidelberg. At the age of sixteen he made his way to London, where he joined an older brother, George, and where he lived for four years, working and learning the English language. Late in 1783 he sailed for America to find another brother, Henry, who was then a butcher in New York City. He had apparently brought with him some musical instruments, presumably made by his brother George in London, and these he sold on commission to earn a bit of cash and to advance his fortunes as he could. After a brief period as a baker's boy, he attached himself to a well-established and successful fur merchant, Robert Bowne. He learned much about fur beating and about fur buying and selling, becoming a competent and respected employee of this man. By the end of 1785, less than two years after his arrival in the United States, Astor had already set his hand and mind to a business that, because of his great industry and shrewd management, was ultimately to rank him among America's financial giants.

His fortunate marriage in 1785 to Sarah Todd, by all accounts a woman of sound sense and unusual business acumen, brought Astor into direct association with certain of her relatives who were engaged in shipping enterprises. Thus he had an opportunity for commercial operations of a larger order than perhaps he had ever dreamed of. In any event, by 1786, while continuing the sale of imported musical instruments in a shop often managed by his astute wife, Astor went into the wilderness of the interior to bargain for furs. By 1788 he apparently had established himself as an independent furrier. One of his biographers, Kenneth W. Porter, says that Astor was listed in the New York City directory in 1790 as a "furr trader, 40, Little Dock Street."[1] He was already sending furs to England and to the continent. He was making money fast.

The year 1800 probably marks the beginning of Astor's trade with the Orient and the beginning also of his investments in commercial shipping on a grand scale. He shipped furs to China and for return cargo purchased teas, nankeens, china, cotton goods, indigo, sugar, ginger, borax—in short, nearly everything that the Orient could ship that was marketable in this country. Meanwhile, Astor may have envisaged himself as a likely competitor of the great Canadian fur companies, particularly of the North West Company which was collecting its furs from the old Northwest (that is, the Mississippi and Missouri valleys), and from which Astor was forced to buy at prices that permitted him no real profit. That, at least, is the traditional interpretation of his manipulations as a fur merchant.

As to the reliability of this interpretation, however, some room for doubt exists. Astor had the most amicable relations with the Montreal men. The South West Company in which Astor had a half interest was managed—profitably for Astor— by his Canadian partners through the War of 1812. It is probable that he had a tacit understanding with the North West

1 *John Jacob Astor* (2 vols., Cambridge, Harvard University Press, 1931), I, 40.

Company men that he would co-operate with them, even as he went ahead with plans to compete with them. At any rate, in 1808 he incorporated the American Fur Company with an initial capitalization of one million dollars. He was himself the company and he furnished the capital. As Kenneth Porter writes, ". . . though he had a board of directors, they were really nominal; the whole business was conducted on his plans, and with his resources. . . ."[2]

Thus by midsummer of 1808, Astor had conceived a business structure the apparent purpose of which was to invade the Canadian monopoly of the fur trade which was conducted within the boundaries of United States territory. As for the fur trade in the Pacific Northwest, however, Astor appears to have tried late in 1808 to reach agreements with the Canadians for co-operative ventures and delimited areas of influence and commerce. But the wintering partners of the Canadian company rejected his proposals. A year later, the Russian consul-general for the United States, Andrew Daschkoff, suggested a joining of the interests of Astor and the Russian American Company at New Archangel. Astor sent the *Enterprise,* under the command of Captain John Ebbets, to explore the possibilities of such an arrangement and to make initial contacts with the Indians on the Columbia River and the Columbia Coast, quite apart from meeting and sealing a bargain with the Russian governor.

For the northwest trade, however, Astor needed men of experience. Though he could not secure the co-operation of his Canadian rivals, he succeeded nevertheless in persuading a number of excellent men of the North West Company to join him in a partnership which he called the Pacific Fur Company. Among them were Duncan McDougall, Donald McKenzie, Alexander McKay, David Stuart, and Stuart's nephew, Robert.

All these plans took time. Not until the spring of 1810 was Astor ready to establish trading posts along the Columbia River. For this purpose he organized two parties. One was a maritime expedition under the leadership of Duncan McDougall, and it

2 *Ibid.*

is with this party chiefly that this account is concerned. The second was an overland party under the command of Wilson Price Hunt, a New Jersey man, who was expected to follow the trail of Captains Lewis and Clark, ultimately to join the maritime party at what today is called Astoria, Oregon.

On June 23, 1810, in New York City, all agreements were concluded among the men who associated themselves with Astor in the daring enterprise planned for an invasion of the Pacific Northwest. Here few white men had ever been. Here were opportunities for adventure, commerce, and fortune.

II

Onto this exciting stage innocently walked an obscure young French-Canadian, a Montreal man, filled with the eager hope of making both fortune and reputation and naïvely unaware that the play might well have a tragic outcome for him—as it was to have for so many of the cast—before the final curtain was to be rung down. This young man was Gabriel Franchère, son of another Gabriel.

Two generations of Franchères had been in Canada before John Jacob Astor reached New York City. Jacques Franchère, the first of his name to come to America, apparently left his native Vitré in France some time in the second quarter of the eighteenth century. He became second surgeon on the sailing ship *Le Fleuve St. Laurent* that put into Quebec and that may have plied between Quebec and Europe. According to the Quebec registry, he married Elizabeth Boissy in September, 1748 or 1749. The first Gabriel was born in Quebec in 1752 and, when he grew to manhood, married Félicité Miron in 1779. Just when the senior Gabriel moved to Montreal is not certain. But move he did, for he became a moderately successful merchant there, a respected citizen, and the father of nineteen children, only eight of whom survived childhood. Gabriel junior was the seventh child and reportedly the third son to be given his father's name.

According to letters once in the possession of the late Dr.

Louis Franchère, of Montreal, some members of the Franchère family were still living in or near Vitré in 1787. Certain maiden aunts wrote from France in the hope that a nephew or two could be persuaded to return to Vitré to "inherit their land, La Batonniere." The letters were signed, variously, *"votre affectionée tante de la Franchère,"* and *"de Latillionnière,"* or *"de Lionnière."*[3] The Canadians preferred their adopted country, however. It appears that there were no other male descendants of Jacques's family left on the Continent, and the property was thereafter divided among the female heirs and their husbands.

Certainly Gabriel senior had no wish to go to France. His own business was flourishing well enough and his family growing almost too rapidly. Félicité died at the age of forty-seven, and he may have found it impossible to consider a move to another country. Gabriel junior, born on November 3, 1786, grew to young manhood in Montreal.

Almost no information about the early life of this son has yet been discovered. His writing in both French and English makes it appear that he had a respectable Latin grammar school education. His propensity for merchandising he may have acquired by working for his merchant father, but in what capacity can only be conjectured. Nor is frequent mention made of his relationships with his brothers and sisters. While young Gabriel was at Astoria, he learned of the death of one of his sisters.[4] In one of his business letters addressed to Ramsay Crooks, dated Montreal, April 24, 1828, he wrote: "I leave town this evening and shall give all my papers to my brother, Mr. J. B. Franchère, St. Paul Street, where they will be subject to your order."[5] This was unquestionably Jean Baptiste Franchère, mentioned as Gabriel's Montreal representative in a letter sent to Gabriel by the Vallée Boyer Company seven years later. Another brother, Louis, was in the lumber business in Milwaukee, Wisconsin, and is

---

[3] So Dr. Louis Franchère wrote me in 1942. His letters are in my possession.

[4] Other exceptions will be noted below. The genealogy of the Franchère family is available at L'Institut Généalogique Drouin, Montreal.

[5] *"Je parts de la ville ce soir et remettrais tous mes papiers à mon frère M. J. B. Franchère, rue St. Paul où ils seront à votre ordre."*

mentioned in a letter to Gabriel from a Michael Dousman [?] on July 13, 1835.[6] Dousman had met Louis in Chicago, to be told that Louis hoped to visit Gabriel at Sault Ste Marie.[7]

It would be a fair guess to say that Gabriel had known and perhaps even courted a Montreal girl, Sophie Routhier, before he joined the Astor expedition. Those romantically inclined may believe that she waited hopefully for his return from the West, despite the generally accepted rumor in Montreal of his death during the massacre of the *Tonquin*'s crew and master and all others aboard. In any event, the records reveal that Gabriel married Sophie, daughter of Jean Baptiste and Henriette Regnault Routhier, in 1815.

These are the scant details of Gabriel Franchère's youth.

Beginning with his adventure at Astoria, much more is known about the young Montreal man. His activities between May, 1810, and September, 1814, he faithfully recorded in his diary, a later version of which is printed in this volume. Having begun his career as a fur trader, he seems to have committed himself to the fur business almost exclusively, though while he was manager of the American Fur Company agency at Sault Ste Marie (as shall be noted later), he dealt in a wide variety of merchandise. Soon after his return from the Pacific Northwest, he became Astor's agent for the American Fur Company in Montreal. Gabriel's letter to Ramsay Crooks on April 24, 1828, shows that he had the business well in hand. Crooks himself, writing a Bernard Pratt in St. Louis, on May 15, 1832, indicates the degree of responsibility with which Franchère carried on the company's enterprise. "Mr. Franchère, our agent at Montreal . . . has no doubt conformed to his instructions in engaging your people especially for your country, and with the clear understanding that they are not to pass by St. Louis. I therefore hope you will this time be exempt from much of the trouble and vexation you

6 Possibly the name is Dourman. In the several copies of this man's letters which are in my possession, I am unable to decipher this one letter of his name.
7 Franchère's papers in the American Fur Company files now in the Clarke Historical Collection, Central Michigan University. See letter of this date, Dousman to Franchère.

experienced with the former importation of Canadians."[8] One of Franchère's duties was to secure boatmen to transport furs from the outposts to the markets in the East, and the files contain many contracts that he drew with Canadian *voyageurs*. Another of his duties was to see that his company did not intrude upon a territory assigned, by mutual agreement, to a competing company. Crooks obviously relied upon Gabriel's business acumen, upon his judgment of men, and upon his complete integrity in all business transactions—a reliance everywhere testified in his letters.

Further evidence of this trust is found in the fact that when Astor sold his American Fur Company in 1834, Crooks, who then became president of the newly formed company, asked Franchère to take over the management of a key agency at Sault Ste Marie. Without question, the American Fur Company papers and Franchère's letter books for the years 1834–42 constitute the most nearly complete record of his activities and the activities of his own family now available; yet his accounts and correspondence form only a part of the total body of data presently housed in the Clarke Historical Collection at Central Michigan University.[9] They reveal the extent of the business that Franchère carried on, the enormous amount of detailed work within his grasp, and the thoroughness and dedication which he applied to his tasks.

The years at the Sault were in some respects happy, in other respects tragic for Gabriel, *fils*. On October 15, 1835, he wrote to his friend and co-worker, William Brewster: "My son [Evariste] goes down to Detroit for the purposes of Education. I have placed him under charge of my friend Vallée—and directed him to present his account monthly or quarterly, for liquidation at your office. The Board Washing & Tuition [*sic*] will come to about 14 or 15 Dollars per month, however I trust entirely to Mr. Vallée's management and economy for his expenses."[10] A

8 Franchère papers. Missouri Historical Society.

9 See also *Calendar of the American Fur Company Papers,* compiled by Grace Lee Nute. Vols. II and III of the American Historical Association *Report,* 1944.

10 See Franchère's Letter Book I, pp. 21–22 (Clarke Historical Collection). Vallée was a close friend and business associate of Franchère for many years. He had

month later (on November 19, 1835), Ramsay Crooks, then in Detroit on company business, informed Gabriel that he had seen the "dear Boy," had found him doing well in his studies; but, Crooks added, "he does not grow any taller." To Franchère, himself of somewhat less than average stature, this fact may have been a small disappointment.

The Sault Ste Marie manager apparently was pleased about the marriage of his daughter Henriette to Captain Charles C. Stanard, commander of the *John Jacob Astor*, a schooner built at the Sault by order of Ramsay Crooks for American Fur Company commerce on the Great Lakes.[11] Franchère wrote Lyman M. Warren at the La Pointe post on February 2, 1836: "My family are all well and have received an addition by the marriage of Captain Stannard [*sic*] to my eldest daughter."[12]

The winters at Sault Ste Marie are almost never moderate. Life at a trading post could not be one of ease and comfort, particularly for women. Communication with the more civilized areas was, after the first of October and until well into the spring, reduced to a trickle. Except for an occasional mail "Express"— correspondence carried overland by runners, sometimes Indians, on snowshoes or on sleds—Franchère's post was very nearly isolated. Indeed, so tenuous and uncertain was the situation that Franchère urged Crooks to close the season's accounts in Sep-

---

moved from Montreal to Detroit and was there during a part of the time when Franchère managed the post at Sault Ste Marie.

11 The schooner was constructed at Sault Ste Marie, under Franchére's supervision. On July 18, 1835, Crooks wrote Franchère from Mackinac, asking him to name the vessel after their former employer. (Clarke Historical Collection).

12 This seems to be the only occasion when Franchère misspelled the name of his new son-in-law, but other letter writers to Franchère's post often made the same error.

Another daughter, Matilda, named in Gabriel's will, married J. B. Chemidlin, apparently in 1840. Chemidlin was himself associated with Pierre Chouteau, Jr., and Company of New York and St. Louis for some time; but he became a partner of his father-in-law about 1857–58. Two other younger daughters I have been unable to account for.

Quaife was wrong about the date of Henriette's marriage to Captain Stanard, listing it as February, 1838—possibly a typographical error. See Gabriel Franchère, *A Voyage to the Northwest Coast of America*, edited by Milo M. Quaife (Chicago, The Lakeside Press, R. R. Donnelley & Sons Company, 1954), *xxiii*.

tember rather than in late October, in order to be sure his reports would reach New York in time for final accounting before the beginning of a new year, a suggestion to which the president of the company agreed.

Franchère did not often mention domestic matters in his business letters, and it must be assumed that his private correspondence was destroyed. Sophie, his wife of twenty-two years, died sometime between Sepember 15 and September 30, 1837. He had been at La Pointe to straighten out some affairs tangled there after the departure of the outpost's manager. In fact, Crooks had suggested that Gabriel himself manage the La Pointe agency; but in any case, Franchère wrote Crooks in an undated letter (probably late September or early October): "Situated as I am since the demise of my late wife, it is quite immaterial where I am located, so far as the company's interest is concerned . . . ."[13]

Upon his return from La Pointe, he found his daughter, Captain Stanard's wife, ill in pregnancy. His two younger daughters were, like his son, in Detroit to further their education. Nine months later, Henriette, too, was dead. In writing to Brewster at the Detroit agency, Franchère said: "The demise of my daughter, the late Mrs. Stanard, compels the Captain to exchange with his brother, in order to take his orphan child to its grandmother at Buffalo . . . "[14] At the same time, Gabriel told Brewster, Stanard was to place the younger Franchère daughters in a school in Ohio, where their board and tuition would be less costly than at Detroit. These are rare instances of the personal and domestic to be found in Franchère's business letters.

Yet despite the severity of these tragic circumstances, Franchère managed his agency with dispatch. Furs were only a part of his trade. He dealt increasingly in fish; but in his account orders are found such items as pork, salt, rice, oil, paint, nails, gunpowder, ship supplies—in short, whatever was in demand and whatever returned a fair profit, he supplied and sold. Interestingly enough, he did not discuss the financial panic of the late 1830's

13 Letter Book I, p. 147 (Clarke Historical Collection).
14 The letter is dated May 8, 1838.

in any of his letters, though he did report to Crooks all fluctuations that he noted in his markets, the nature and extent of his competition, the arrival and departure of his commercial schooners and brigs, and their readiness or unreadiness to transport merchandise to the several agencies in the Great Lakes area. When the federal government invested $5,000 in the construction of habitations for local Indians, he was quick to note that most of the money would be spent in his stores for supplies. That he could vastly expand his business operations yet find time to see that even the watches of friends and employees were sent to Detroit for repairs testifies to his grasp of detail and his close attention to the management of his affairs.

Two years after Sophie's death, Gabriel met and married Mrs. Charlotte Prince, of Detroit, a widow and the niece of Colonel Stephen Mack, a man well known in the Detroit community. Whether his newly acquired wife remained in Detroit while he traveled about the Middle West or accompanied him on his journeys is not known. In any case, the president of the American Fur Company, respecting Franchère's ability and increasingly depending upon him, sent him to oversee several agencies, including the Evansville and the Detroit posts, and finally brought him to the New York office in 1842. There he was to witness, perhaps in a measure to preside over, the failure of the company that occurred in 1848.

As Mr. Quaife reported in 1954, in his introduction to his edition of the Franchère narrative, Gabriel Franchère behaved honorably in assuming a portion of the indebtedness of the American Fur Company following its demise. No concrete evidence has so far appeared to show that he was a partner in the company. One can only assume that since he accepted responsibility for its losses he must have been an owner of some of its properties. For a time afterward he was associated with Pierre Chouteau, Jr., and Company, of New York and St. Louis; but in December, 1857, he established his own fur commission office, carrying on his own business until his death.

During those last years Gabriel several times visited the

No. 17 BROADWAY,
NEW-YORK, 15th December, 1857.

Mess. Ewing & Miner

Fort Wayne Indiana

The house of Messrs. P. CHOUTEAU, Jr., & CO., of this city, having declined to continue the FUR BUSINESS, I beg to inform you that, as their successor, it is my intention to continue the same on my own account, in the premises lately occupied by them.

My long connection with that house, and also with the old "AMERICAN" FUR COMPANY, (now exceeding a period of forty years,) together with the repeated solicitations of many parties now engaged in the FUR TRADE, induce me to open a COMMISSION HOUSE, for the sale, in this market, (or if preferred, for sale in Europe,) of such consignments of Furs as you may send to me.

Intending to confine myself exclusively to effect sales, and being wholly unconnected as a buyer, I shall at all times be prepared to furnish accurate and reliable weekly advices of the prices paid in this market, to those correspondents who may desire such information for their guidance in making purchases.

To those engaged in the TRADE, who know me, personally or by reputation, it is hardly necessary to say more than that due justice will be done to them in the assorting and disposal of their consignments; and all others I beg to refer to the well-known houses of Messrs. P. CHOUTEAU, Jr., & CO., of this city, and the same firm at St. Louis, Missouri.

In soliciting your patronage, I beg to state that I am prepared to make liberal advances on consignments, charging a regular commission on sales, and that all returns will be promptly remitted.

Respectfully,

Yours, &c., &c.,

GABRIEL FRANCHERE.

Franchère's announcement of his new fur commission business.

home of his stepson, John S. Prince, in St. Paul, Minnesota. Young Prince had himself been engaged by the Chouteau company as an agent, and he later became mayor of St. Paul. It was on one of his visits to Prince's home that Gabriel died—April 12, 1863. In Brooklyn he had maintained his residence at 237 Schermerhorn; his offices were located severally at 40 and 17 Broadway and, from as early as January, 1859, at 12 Broadway.[15] New York directories for the period list him as "merchant" and "fur dealer."

His wife, Charlotte S. Franchère, and four children—Evariste, Matilda, Sophia, and Celina [?]—survived him.[16] Interestingly enough, the story prevails among Evariste's descendants that when Evariste married a Protestant, Martha Cross, in California, Gabriel wrote his only male heir that he no longer regarded him as his son. The tale was repeated by Martha herself, not only to her children but also to her grandchildren. And it is quite believable, because Gabriel was a devout Roman Catholic. However that may be, in his last will and testament, drawn in Brooklyn in November, 1862, he specifically included his erring son. In the second clause of this will, he named his "beloved wife" as heir to all his property, "without power of alienating or dispossessing of the same in her own right." In the third clause the following appears: "I give unto my children Evariste, Matilda, Sophia, and Celina all that I may be possessed of or which may remain after the decease of my wife aforesaid Charlotte S. Franchère to be divided amongst them share and share alike."[17] And, in a later clause, he designated small but specific sums of money (more to Evariste than to the daughters) to each of his children

---

[15] The letterhead of Gabriel Franchère and Company, Commission Merchants in Furs, Skins, Etc., reveals the names of G. Franchère and J. B. Chemidlin on opposite sides of the heading, with No. 12 Broadway, the address, below. A letter with his heading, dated January 5, 1859, was addressed to the Ewing and Miner Company, of Fort Wayne, Indiana. See Franchère papers, Indiana State Library Collection.

[16] "Celina" seems to be correct, though the name is somewhat blurred in my copy of the Franchère will.

[17] The will was witnessed in the King's County Surrogate Court, Brooklyn, in November, 1862, and probated, following Franchère's death, on July 9, 1863. Franchère's son-in-law and partner, J. B. Chemidlin, was one of the two witnesses.

"besides," the will further prescribes, "the Book debt on my Ledger." Thus, although the story of Evariste's being "disinherited and disowned" was true enough at the time of the young man's marriage, Gabriel evidently had a more sophisticated and certainly a more compassionate attitude toward his only son in later years.[18] Unfortunately, no evidence has so far been discovered to show that Evariste knew about the will or that he ever received his portion of the inheritance.

By all known accounts, Gabriel was the last of the famed Astorians. (Possibly some record may yet be found of the later deaths of François Benjamin Pillet, of Montreal, or of Alfred Seaton, of New York.) It is a matter of accounting record that a vast wealth of furs passed through his hands as agent, or possibly part-owner, of the American Fur Company, and later in his own right as a fur commissioner in New York City—all in an age when the fur business was an important segment of the American as well as of the Canadian economy. Despite the losses that he suffered in 1848, he did not capitulate, but strove, even late in life, to mend his fortunes. No matter that when he died he was far from being a wealthy man; he was a prime mover in great enterprises. He was a man of simple habits and tastes, of honesty and probity, of dedication and loyalty to his associates.

He is not forgotten today. His portrait, painted by his nephew, Joseph-Charles Franchère, is one among a number of Canada's illustrious citizens hanging in the Portrait Gallery of the Chateau de Ramezay, in Montreal. In Alberta Province both a mountain and a town are named after him. During World War II a supply ship, constructed in Portland, Oregon, was christened the *Gabriel Franchère*. His name is likewise honored by the Society of St. John the Baptist; for while he was a citizen of New York, he led in the establishment of that excellent association and has for years been regarded as its founder. He was awarded

18 The story of Evariste's being disowned is accepted by all of Gabriel's descendants, but the conditions of the will have not heretofore been known by any of the Franchère family. Quaife told the story as it was related to him by my cousin Dr. Frederick W. Franchère, of Lake Crystal, Minnesota. See Franchère, *Voyage*, edited by Quaife, *xxiv*.

the John Jacob Astor medal for his distinguished services. He gave the medal to his son before Evariste left for California during the Gold Rush of 1850. Evariste, in turn, willed it to his older son, William. The medal was finally willed to my cousin, Dr. Frederick Franchère, and is now held by the Minnesota Historical Society. Gabriel was buried in Calvary Cemetery, St. Paul, in the Prince family lot. A modest stone marks his grave.

III

A brief history of the Franchère narrative needs to be recounted. During his four-year adventure with the Astor expedition, as has been noted, Gabriel *fils* kept a diary of his experiences and observations. Urged by his friends, in 1819 he expanded this record, making it into a journal which was published in 1820, bearing the French title: *Relation d'un Voyage à la Côte du Nord-Ouest de L'Amérique Septentrionale, dans les Années 1810, 11, 12, 13, et 14*. It was printed in Montreal by C. B. Pasteur and was edited by Michel Bibaud, the latter a reputable journalist and poet and a man far better educated than Franchère.

It is important to record here what Milo M. Quaife said about Bibaud and the Franchère journal following his examination of the manuscript that Franchère wrote in 1819: "Although Bibaud was evidently a conscientious editor, he treated Franchère's copy with a degree of freedom which would not meet the approval of present-day historical scholars. In particular he subjected it to an enormous number of transpositions, ranging from single sentences to entire chapters."[19] The *Journal* manuscript, a simple and straightforward narrative, Franchère did not divide into chapters. It was Bibaud who rearranged the text to suit his editorial pleasure. Nevertheless, I have found some awkward contradictions in what Mr. Quaife and at least one other scholar have said as they compared the manuscript with the Bibaud text. For example, Mr. Quaife states in a footnote on page 171 of his edition: "The remainder of this chapter was written by Bibaud, editor of the 1820 edition. Chapters 18, 19, and 20 which follow

19 *Ibid., xxxiii.*

[they are translated and included in Part III of the present volume] were transferred by him to this place from the much earlier position they occupy in the manuscript. In the latter, the opening sentence of Chapter 21 follows at this point." On the other hand, the head of the Canadian History and Manuscript Section of the Toronto Public Library, Edith G. Firth, wrote me on March 10, 1964, saying, among other things, "The descriptive passages about Astoria (pp. 171–98 in the Quaife edition) are not in the manuscript at all."

Some time ago I made an extensive but futile search for the original diary that Franchère kept on his westward journey, even for fragments that might possibly be found. Failing that, in 1958 I requested permission of the Toronto Public Library to make a translation of the original manuscript which is domiciled there; for, having examined all the known texts and reprints of the Franchère narrative, I believed that from the historical point of view such a translation was sorely needed. However, my request was denied. Again last year I asked for a copy of the *Journal* manuscript so that I might make a collation of that text with the Bibaud and Huntington editions. I was again refused permission to have a copy, "or to use the full text, for publication purposes." The Chief Librarian wrote that "the manuscript was acquired by the Board with a view to its eventual publication and this has always been the intention of the Board."[20] The Toronto Public Library acquired possession of the *Journal* manuscript in 1890. Be that as may be, in taking this action, the Toronto Public Library has overlooked an important condition of the common law: the literary rights in original manuscripts and letters inhere in the descendants of the writer, in the absence of a clear conveyance of such rights with the deposit of a manuscript or letters.

However, I am assured that despite the numerous transpositions of textual material which Bibaud made, most of the manuscript is, in its basic form, close to the 1820 publication. In any case I have, following Mr. Quaife's footnotes, carefully annotated Bibaud's alterations. J. V. Huntington translated the French

[20] Letter to me dated April 22, 1966.

text in 1854, apparently under Franchère's supervision, and the book was published in New York by the Redfield company. For this edition Franchère wrote a second Preface, and he added a chapter as well as an Appendix. So far as I can judge, he made these additions with three purposes in mind: to note the changes that had occurred both to the areas he had visited and lived in during his travels and to the people who had inhabited these areas; to give an account of the "fate of some of the persons who left Astoria before and after its sale or transfer to the British"; and to refute some of the charges made by Washington Irving regarding the French fur traders who went on the hazardous adventure to the Pacific Northwest. For Irving had published his *Astoria; or Anecdotes of an Enterprise Beyond the Rocky Mountains* at Philadelphia, in 1836, and Gabriel was one of the first (but by no means the only one) to find flaws in the Irving account of the western adventure.[21]

Washington Irving wrote his *Astoria* at the instigation of John Jacob Astor, his friend for many years and his benefactor and patron. But Irving had not himself been on the West Coast; thus he was dependent upon direct sources such as the published journals of Lewis and Clark, Franchère, Wilson P. Hunt, and Ross Cox, the last of whom had published his *The Columbia River* in England in 1831. Moreover, Irving had access to an apparently rich supply of records and letters belonging to Mr. Astor. Yet, as Edgeley Todd pointed out in his excellent scholarly edition of *Astoria,* Franchère's narrative was the "most important" of Irving's published sources of information.[22] Two charges are often made against Irving today. First, that he cavalierly dismissed those to whom he was most indebted for his information, saying that he had made only occasional use of their works; and second, that he so closely followed some passages from his sources

21 An excellent scholarly edition of *Astoria*, edited by Edgeley W. Todd, was published in 1964 as a volume in the American Exploration and Travel Series (Norman, University of Oklahoma Press).

22 See Mr. Todd's Introduction to *Astoria, xxx.* Mr. Todd makes a thorough analysis of Irving's sources, *xxxiv* ff.

as, by modern standards at least, to have been guilty of plagiarism.

Nevertheless, Gabriel Franchère's justifiable grievance over Irving's book was of another nature, though he was doubtless aware of Irving's indebtedness to him. For one thing, he resented the New Yorker's uncritical acceptance of Captain Thorn's "illiberal remarks" about Astor's partners aboard the *Tonquin* and particularly about the clerks, artisans, and *voyageurs* employed for the expedition. The clerks were to Thorn "mere pretenders," of no higher rank than "barkeeper of a tavern or marker of a billiard table"; the artisans and others were "culprits who fled from Canada on account of their misdeeds . . . ."[23] It was this kind of statement that Franchère sought to refute in the Appendix to his 1854 edition. But it must be noted that he did so quite gracefully and that he exonerated Irving from any intent to prejudice the minds of his readers. It is even then difficult to accept Mr. Todd's defense of Irving on the ground that these passages "were clearly intended to show how Thorn's poor judgment and prickly attitude contributed to the disharmony that prevailed on the ship [*Tonquin*]."[24] Irving was, after all, an established and popularly read author; only the most perceptive readers could be expected to note the subtle exposure of the Captain, if, in fact, Irving was unsympathetic to Thorn's temperament. Franchère, in any event, did not so view the criticism of his fellows on the expedition, and thus recorded his objections with a statement of plain facts.

In his Preface to the second edition Franchère also recorded his part in the settlement of the Oregon Boundary issue. Senator Thomas H. Benton, of Missouri, called him to Washington to testify during the debate on the Senate floor. Franchère was

23 *Ibid.*, 51–52.
24 *Ibid.*, 52n. However, Todd notes that Irving and Thorn had once been acquainted, a fact which "may help to explain Irving's efforts here and earlier in Astoria to exonerate Thorn's behavior." *Ibid.*, 115n. It would seem to me that this latter position is closer to the mark so far as Irving's attitude toward Thorn is concerned.

cordially received in the capital and had the pleasure of meeting many distinguished legislators, including the great Clay and Webster. He was glad to find himself of service to his adopted country and proud, of course, of the recognition given him. Indeed, Senator Benton's mention of the fact that Franchère's account of activity in the Pacific Northwest was known only in a French edition served as a spur to the fur trader to produce an English translation of his work. But, as can be seen, his "reperusal" of Irving's *Astoria* inspired him "with an additional motive"; for he believed that Irving's work was filled with "inaccuracies, misstatements (unintentional of course), and a want of chronological order" that to him, as one entirely familiar with what actually happened along the lower Columbia, necessitated an English version of his narrative for the American reading public.

Be that as may be, the 1854 edition, translated and edited by J. V. Huntington, reveals at least 167 additions, deletions, or variations when compared with the Bibaud publication of 1820. Most of these differences appear to have been made for one of three reasons: Huntington added a number of details in order to clarify or explain whatever may have appeared to be oversimplified in the Bibaud text; in a few instances he added some passages in an attempt, apparently, to intensify and make more dramatic whatever situation is being described; and in two or three passages he added some details in an effort further to negate Irving's position on Captain Thorn—to show that Thorn was, in effect, a veritable Bligh.[25] On the other hand, the 1854 edition omits the superb description of the Indian medicine man at work with his cures, the fine description of the fishing practices of the Columbia River Indians, and the ingenuously devised vocabulary of the Chinook language to be noted at the end of Chapter

[25] Franchère's statements were severe enough, though not filled with the bitter invectives sometimes appearing on the pages of Alexander Ross in his *Adventures of the First Settlers on the Oregon or Columbia River*, edited by Milo M. Quaife (Chicago, The Lakeside Press, R. R. Donnelley and Sons, 1923), hereafter referred to as Ross, *First Settlers*.

20 in Bibaud and translated for the reader in Part III of the present volume.

It was the Huntington translation that, at the turn of the century, Reuben Gold Thwaites reprinted verbatim and edited as a part of Volume VI of his *Early Western Travels*.[26] Thwaites made some useful annotations, especially in regard to the names of people mentioned in Franchère's work but whose identity Franchère had not established for his readers. However, so far as annotations in the 1854 edition were concerned, Thwaites did not distinguish between the Bibaud and the Huntington renderings. A more extensively edited printing of the 1854 translation was published by Milo M. Quaife in 1954.[27] As Mr. Quaife stated in his introduction, his presentation is "basically a reprint" of Huntington's text; and though he maintains that he made no pretense of publishing a verbatim copy, the changes he made, it seems to me, are negligible. He went far beyond Thwaites, however, in his search for related materials such as those he found in the American Fur Company papers then housed in the Carnegie Library at Sault Ste Marie, as well as in other papers at the Detroit Public Library and at the Minnesota Historical Society. He was dependent, moveover, upon my cousin, Dr. Frederick Franchère, of Lake Crystal, Minnesota, for many details regarding Gabriel and Gabriel's descendents. Even then, Mr. Quaife did not by any means exhaust the possible sources of information, and he made some errors that are corrected in this volume. However, he was permitted at least to examine the original manuscript in the Toronto Public Library, carefully annotating those variations that he found in the Bibaud text. I am thus greatly indebted to him for my own footnotes concerned with the original manuscript; and, failing to secure a copy of it for the purposes of collation, I have been guided by his notes.

Therefore, in order to bring to American readers the closest possible approximation to Franchère's original journal in a form

26 Cleveland, Ohio, The Arthur H. Clark Company, 1904.
27 Listed above.

that might reach a far wider audience than has had access to it so far, I have made a new translation of the French edition published at Montreal in 1820. I have, moreover, attempted a close collation of all three texts: the original manuscript (insofar as I have been able to acquire the facts), the Bibaud edition, and the Huntington translation. My annotations will thus allow my readers to see how vast a difference exists between Franchère's original composition and the 1854 translation. Except for his numerous additions, Huntington's translation is a quite literal rendering of the French version. In my own work I have sought to render the French into modern English while remaining faithful to the basic substance of the French version. Gabriel's French is heavily endowed with Latin constructions, and an over-use of the Latin ablative absolute, for example, makes hard going in English, as one may surely note in the Huntington translation. However, the essentially dramatic nature of the Franchère narrative cannot easily be lost, even in its English form. As a simple chronicle of events it moves rather briskly, relating with candor, yet with warmly human understanding and sensitivity, the struggles of those men who dared risk their lives—several losing them —in an adventure that came to have much significance in the history of Oregon and of the Northwest generally.[28]

Two other Astorians, one-time fellows of Gabriel Franchère, years later wrote of their experiences in the West. In 1831, Ross Cox, as earlier noted, completed his *Adventures on the Columbia River;*[29] and in 1849, Alexander Ross published his *Adventures*

[28] For the purposes of collation I am using the following texts throughout the present volume: Gabriel Franchère, *Relation d'un Voyage à la Côte du Nord Ouest de l'Amérique Septentrionale, dans les Années 1810, 11, 12, 13, et 14,* edited by Michel Bibaud (Montreal, De L'Imprimerie de C. B. Pasteur, 1820).

Gabriel Franchère, *Narrative of a Voyage to the Northwest Coast of America in the Years 1811, 1812, 1813, and 1814; or, the First American Settlement on the Pacific,* translated and edited by J. V. Huntington (New York, Redfield, 1854).

Gabriel Franchère, *A Voyage to the Northwest Coast of America,* edited by Milo M. Quaife (Chicago, The Lakeside Press, R. R. Donnelley and Sons Company, 1954).

[29] London, Colburn. An excellent edition of the Cox book, *The Columbia River,* edited by Edgar I. and Jane R. Stewart (hereafter referred to as Cox, *Columbia River),* is one of the volumes in the American Exploration and Travel Series (Norman, University of Oklahoma Press, 1957).

of the First Settlers on the Oregon or Columbia River.[30] Although Franchère's narrative was late to be translated and was known chiefly in Canada until 1854, it is probably the most significent of these three documents in its treatment of the lives of the early fur traders along the lower Columbia and in its graphic representation of the Indians in that area. Certainly, as a record of an overland journey in the early nineteenth century it is scarcely surpassed.

IV

Something remains to be said concerning Astor's great action to capture the fur trade of the West, and something besides about the leaders in the enterprise. For great action it was, despite the fact that, owing to accidents of time and circumstance and the unfortunate conflicts of some personalities involved, it was also a failure.

Counting those who died on the overland expedition, more than sixty lives were lost from that group of men called the Astorians. Franchère does not by any means count the total of the dead in his narrative, though he says a good deal about the men he knew who were drowned while taking soundings at the Columbia River mouth or while returning to Montreal. Lost, as well, was a large sum of money that Astor invested in ships. Two of these, the *Tonquin* and the *Lark*, were destroyed: the former was blown up at Newettee; the latter capsized in heavy seas not far from Hawaii, five men perishing in the disaster. Although she was righted, her rigging had been torn away and she maneuvered for a time half-submerged. The crew swam ashore at Maui in the Islands, but the natives took their clothes and other possessions and claimed the cargo, most of which floated up on the beach. The ship washed onto the sands and was shattered by the waves. Franchère tells the story of these losses, but he says nothing of the

---

[30] London, Smith, Elder and Company. An admirable edition of the Ross narrative, Alexander Ross, *The Fur Hunters of the Far West*, edited by Kenneth A. Spaulding (hereafter referred to as Ross, *Fur Hunters*), is also a volume in the American Exploration and Travel Series (Norman, University of Oklahoma Press, 1956).

financial failure sustained by the *Beaver* when it put into the Canton harbor in China.

Nevertheless, as G. W. Fuller has pointed out in his *History of the Pacific Northwest*, Astor's loss was the nation's gain.[31] Wilson Price Hunt's trek to the West Coast proved that the Snake River route was far too hazardous for fur traders, while Robert Stuart's party returning to St. Louis found the South Pass through the Rockies and thereby traced a large part of the Oregon trail as it is known today. The rich promise of the Willamette Valley was discovered, and Irving's *Astoria* awakened American interest in Oregon and in the Northwest generally. The $40,000 that Astor received from the transfer of his properties to the North West Company did not erase the red ink on his Pacific Fur Company ledger, but the whole country profited from his venturesome enterprise.

Of Astor's partners, the leaders in his maritime expedition, perhaps Alexander McKay stands first. It was he who signed Gabriel Franchère as clerk of the Pacific Fur Company in the spring of 1810. The date of his birth is unknown, but he came from Upper Canada and had been an employee of the North West Company for some years before 1791. He went overland with Sir Alexander Mackenzie to the Pacific in the years 1792–93, returning to Portage la Prairie in the following year. He became a partner in the company in 1799 and retired in 1808. Two years later, however, he joined Astor, and the reader of Franchère's narrative learns how this able and kindly figure met his tragic end at Newettee.[32]

Two other partners, David and Robert Stuart, emigrated from Scotland—David at some time before 1800, Robert in 1807. The former was born about 1765, and may have been employed

---

31 (New York, Alfred A. Knopf, 1958. Second Edition Revised), 109.

32 See *Dictionary of Canadian Biography* (Toronto, The Macmillan Company, 1963). McKay's wife, a half-blood woman, bore him at least one son, Thomas. After her husband's death, she married Dr. John McLoughlin, one of the great leaders in early Oregon and factor for a number of years at Astoria. McKay's sister, Catherine, married another famous Northwester and explorer, Simon Fraser.

by the North West Company before 1810; but he joined Astor in that year and remained loyal to Astor's interests thereafter. It was he who went with Alexander Ross on the first trek of the Astoria men to the interior, where they founded the post at Okanogan. While Ross maintained the new quarters, then only a small hut built of driftwood from the Okanogan River, Stuart explored the river's headwaters. He was gone six months. Meanwhile, Ross managed to keep peace with the neighboring Indians.[33] Okanogan became one of the principal fur-trading posts not only for the Pacific Fur Company but also for the North West Company and, later still, the Hudson's Bay Company. It was maintained until 1859.

Upon returning to the Middle West, David Stuart continued his employment with Astor's American Fur Company, retiring in 1833. He died at Detroit in the home of his nephew's widow, on October 18, 1853.

Robert Stuart, like his uncle, remained with Astor throughout his career. Although he was with the maritime party on the *Tonquin*, he stayed at Astoria only until June, 1812. At that time, along with Ramsay Crooks and Donald McClellan, he was sent back to St. Louis with dispatches to be forwarded to Astor's headquarters. Franchère tells of the departure of these men, just as he tells about John Reed's departure previously on an earlier, though disastrous, attempt to return to the Middle West. But Franchère did not know of the severe hardships these men endured in the eleven long months of privation they suffered— hazards surpassed only by those that Hunt and Crooks had faced on their way westward. Robert served as Astor's agent at Michilimackinac from 1819 until 1834, when he retired from the trade. He died in Chicago on October 28, 1848.[34]

Possibly the most colorful of the four partners in the maritime party was Duncan McDougall, yet less is known about this man than about the others. He was put in charge of the fort at

[33] See Ross, *Fur Hunters*.
[34] Robert Stuart's narrative of his overland journey with Crooks and McClellan was edited by P. A. Rollins under the title *Discovery of the Oregon Trail*, and published in New York in 1935.

Astoria and entered the service of the North West Company when the Astor property was sold in 1813.[35] Franchère makes no mention of complaints raised by Alexander Ross about McDougall's management of the enterprise, nor does he give an account of McDougall's marriage to an Indian princess, a daughter of Chinook chieftain Concomly, an interlude that Irving treated with eminently good humor.[36] In any event, McDougall remained at Astoria until 1817, leaving there to take charge of the North West post at Fort William. Thus the record of this man extends only from 1810 to 1817, and aside from Franchère's statement that McDougall died a "miserable death," nothing is known, not even the date or place of his death.

These four were Astor's partners who led in the establishment of the fur-trading post at the mouth of the Columbia. With the possible exception of Alexander McKay, who had already achieved an excellent reputation before he joined Astor and whose early death deprived the fur trade of an able and knowledgeable leader, none of these men lived to match the significant record of Ramsay Crooks, another Scottish *émigré*, who came to Montreal in 1803 at the age of sixteen. Crooks served three of those early years as a clerk of Robert Dickson at Mackinac, then went to St. Louis where he joined Robert McClellan as a partner in several trading expeditions.

When that partnership dissolved in 1810, Crooks went once again to Montreal, where, persuaded by Wilson Price Hunt, he joined the Astor expedition, serving as one of the two leaders in that miserable overland struggle to Astoria. Indeed, for a time Crooks was ill from the privations he and his men had endured en route. It is possible that he was in no condition either mentally or physically, to be elated over what he saw at Astoria. Despairing over the prospects of the Pacific enterprise, he sold his shares in the Astor partnership and returned, as has been noted earlier, to St. Louis in 1812–13.

35 Fuller maintains that McDougall "showed himself to be an irritable person of second-rate ability." Fuller, *History*, 98.
36 Irving, *Astoria*, edited by Todd, 461–62.

However, Crooks remained in Astor's employ, and was actually, though not nominally, in charge of all the activities of the American Fur Company from 1822 until 1834, when Astor retired. He then became president of the company, serving in that capacity until it collapsed in 1848. He made yearly trips from New York to Mackinac and St. Louis, always displaying the utmost vigor in the pursuit of his business ventures. He had an outstanding grasp of detail and a reputation unsurpassed for integrity in all relationships with both partners and agents—in a trade in which shady practices were commonplace. Meantime, too, he became a citizen of note. He was president of the Mohawk Railroad until 1835, later a trustee of the Astor Library, and a member of many learned societies. In short, he is a prototype of the successful American entrepreneur.

The correspondence between Gabriel Franchère and Ramsay Crooks, that is, between Sault Ste Marie and New York—from 1834 until 1842 when Franchère joined Crooks in New York—reveals a growing mutual respect between these men, a great dedication, and a high degree of loyalty in both.[37] It is unfortunate that after the demise of the American Fur Company Franchère did not make a record of his experiences with Crooks, just as he had made a record of his travels to the West Coast of America in the years when their association had its first tenuous and nearly tragic beginning.

In all his extant correspondence acquired by the present editor, Franchère seems not to have been involved with the Stuarts, who lived in Detroit all through the period of his management of the Sault Ste Marie agency. He has no word for Wilson Price Hunt, who lived out his life in St. Louis, or for Donald McKenzie, one of Hunt's partners in the overland expedition. Indeed, of all the hardy fellows who joined Astor in 1810 for one of the most daring and imaginative enterprises of the early nineteenth century, only Ramsey Crooks remains to figure in Franchère's accounts.

[37] Franchère Letter Books, The American Fur Company Papers, Clarke Historical Collection, *passim.*

Contents

﷽﷽﷽﷽﷽﷽﷽﷽﷽﷽﷽﷽﷽﷽﷽﷽﷽﷽

Illustrations

ADVENTURE AT ASTORIA, 1810–1814

Author's Preface

When I was writing my journal on board the ship that carried me to the northwest coast of North America and into the wilderness of this continent, my last thought was that it would one day be put before the eyes of the public. I had no other intent in writing but to produce for my family and friends a more precise and coherent account of what I had seen or learned on my journey than it would have been possible for me to make by telling it orally. Since my return to my native city, my manuscript has passed through different hands and has been read by different people. Several of my friends advised me to print it. But it is only recently that I have let myself be persuaded that though he may not be a naturalist, a competent geographer, or a profound moralist, a traveler can still interest [readers] by a faithful and succinct account of the situations in which he has found himself, of adventures in which he has been involved, and of incidents to which he has been witness. If a simple and ingenuous narrative, lacking the merit of science and the grace of diction, should prove less tasteful to the man of letters or to the scholar, it nevertheless might have the compensating advantage of being an open door to a larger number of readers. Finally, a man's wish to write for the entertainment of his countrymen, according to his ability and without any mixing of his vanity or material interest, ought to be a sufficiently just reason for their indulgence. Whether I have done well or badly in yielding to these suggestions—suggestions that I must regard as those of friendship or of good will —it is for the impartial and disinterested reader to decide.

xx

Author's Introduction

SINCE THE INDEPENDENCE of the United States of America, merchants of this industrious and enterprising nation have, along the northwest coast of the continent, carried on an extremely advantageous trade. In the course of their voyages they have made a great many discoveries that they have not thought wise to make public—no doubt for fear of revealing too much to their competitors and thereby losing some of their profits.[1]

In 1792, Captain Gray, commander of the ship *Columbia*, from Boston, discovered the entrance to a great bay at 46° 19" North Latitude. When he sailed into it, he realized that it was actually a large river, because he found fresh water a short distance from its mouth. He went upriver eighteen miles and dropped anchor on its north bank at the entrance to a rather deep bay. There he drew a map of what he had seen of the river and of the neighboring countryside. And after he had traded with the natives (trade was his reason for making these expeditions), he returned to the sea.

Soon he met Captain Vancouver, who was sailing under orders of the British government, trying to make new discoveries.[2]

1 Huntington varies the sentence to conclude with the following: ". . . no doubt to avoid competition in a lucrative business" (p. 17).

2 Captain Robert Gray and Captain George Vancouver met on April 28, 1792, before Gray had entered the Columbia River. Vancouver then set sail for Puget Sound and Nootka. Gray put into the mouth of the Columbia on May 11

Mr. Gray informed him of what he had done and showed him the map he had drawn. Vancouver sent First Lieutenant Broughton upriver about 120 miles to take possession of this territory in the name of the British crown. He named the river Columbia, and the bay where the American captain had stopped, Gray's Bay. Since that time, the country has been visited frequently, chiefly by Americans.

In his second journey overland, Sir Alexander McKenzie [Mackenzie] attempted to reach the western ocean by way of the Columbia River. He believed that he had succeeded when he emerged six degrees to the north, at the lower end of a bay called Puget's Sound.

In 1805, the American government sent Captains Lewis and Clark who, with about thirty Kentucky riflemen, paddled and sailed up the Missouri, crossed the mountains at the source of that river, and went down the Columbia to the shores of the Pacific Ocean, where they were forced to spend the winter. The report they made of their journey aroused great interest.[3]

Mr. John Jacob Astor, a New York merchant who almost alone carried on a fur trade south of the great lakes Huron and Superior and who had acquired a prodigious fortune by that business, believed that he could further augment his fortune by forming on the banks of the Columbia River an establishment whose supply house would be at its mouth. He explained his views to agents of the North West Company. He even wished to form this establishment in partnership with them. But after some negotiations, the North West partners rejected his proposals and Mr. Astor decided to make the attempt alone.

To succeed in this endeavor he needed men long accustomed to trading with the Indians, and he soon found them. Mr. Alexander McKay (the same man who had accompanied Sir Alexander Mackenzie on his journeys), a hardy and enterprising man,

of that year. His sketches of the river's entrance he gave to Quadra, Spanish governor at Nootka, on May 20; Quadra, in turn, gave them to Vancouver, who visited the Columbia during the following October.

3 Huntington, ". . . created a lively sensation" (p. 19).

6

joined him. Soon afterward, Messrs. Duncan McDougall, Donald McKenzie (formerly in the service of the North West Company), David Stuart, and Robert Stuart, all of Canada, did the same. Finally, in the winter of 1810, a Mr. Wilson Price Hunt, of St. Louis, on the Mississippi, also joined them. They determined that an expedition should be undertaken the following spring.

It was during the course of this winter that one of my friends told me, in confidence, about the plans of these gentlemen, with a plea to keep the news a secret. The desire to see other countries joined with the wish to make a fortune made me decide to seek employment with the new company. On May 20, I went to the home of Mr. Alexander McKay, with whom I arranged the preliminaries; and on the twenty-fourth of the month, I signed a contract for a period of five years.

When the associates had engaged a sufficient number of Canadian *voyageurs*, they equipped a bark canoe under the command of Messrs. Hunt and McKenzie, with a Mr. Perrault, clerk, and fourteen men. Messrs. Hunt and McKenzie were expected to proceed to Mackinac by the Grand River, there to engage as many men as they could. They were then to go to St. Louis in order to travel up the Missouri River to its source and, following the route taken by Captains Lewis and Clark, reach the mouth of the Columbia.[4] I shall have occasion to speak of the success of that expedition in the course of this work.

---

4 Huntington inexplicably alters this passage to ". . . they were to ascend the Missouri to its source, and there diverging from the route followed by Lewis and Clark, reach the mouth of the Columbia to form a junction with another party, who were to go round by way of Cape Horn. In the course of my narrative I shall have occasion to speak of the success of both these expeditions" (p. 22). It appears that Franchére had access to supplementary data about Messrs. Hunt and McKenzie; otherwise he had inaccurate information for his 1820 edition.

❈❈

PART I

Westward Sailing

CHAPTER 1

WE REMAINED in Montreal the rest of the spring and part of the summer. At last all arrangements for the journey were completed. We received orders to get ready to depart; and on July 26 [1810], accompanied by my family and a few friends, I went to the place of embarkation where a bark canoe manned by nine men was moored. The feelings that I experienced at that moment would be as difficult to describe as they were painful to bear. For the first time in my life I was leaving my birthplace and separating myself from devoted parents and intimate friends. My only consolation was the faint hope of seeing them again one day.

We embarked about five o'clock in the afternoon and arrived at La Prairie de la Madeleine at eight. We slept in this village; and very early the next morning, with our canoe on a cart, we got under way and arrived at St. Johns, on the Richelieu River, a little before noon. We relaunched our canoe, crossed Lake Champlain, and arrived at Whitehall on July 30. There we were joined by Mr. Ovide Montigny and Mr. Paul D. Jeremie, who were to be members of our expedition. Again we placed our canoe on a cart and continued along our route, arriving on August 1 at Lansingburg, a small village situated on the banks of the Hudson River. Our canoe in the water once more, we paddled past Troy and Albany, where we were graciously welcomed, but where the Americans took our *voyageurs* for Indians. We arrived at New York on August 3 at eleven o'clock at night. We had landed at the north end of the city, and the following morning, which was Sunday, we re-embarked and were obliged to go around the entire city in order to reach our lodgings on Long Island. We sang as we rowed, and our singing, along with the sight of our bark canoe, drew a crowd of people to the wharves. On Long Island we found some young men who had left Canada before us and who had entered the service of the Astor Company.

The ship on which we were to sail was not ready. I should have found myself completely isolated and a stranger in the big city of New York but for a letter of introduction to a Mr. G———, that his sister had given me before I left Montreal. I had met this man when he visited Montreal in 1801, but as I was then very young, he probably would have had great difficulty in recognizing me without the letter from his sister. He introduced me to several of his friends, and during the five weeks that passed from the time I arrived in New York until I boarded ship, I enjoyed myself immensely.

I shall not undertake a description of New York. I shall say only that the elegance of the buildings, public and private, the cleanliness of the streets, the shade of the poplars that border them, the public walks, the markets always abundantly supplied with all kinds of commodities, the business then flourishing, the great number of ships of all nations that lined the quays—all, in a word, conspired to make me feel the difference between this great port city and my native town, which I had never left before and which was not then nearly what it is today.

New York has never been a fortified city. However, one can see there several batteries and fortifications, of which the greatest are on the Narrows, or the channel which forms the mouth of the Hudson River. Governor's Island and Gibbet Island also were strongly fortified. On the first, located west of the city and about a mile away, barracks large enough to accommodate several thousand soldiers had been constructed, as well as a stronghold with three tiers of cannon, all bombproof. These fortifications were enlarged during the War of 1812.

There were eight markets, of which the largest was called the "Fly-market."

The Park, the Battery, and Vauxhall Garden were the principal public walks [then called "promenades"]. In 1810, there were thirty-two churches, two of which were devoted to Catholic worship. The population numbered about ninety thousand inhabitants, of whom ten thousand were French. It is believed that since that time the population has increased by nearly thirty thousand.

During my stay in New York, I lodged in Brooklyn, on Long Island. This island is separated from the city by a sound, a narrow arm of the ocean. Here there was an attractive village, and a short distance away was a dock onto which some gunboats had been hauled up almost high and dry. Some barracks had been built and a guard was maintained there.

Perhaps I should mention that during our stay in New York Mr. McKay thought it wise to see the British minister, Mr. Jackson, to inform him of the object of our expedition and to ask his advice about what we should do in the event of war between England and the United States. He explained to the minister that we were all British subjects, but that we were trading under the American flag.

After some moments of reflection, Mr. Jackson replied that we were planning to establish a trading post at the risk of our lives; that he could promise us only that in case of war between our two countries we should be respected as British subjects and merchants. This response seemed satisfactory and Mr. McKay thought that we had no reason to be apprehensive about the matter.

The ship on which we were to sail was the *Tonquin*, of 286 tons burden, commanded by Captain Thorn, who had twenty-one crew members. The passengers numbered thirty-three. Here are the names of both:

Passengers

Owners

Alexander McKay David Stuart

Duncan McDougall Robert Stuart

Clerks

James Lewis Donald McLennan[2]

Russel Farnham W. W. Matthews

Alexander Ross W. Wallace

J. B. Pillet[1] Thomas McKay

Donald McGillis G. Franchère

Ovide Montigny

Voyageurs

Olivier Roy Lapansée Joseph LaPierre

Ignace Lapensée Joseph Nadeau

Basil Lapansée J. Bte. Belleau

Jacques Lafantaisie Louis Brulé

Benjamin Roussel Antoine Belleau

Michel Laframboise P. D. Jeremie

Giles Leclerc

Johann Koaster, a ship carpenter, Russian

George Bell, a cooper

Aug. Roussil, a blacksmith

---

[1] Franchère erred in the 1820 edition. Pillet's name was François Benjamin Pillet. It is interesting to note that over the years the name mutated to Payette. Mr. B. C. Payette, of Montreal, editor of several documents concerned with the history of the Northwest and of the fur trade, is a great-grandson of F. B. Pillet. It was Pillet–Payette's name that was given to both city and river in the state of Idaho.

Ross Cox relates that when he returned to Montreal in 1817, at the Lake of the Two Mountains not far west of the city he "found another old friend from the Columbia, Mr. Pillet, with whom we stopped a couple of hours. He had a snug farm, a comfortable house, a handsome wife, and two pretty children, and altogether appeared to be in happy circumstances." Cox, *Columbia River*, 352.

[2] In the 1820 edition Franchère listed Donald McLellan, but so far as can be discovered no such name appears in the records of the Astor enterprise. Franchère meant to write the name of Donald McLennan and he corrected his error in the Huntington text of 1854. McLennan was a member of the maritime party with Franchère. Robert McClellan was with Wilson Price Hunt on the overland expedition.

11

Job Aikin (Aitken), rigger and calker
Guilleaume Perrault, a boy

Crew

J. Thorn, captain	John White, sailor
E. D. Fox, First mate	Adam Ficher, same
J. D. Mumford, second mate	Peter Vershel, same
	Edward Aymes, same
John Anderson, boatswain	Robert Hill, same
Egbert Vanderhuff, tailor	Jos. Johnson, same
John Weeks, carpenter	Charles Robert, same
Stephen Weeks, armorer	John Martin, same
John Coles, sailmaker	A mulatto, cook

and three or four other men whose names I have forgotten.[3]

CHAPTER 2

When all was ready for our departure, we boarded the ship and weighed anchor on the morning of September 6. The wind soon fell off, however, and we spent the day drifting and tacking near Staten Island, where we stayed the night.[1] On the following morning we weighed anchor again; but again we experienced a dead calm and were forced to anchor near the lighthouse at Sandy Hook. On the eighth we weighed anchor for the third time, and with the aid of a fresh breeze from the southwest, we managed to pass the bar. Our pilot left us at eleven o'clock and soon afterward we lost sight of the coast.

One must experience it himself in order to understand the sadness that overwhelms the spirit of a sensitive person at the moment when he leaves his country and the civilized world to live among strangers in savage and unexplored lands. I should find it impossible to give my readers more than a vague idea of the painful heart-sinking that I suddenly felt, and of the gloomy

---

[3] Quaife states: "The Manuscript lists the names of 17 members of the crew, which totaled 21. An open space follows, to fill which the Editor has supplied the line 'and three or four others whose names I have forgotten.'" Apparently it was Bibaud who inserted the line, and Huntington reprinted it in the 1854 edition.

[1] Huntington varies the reading, but makes no substantive change in the text.

picture I envisaged of the future because it offered nothing but confusion and uncertainty. A new scene opened out before me, but it was a monotonous one, and hardly designed to lessen the melancholy by which my mind was depressed.

For the first time in my life, I found myself sailing on the open sea with nothing between the depths of the water and the immensity of the sky on which to fix my eye or to attract my attention except the frail machine that bore me. For a long time I remained with my eyes straining toward the coastline that I could no longer see and that I despaired of ever seeing again. I engaged in serious reflections on the nature and the consequences of the enterprise into which I had plunged so recklessly. And I confess that if at that moment release had been offered me, I should have abandoned my contract wholeheartedly.

It is true also that the crowding of the ship, the great number of strangers among whom I found myself, the brutal manner in which the captain and his subalterns abused our young Canadians—everything, in a word, conspired to make me anticipate a troublesome and disagreeable voyage. What follows will show that I was not mistaken in this view.

We soon saw, in the southwest, a ship that bore directly toward us. She made a signal that our captain understood, and we hauled in sail and drew longside her. She proved to be the American frigate *Constitution*. We sent our longboat to board her; and we sailed in her company until about five o'clock when, our papers having been returned to us, we separated.

The wind had increased and the rolling of the ship made us seasick—at least those of us who were for the first time at sea. Nevertheless, the weather was fine. At our departure we had been so encumbered that we could scarcely get into our hammocks, and the ship had been difficult for us to manage. Now, gradually, we became better organized and soon found ourselves more comfortable.

On the fourteenth we began to capture flying fish. On the twenty-fourth we saw a great number of dolphins. We prepared our lines and caught two of them, which we cooked. The flesh of this fish seemed excellent to me.

From the time of our departure from New York until October 4, we headed southeast. On that day, however, we struck the trade winds and changed course to SSE. We were, according to our observations, at 17° 43″ Latitude and 22° 39″ Longitude.

On the morning of the fifth we came into sight of the Cape Verde Islands, bearing west northwest, about fifteen or sixteen miles away, with the coast of Africa lying to SSE.[2] We should have been happy to touch at these islands to get fresh water; but since our ship was American and had on board a number of British subjects, our captain thought it wise not to risk meeting the British warships that frequented these waters and would not have failed to make a thorough search, relieving us of the better part of our crew. Such a thing surely would have made it impossible for us to follow the course on which we had embarked.[3]

As long as we were near the coast of Africa, we had variable winds and extremely hot weather. On the eighth we had a dead calm, and saw several sharks around the ship. We caught one of them and ate it. I found it to taste a little like sturgeon. On that day, too, we experienced excessive heat, the mercury rising to 94° Fahrenheit. From the eighth to the eleventh we had on board a canary that we carried a great distance, but it deserted us, nevertheless, probably to go to a certain death.

The closer we came to the equator the more we felt the heat. On the sixteenth, at 6° Latitude and 22° Longitude west of Greenwich, the mercury stood at 108. On the same day, we discovered a sail bearing toward us. The same sail appeared the next morning and came within cannon shot of us. We saw that

---

[2] Huntington says eight or nine miles. Bibaud says ". . . *à cinq ou six lieues de distance.* . . ."

[3] For the 1854 edition Franchère prepared a paragraph about rations. Quaife says: "This long paragraph is not found in this place in the Manuscript. Because of the very frequent transpositions of sections of the narrative made by Bibaud, the original editor, it is perhaps hazardous to affirm that it does not occur at some other place" (p. 14n).

she was a large brig, carrying, apparently, twenty pieces of cannon. The two of us ran in company with a good wind—all sails spread—but toward evening we left her behind and she changed course to SSE.

On the eighteenth, at daybreak, the watch alarmed us by announcing that the same brig that had followed us the day before had appeared leeward, within a cable's distance, and seemed to want to know who we were, without, however, showing her own colors. Our captain was alarmed. And since he thought she was a better sailer than our ship, he summoned all the passengers and crew on deck and we pretended to make preparations for battle. It should be said that our ship mounted ten cannon and was pierced for twenty. The portholes were painted with sham guns. However, at ten o'clock the wind freshened and we drew away from the brig, which had changed her course.[4]

Nothing remarkable happened to us until the twenty-second, when we crossed the equator at 25° 9″ Longitude. Following an old custom, the crew baptized those of us who had not been over the line before. That day was a holiday for them. About two o'clock in the afternoon, we sighted a ship SSW. We were not a little alarmed. We thought she was the same brig that we had seen several days earlier, for she was lying to and appeared to be waiting for us. We soon approached her; and, to our great satisfaction, we saw that she was a Portuguese ship. We hailed her and found that she had come from South America and was bound for Pernambuco [Recife] on the coast of Brazil.

Soon we began to see what the navigators call the Clouds of Magellan. These are three little specks that one perceives in the sky soon after crossing the equator. They are located SSW.

On November 1 we saw the first of a great number of aquatic birds. Toward three o'clock in the afternoon we discovered a ship to starboard, but we did not come near enough to speak to her.[5] On the third we saw two more sails headed SE. Making

4 Huntington writes: "Whether it was our formidable appearance or no, at about ten A. M. the stranger again changed her course, and we soon lost sight of her entirely" (p. 38).

5 Huntington translates it as "larboard." Bibaud used Franchère's term

good headway, we passed the Tropic of Capricorn on the fourth, at 33° 27″ Longitude. We lost the trade winds; and as we gradually moved southward, the weather became cold and rainy. On the eleventh we experienced a calm, although the swell was very heavy. We saw several turtles; the captain lowered a small boat into the water and we caught two of them.

During the night of the eleventh the wind changed to NE and brought a furious storm in which wind, rain, lightning, and thunder seemed to have conspired our destruction. The sea was all afire and our ship the plaything of the winds and waves. We battened down the hatches, but we could not escape some very bad nights while the storm lasted, for the intense heat we had experienced in the tropics had so dried out our deck that every time the waves washed overboard the water leaked in quantities onto our hammocks below.

On the fourteenth the wind changed to SSW and we were obliged to tack about. During the night we were struck by a tremendous sea. Our rudder seemed to be unmanageable. The man at the helm was thrown from one side of the deck to the other and so bruised that he had to be confined to his berth for several days.[6]

At 35° 19″ Latitude and 40° Longitude the sea seemed to be covered with marine plants, and the change that we noticed in the color of the water, along with the great number of gulls and other water birds we could see, proved that we were not far from the mouth of the Río de la Plata. The wind continued to blow with force until the twenty-first, when it fell off a little and the weather cleared. On the twenty-fifth, at 46° 30″ Latitude, we saw a penguin.

We began to feel keenly a need for water. Since we had passed the Tropic of Capricorn, the ration had continually diminished, and we were now reduced to three gills a day. That

---

"stribord" or "tribord." Both mean starboard. Quaife followed the text of the 1954 edition.

6 Huntington says the man broke two of his ribs and was confined to his berth for a week (pp. 40–41).

was little enough, since we had only a salt-meat diet. We had, in fact, a still which served to render sea water drinkable; but we distilled only what was needed for daily use in the kitchen. To distill more would have required a great quantity of wood and coal. As we were not more than three hundred miles from the Falkland Islands, we resolved to cast anchor there and try to find water. The captain therefore had the anchors made ready.

We had contrary winds from November 27 until December 3. But on the evening of that day, we heard one of the officers who was high on the mast shout, "Land! Land!" However, darkness soon prevented our seeing the rocks we had before us, and we lay to.

CHAPTER 3

On the morning of 4 [December], I hurried to mount the deck to fill my eyes with the sight of land. Only those who have been three or four months on the high seas know how to appreciate the pleasure one then feels upon seeing lands even as barren as the Falkland Islands. We soon drew near to these rocks and entered between two of the islands, where we anchored in a good depth. The second mate was sent ashore to look for water, with several of our gentlemen accompanying him. They returned in the evening with the disappointing news that they had not been able to find fresh water. Nevertheless, they brought us, as compensation, a number of wild geese and two seals. Then, the weather appearing to threaten, we weighed anchor and put out to sea.

The night was stormy, and by the morning of the fifth we had lost sight of the first islands. An offshore wind was blowing and we found it necessary to tack about all day, but by evening we found ourselves near enough to the shoreline and we lay to for the night.

The sixth brought us a clear sky, and with a fresh breeze we succeeded in gaining a good anchorage, which we took to be Port Egmont, and there we found good water. On the seventh we sent our water casks ashore, as well as the cooper to fill them and the blacksmiths who were occupied with some repairs required by the ship. For our part, we erected a tent near the springs, and while they were taking in water we scouted the islands. We were provided with a small-boat accommodation and every day killed a great many wild geese and ducks. These birds differ in plumage from those which are seen in Canada. We also killed a great many seals, which ordinarily keep upon the rocks. We also saw several foxes of the species called Virginia fox. They seemed ill-tempered enough to us and they barked like dogs. Penguins, aquatic birds, are numerous on the Falkland Islands and have a fine plumage that resembles the loon; but they do not fly and have only little stumps of wings that they use to help themselves in waddling along. When they waddle they resemble little dwarfs. They are somewhat shy and timid; yet far from fleeing, they tried to pick at us with their beaks which are very sharp.[1] The flesh of the penguin is black and tough and one must be extremely hungry to persuade oneself to eat it. It was the time of egg-laying and we found a great quantity of eggs.

The French and English had both attempted to form establishments on these rocks, and we tried coursing to find some vestige of them.[2] The tracks that we met everywhere made us hope to find goats also, but our search was quite fruitless. All that we discovered was an old fishing cabin, constructed of whalebone, and some sealskin moccasins. These rocks offer not a single tree to the view and are frequented only by the whaling ships in the southern seas. We found, however, two headboards with inscriptions in English, marking the spot where two men had been buried. As the letters were nearly obliterated we carved new ones.

This attention to two dead men nearly proved fatal to a great number of the living; for when all the casks had been filled and sent aboard, the captain gave orders to re-embark. Without troubling to find out whether this command had been executed,

[1] Huntington adds: "The rocks were covered with them . . . ." and he varies the Bibaud text by saying "They are not wild or timid . . . ." and "We got a great quantity of eggs by dislodging them from their nests" (p. 47).

[2] Quaife maintains that "The Manuscript reads 'Portuguese' instead of 'French and English'" (p. 21n).

he ordered the anchor weighed on the morning of the eleventh, while some of my companions and I were engaged in erecting the inscriptions of which I have spoken. Others were cutting grass for the hogs. Mr. McDougall and Mr. David Stuart had gone to the south side of the island to look for game.

These two men had not heard the boarding signal and did not rejoin us until later, when the ship was already in the open sea. However, we then lost no time, but pushed off, eight in number, in our little boat, which was no more than twenty feet in length. After having run some danger and having rowed extremely hard for nearly three and a half hours, we succeeded in regaining our ship and went aboard at three o'clock in the afternoon.

Having related this trait of malice on the part of our captain, I shall allow myself to make some remarks on his character. Jonathan Thorn was brought up in the service of his country, and had distinguished himself in a battle fought between the Americans and the Turks at Tripoli some years before. He held the rank of first lieutenant. He was precise and rigid in mind, with a quick and violent temper; he was accustomed to exact obedience, being obeyed at the smallest demand, and was concerned with duty only. He ignored the murmurs of his crew, taking counsel of no one and following Mr. Astor's instructions to the letter.[3]

Such was the man who had been selected to command our ship. His haughty manners, his brusque and arrogant disposition, had lost him the respect and esteem of most of the crew and of all the passengers. He knew this, and in consequence always sought an opportunity to embarrass us. It is true that the passengers had some reason to reproach themselves. But he had been the aggressor, and nothing could excuse the acts of cruelty and barbarity of which he was guilty in leaving us upon those barren rocks of the Falkland Isles, where inevitably we should have died. This lot had been ours but for the bold decision of

[3] Huntington varies this passage slightly, calling Thorn a "strict disciplinarian" (p. 48). The remainder of the description follows Bibaud rather closely.

Mr. Robert Stuart, whose uncle was of our party. Seeing that the captain, far from waiting for us, continued his course, Mr. Stuart threatened to blow his brains out unless he hove to and took us on board.[4]

We pursued our course, sailing SSW, and on the fourteenth, at 54° 1″ Latitude, and 64° 13″ Longitude, we marked sixty-five fathoms and noticed a sail to the south. On the morning of the fifteenth we discovered before us the high mountains of Tierra del Fuego, which remained in view until evening, when the weather thickened and we lost sight of them. We encountered a furious storm that drove us to the 56° 18″ Latitude. On the eighteenth we were only about forty-five miles from famed Cape Horn. A dead calm followed, and the current carried us within sight of the Cape, fifteen or sixteen miles away. This cape, forming the southern extremity of Tierra del Fuego, or rather the continent of South America, has always been an object of terror for navigators who have to pass from one sea to the other. Several, in order to avoid doubling it, have exposed themselves to the long and dangerous passage of the Straits of Magellan, especially when it was a question of entering the Pacific Ocean. When we found ourselves, so to speak, under the Cape, we felt no other desire than to withdraw promptly, so frightening were the rocks there, even for men who had been several months at sea! And by the help of an offshore breeze, we succeeded in standing out to sea.[5]

[4] Ross Cox writes concerning this action on Thorn's part: "The gentlemen on board expostulated in vain against this act of tyrannic cruelty, when Mr. Robert Stuart, nephew of the old gentleman who had been left on shore, seized a brace of pistols, and presenting one at the captain's head, threatened to blow out his brains if he did not instantly order the ship to lay to and wait for his uncle's party. Most part of the crew and officers witnessed this scene; and as they appeared to sympathize deeply with young Stuart, the captain thought it more prudent to submit, and gave orders accordingly to shorten sail, and wait the arrival of Mr. Stuart's party." Cox, *Columbia River*, 52. It should be remembered, of course, that Cox was not with this expedition and did not sail for the Columbia until a year had passed. He had his information from others who rounded Cape Horn on the *Tonquin*. Alexander Ross tells a similar story, but in a less expanded treatment. See Ross, *First Settlers*, 18.

[5] Huntington adds: "While becalmed here, we measured the velocity of the current setting east, which we found to be about three miles an hour" (p. 50).

The wind soon changed and a storm followed. We sailed in view of the Diego Ramírez Islands and saw a schooner. The distance that we had come since our departure from New York was, according to the calculation that I had made of the ship's course, some 9,165 miles.

We had frightful weather until December 24, when we found ourselves in 58° 16″ of South Latitude.

Although we were then in the very midst of summer [in the Southern Hemisphere], and the days were much longer than they are in Quebec on June 21, the cold was nevertheless greater and the air very humid.[6] For several days the mercury stood at four degrees below zero, by the Fahrenheit thermometer. If such is the temperature in these latitudes at the end of December, what must it be at the end of June—that is to say, during the shortest days of the year. And where then can the Patagonians [who live at the southern tip of South America], or the inhabitants of the Archipelagoes take refuge—so improperly named, the Land of Fire!

The wind that until the twenty-fourth [of December] had been contrary, swung to the south and we sailed westward. The next day, Christmas Day, we had the satisfaction of learning that we were west of the Cape [that is, in the Pacific Ocean]. Until that day we had but one man attacked with scurvy, a malady to which those who make long voyages are subject, and which is occasioned by the constant use of salt provisions, by the humidity of the vessel, and by inaction.

From December 25 until January 1 [1811] we were favored with a good wind and ran eighteen degrees to the north in that short space of time. Although it was still cold, the weather was nevertheless agreeable enough.

On the seventeenth, at 10° 50″ South Latitude, we caught several bonitas, an excellent fish.

6 Bibaud adds a footnote: "The nights, which are extremely short, are no darker than those in Canada when the moon is on the horizon and the sky is slightly overcast" (p. 34).

Huntington interpolates parenthetically: "we could read on deck at midnight without artificial light" (p. 50).

We passed the equator on the twenty-third, at 128° 14″ West Longitude. A great many porpoises came round the ship. A storm arose on the twenty-fifth and lasted until the twenty-eighth. The wind shifted to the ESE, scudding us northward, and we drove 222 miles in the next twenty-four hours. Then we had several days of contrary wind. It swung to the SE on February 8, and on the eleventh we saw the peak of a mountain covered with snow, which the first mate, who was familiar with these seas, told me was the summit of Mona-Roah [Mauna Loa], a high mountain on the island of Ohehy [Hawaii], one of those which circumnavigator Cook named the Sandwich Islands and where he met his death in 1779.[7] We headed toward the land all day, and although we made eight or nine knots an hour, it was not until evening that we were near enough to distinguish the huts of the islanders—a fact sufficient to prove how high Mauna Loa stands above level of the sea.

CHAPTER 4

We were ranging along the coast with the aid of a fine breeze, when the boy, Perrault, who had mounted the shrouds the better to distinguish the view of the island, unhappily fell into the sea.[1] We witnessed his fall and threw chairs and barrels

[7] It is interesting to note that Ross Cox used some spellings similar to Franchère's in speaking about Hawaii and its people and countryside, though his variations seem to be an attempt at a phonic spelling on some occasions. See Cox, *Columbia River*, 23ff. The same is true of Alexander Ross's account. See Ross, *First Settlers*, 34ff.

[1] Huntington adds: ". . . and being to windward when the shrouds were taut, rebounded from them like a ball some twenty feet from the ship's side into the ocean" (p. 53). Besides chairs and barrels, Huntington adds "benches, hencoops, in a word everything that we could lay hands on; then the captain gave the orders to heave to; in the twinkling of an eye the lashings of one of the quarterboats were cut apart, the boat was lowered and manned: by this time the boy was considerably astern. He would have been lost undoubtedly but for a wide pair of canvass overalls full of tar and grease, which operated like a lifepreserver. His head, however, was under when he was picked up. . . ." (pp. 53–54). This is only one of a number of instances in which Huntington's addition to the story seems intended to make a scene more dramatic.

Ross's account is somewhat briefer and follows Franchère's. But Ross calls the "boy" Joseph La Pierre, whether an intentional bit of purposed humor one cannot say. See Ross, *First Settlers*, 32.

to him. Then the captain gave the order to put about and we lowered our boat. The boatswain and four others embarked in this and managed to save the young man, about a quarter of an hour after he had fallen into the water. They brought him onto the ship unconscious and lifeless. However, we succeeded in bringing him around quickly enough, and in a few hours he was able to run upon the deck.

The coast of the island, seen from the sea, offers the most picturesque and happiest of views. From the beach to the mountains the land rises gradually, like an amphitheater. All along it is a border of lower country covered with coconut trees and bananas through which one perceives the huts of the islanders. The valleys that cut the more distant hills seemed to be well cultivated; and the mountains themselves, though exceedingly high, are completely covered with woods.

As we ran along the coast, some canoes left the beach and came alongside with vegetables and coconuts; but as we wished to profit by the breeze to gain the anchorage, we did not think it best to stop. We coasted along during a part of the night, but a calm came on and lasted until the next morning. Since we were lying opposite the Bay of Kealakekua, the natives came out again in greater numbers in their canoes, bringing us cabbages, yams, bananas, taro, watermelons, poultry, etc., and we traded with them.[2] Toward evening, by the aid of a breeze that rose from seaward, we got inside the bay, where we anchored on a coral bottom in fourteen fathoms of water.

The next day the islanders visited the ship in great numbers all day long, bringing, as on the day before, fruits, vegetables, and some pigs, in exchange for which we gave them glass beads, iron rings, needles, cotton cloth, and so forth.

Some of our gentlemen went ashore and were astonished to find a native occupied in the construction of a small sloop of about thirty tons. The tools that he used consisted of a worn-out ax, a wretched adz with about a two-inch blade, and an augur

[2] Throughout this chapter, present-day spellings of Hawaiian place names have been utilized.

that was nothing more than an iron rod which he heated red-hot. He must have had great patience and dexterity to accomplish anything with such instruments. He was apparently not deficent in these qualities, for his work was already well advanced. Our people took him on board and we gave him some suitable tools, which he appeared extremely happy to have.

On the morning of the fourteenth [February, 1811], while the ship's carpenter was engaged in replacing one of the catheads, two large composition sheaves fell into the sea. As we had no others to replace them, the captain proposed to the islanders, who are excellent swimmers, to dive for them. He promised a reward if they found them. Immediately two offered themselves to try. They plunged several times, and each time brought up shells to prove that they had been to the bottom. We had the curiosity to hold our watches while they dived and were astonished to find that they remained four minutes under water. This exertion appeared to me, however, to fatigue them a great deal—to such an extent that the blood streamed from their noses and ears. At last one of them brought up the two sheaves and received the promised recompense, which consisted of four yards of cotton.

The Bay of Kealakekua, where we had anchored, is possibly three-fourths of a mile deep and a mile and a half wide at its entrance. The entrance itself is framed by two low points of rock that appear to have poured down from the mountains in the form of lava, following some volcanic eruption. On each of these points is a village of moderate size. The bay is bounded by a rocky, precipitous slope about two hundred feet high, on the top of which grows a lonely coco palm.[3]

In the evening I went ashore with some other passengers, and we landed at a village situated at the western end of the bay that I have just described. The inhabitants entertained us with a dance executed by nineteen young women and one man, all singing together, and in good time.[4] An old man showed us the spot

[3] Huntington says "four hundred feet" (p. 57).
[4] Ross indicates that a number of sailors attempted to desert the ship at Hawaii, hating the tyranny of Captain Thorn. One sailor, with the improbable

24

where Captain Cook was massacred on February 14, 1779, with the coconut trees pierced by the balls fired from the boats that the navigator commanded. This old man, whether it was feigned or real feeling, seemed extremely affected and even shed tears while showing us these objects. As for me, I could not help finding it a little singular to see myself, by mere chance, upon this spot on February 14, 1811; that is, thirty-two years to the day after the catastrophe that made it forever remembered.

I drew no sinister augury from the coincidence, however, and returned to the ship with my companions as gay as I had left it. When I say "with my companions," I ought to except the boatswain, John Anderson. For he had had several altercations with the captain on the passage and now deserted the ship, preferring to live with the natives rather than to obey so discourteous a superior any longer. A sailor also deserted, but at the request of the captain, the natives brought him back. They offered to bring back the boatswain, but the captain refused.

We found no good water near Kealakekua Bay. What the natives brought us in gourds was brackish. We were likewise greatly in need of fresh meat, but could not get any at all. The king of these islands had strictly forbidden his subjects to procure it for any ships that might touch there. However, one of the chiefs sent a canoe to Kailua Bay to try to obtain from the governor of the island, who lived there, permission to sell us some pigs. The messengers returned the next day, bringing us a letter in which the governor requested us to proceed without delay to the island of Oahu where the king resided. We were assured that there we should find fresh water and everything that we needed.

We got under way on the sixteenth, and with a light wind coasted the island as far as Kailua Bay. The wind then dropped away entirely, and the captain, accompanied by Mr. McKay and Mr. McDougall, went ashore to pay a visit to the governor. He was not a native, but a Scotsman by the name of John Young,

name of Jack Tar, went overboard and was never seen again; others were caught and flogged or put in chains below deck. Ross maintains that the fur traders were in this case sympathetic to Thorn and helped man the ship until order could be restored. See Ross, *First Settlers*, 35–36.

who tarried on these islands some years after the death of Captain Cook. He had married a native woman and had so gained the friendship and confidence of the king as to be raised to the rank of chief and made governor of Hawaii, the largest of the Sandwich Islands, both by its extent and by its population.[5] His Excellency explained to our gentlemen why the king had prohibited the trade in hogs to his subjects—His Majesty wished to reserve to himself the monopoly of that branch of commerce in order to have the total profits.

The governor also informed them that no rain had fallen on the south part of Ohehy for three years, a fact that explained why we found so little fresh water. He added in the course of the conversation that the north part of the island was more fertile than the south, where we were; but that there was no good anchorage, for that part of the coast is rimmed by sunken rocks which form heavy breakers. At last the governor dismissed our gentlemen with a present of four fine, fat hogs. We, in return, sent him some tea, coffee, chocolate, and several gallons of wine.

We experienced a calm nearly all the night and on the seventeenth we found ourselves opposite Mona Ouhoroaye [Mauna Kea?], a mountain then covered by snow, like Mauna Loa, but which seemed to me not so high as the latter.[6] A number of natives visited us, as others had earlier, with some curious objects and some small fresh fish. The wind blew up on the eighteenth and we sailed past the western extremity of Ohehy and a short distance from Mowhee and Tahouraha, two other islands of this group said to be quite densely populated. The first presents a very picturesque scene, filled as it is with hills that rise like sugar loaves and are covered by coconut and breadfruit trees. Finally, on the twenty-first, we approached Oahu and cast anchor opposite the bay of Waikiki at a distance of nearly two miles from land.

[5] Huntington interpolates: "after the conquest of Wahoo [Oahu] by King Tamehameha" (p. 60).

[6] Quaife says that the Manuscript reads "'Mont Kea' in place of 'Mona Roah'" (p. 34n). Unaccountably, Bibaud uses the latter spelling.

CHAPTER 5

There is not a single good anchorage in Waikiki Bay outside the reef.[1] Moreover, our captain preferred to remain in the roadstead rather than to expose the ship to the temptation of the natives by lying to inside the reef, whence he could not get out easily. For the rest, the environs of this bay are even more beautiful than those at Karakakona. The mountains in the background are not so formidable, and the soil appears to be more fertile.

Tameamea [Kamehameha], whom all the Sandwich Isles obeyed when we were there in 1811, was neither the son nor the relative of Tierrobou [Kalaniopuu], who reigned in Hawaii in 1779, when Captain Cook and some of his men were massacred. He was then a chief of moderate power; but being skillful, intriguing, and full of ambition, he soon succeeded in gathering a numerous following, and finally gained for himself the sovereign power. As soon as he found himself the master of Hawaii, his native island, he dreamed of subjugating the leeward islands, and in a few years he did so. He even landed on Kauai, the most remote of all, and defeated the ruler of it, but contented himself with imposing an annual tribute upon him. He had established his residence at Oahu because, of all the Sandwich Isles, it was the most fertile, the most picturesque—in a word, the most worthy of the presence of a sovereign.

Upon our arrival, we were visited by a canoe manned by three white men, Davis and Wadsworth, Americans, and Manini, a Spaniard. This last man offered to serve as our interpreter during our stay in Waikiki, an offer that we accepted.

Kamehameha presently sent to us his prime minister, Craimocou [Karaimoku], to whom the Americans have given the name of Pitt because of his skill in affairs of government. Our captain, accompanied by some of our gentlemen, went ashore immediately to be presented to Kamehameha. About four o'clock in the afternoon we saw them returning, accompanied by the

[1] Huntington varies this passage slightly, but makes no substantive changes (p. 62).

king and his suite in a double pirogue. We ran up our colors and saluted his majesty with four cannon shots.

Kamehameha was above average height, well made, robust, and inclined to corpulence, and had a majestic carriage. He appeared to me to be between fifty and sixty years old. He was clothed in the European style, and wore a sword as a side arm. He walked a long time on the deck, asking explanations of those things he had not seen on other ships that were found on ours. A thing that appeared to surprise him was that we could render the sea water fresh by means of the still attached to our canteen. He could not imagine how that was done. We invited him into the cabin and, having regaled him with some glasses of wine, began to talk of business matters. We offered him merchandise in exchange for hogs, but were unable to conclude the bargain that day. His Majesty re-embarked in his double pirogue about six o'clock in the evening. This pirogue was manned by twenty-four men. A large chest containing firearms lay over [straddled] the double canoe, and upon this Kamehameha sat, his prime minister beside him.

We sent our water casks ashore and filled them with good water on the morning of the twenty-second. At midday, His swarthy Majesty paid us another visit, accompanied by his three wives and his court favorite. These females were extraordinarily fat and of unmeasurable size. They were dressed in the fashion of the country, having nothing but a piece of bark-cloth, about six feet in length and about two feet in width, wound about their hips. We resumed the negotiations of the day before and were more successful. I noticed that when the bargain was concluded, the king insisted that part of the payment should be in Spanish dollars. We asked the reason, and he replied that he wished to buy a frigate from his brother, King George, meaning the King of England. The bargain concluded, we prayed His Majesty and his suite to give us the honor of dining with us. They consented, and toward evening retired, apparently well satisfied with their visit and our reception of them.

In the meantime, the natives surrounded the ship in great

numbers, with hundreds of canoes, offering us their goods in exchange for merchandise.[2] But they had also brought intoxicating liquors in gourds, and some of the crew got drunk. The captain was obliged to suspend the trade, and forbade anyone to traffic with the islanders except through the first mate, who was alone charged with that business.

I landed on the twenty-second with Messrs. Pillet and Mc-Gillis. We spent the night ashore, and on the following morning we strolled all over the bay area, followed by a crowd of men, women, and children.

Waikiki, where Kamehameha resides, and which consequently may be regarded as the capital of his kingdom, is, or at least was then, a moderate-sized town or rather a large village. Besides the private houses, of which there were perhaps two hundred, there were the royal palace, which was nothing magnificent; the king's storehouse, of two stories, one stone and the other wood; two morais [burial grounds]; and a little wharf. Near the latter we found an old ship, the *Lilly Bird* [*Lelia Byrd*], which some American navigators had given in exchange for a schooner. It was the only large ship that King Kamehameha possessed, and was worth nothing. As for schooners, he had forty of them, in size from twenty to thirty tons. These served to transport the tributes in kind paid by his vassals in the other islands. Before the arrival of Europeans among these savages, they could not communicate from one island to another except by means of their canoes, since the islands are not in sight of each other. Near the king's palace we found an Indian from Bombay busy making a twelve-inch cable for use by the ship that I have just mentioned.

Kamehameha kept a guard of twenty-four men constantly round his house. As a uniform these soldiers wore a long blue coat faced with yellow, and each had a musket. In front of the house, on a square in the parade ground, were fourteen four-pound cannons, mounted on their little carriages.

The king exercised absolute authority and himself judged

2 Huntington interpolates: "in the shape of eatables and the rude manufactures of the island . . ." (p. 66).

the differences that arose among his subjects. We had occasion to witness this fact on the day after we landed on the island. A Portuguese had quarrelled with a somewhat intoxicated native, going so far as to strike him. Immediately the compatriots of the latter, who had, after all, been the aggressor, gathered in a crowd to stone the poor foreigner. The poor foreigner fled as fast as he could to the king's house, followed by the mob of furious island-ers, who stopped some distance [from the king's house] while the Portuguese, out of breath, crouched in a corner. We were on the esplanade, just opposite the royal palace. We stood close to His Majesty, who, having learned of the nature of the quarrel and having listened to witnesses for both parties, condemned the native to work four days in the garden of the Portuguese and to give him a pig. A young Frenchman from Bordeaux—tutor for the king's sons, whom he taught to read–who knew the native tongue, served as interpreter for the Portuguese and explained to us the sentence that had been handed down.

I cannot say whether our presence influenced this judgment, or whether, under other circumstances, the Portuguese might have been treated less favorably. We were given to understand that Kamehameha was pleased to have white men settle in his domain, but that he esteemed only those who had a trade and looked upon idlers and drunkards with contempt. At Oahu we saw about thirty of these individuals, from all nations, and most-ly people without recognition and without character. They had remained in these islands because of idleness, or drunkenness, or debauchery. They had managed to procure a small still and furnished the natives with liquor.

The first European navigators found only four kinds of quadrupeds on the Hawaiian Islands: dogs, pigs, lizards, and rats. Since then sheep, horses, and cattle have been brought there and these animals have multiplied.

The chief vegetable crops of these isles are the sugar cane, the banana, the bread-fruit tree, the watermelon, the muskmelon, the taro, the ava, the Pandanus, the pumpkin, and so forth. The bread-fruit tree is about the size of a young apple tree. The fruit resembles an apple and is about twelve or fourteen inches in circumference. The rind is rough, like a melon, and when cut transversely it is found to be full of sacs, like the inside of an orange. The pulp has the consistency of watermelon and is cooked before it is eaten. We saw orchards of bread-fruit trees and bananas and fields of sugar cane back of Waikiki.

The taro grows in the lowlands and demands much care.[3] This dry root, ground and reduced to a *flom* (or meal) makes, along with the bread fruit, the principal food of the natives. Sometimes they boil the taro roots and reduce them to a kind of thick soup that they allow to sour. This they put into jars and serve as they need it. The skill these natives have in preparing food is extraordinary. In our presence they caught a suckling pig, killed it, and roasted it—all in an hour and a half.

The ava is a plant more injurious than useful to the inhabitants of these islands. They use it only to make a dangerous and intoxicating drink that they also call ava. Here is the way they make this beverage: they chew the root, and spit the juice into a jar; the juice thus obtained is exposed to the sun to ferment, after which they let it trickle into another jar. The ava is then made, and they drink it, on occasion, to drunkenness. Too frequent use of this disgusting liquor causes the loss of their sight and gives them a sort of leprosy which can be cured only by abstaining from the ava and by bathing frequently in the water of the sea. This leprosy turns their skin white. We saw several of the lepers who were also blind, or nearly so.

The natives are also fond of smoking. Tobacco grows in the islands, but I think it has been transplanted from elsewhere. The bark of the mulberry tree furnishes the most common cloth, and the leaves of the Pandanus, or pine, serve as their mats.[4]

The men are generally well made and tall. They wear for

[3] At this point Huntington adds a full paragraph about the nature of taro and about its culture as a basic food of the natives. His explanation regarding its preparation for consumption varies from the Bibaud rendering (See pp. 71–72).

[4] Huntington adds: "They have also a kind of wax-nut, about the size of a dried plum of which they make candles by running a stick through several of them. Lighted at one end, they burn like a wax taper, and are the only light they use in their huts at night" (p. 73).

31

their entire clothing a garment they call a *maro*. It is a piece of figured or white tapa, two yards long and a foot wide, which they pass around the loins and between the legs, tying the ends on the hips. At first sight I thought that they painted their bodies red, but soon perceived that red was the natural color of their skin. The women wear a kind of skirt made from the same material as the *maro*, wider and longer, but not reaching below the knees. They have sufficiently regular features and but for their color may pass, generally speaking, for beautiful women. Some, to heighten their charms, dye their hair, forming around the head an inch-wide strip of white resembling, at a distance, a bow of ribbons.[5] They are quite wanton and display almost no modesty, especially with strangers.[6] As for articles of mere finery, it is said that they are not the same on all the islands.

I did not see them dressed in their war gear or in their ceremonial clothing. But I had occasion to see them paint their tapa, or bark-cloth, an occupation with which they take great care and patience. Their paints are made from the juices of trees, prepared with the oil from the coconut. Their brushes are little bamboo canes, at the ends of which they ingeniously carve various sorts of flowers. First they coat the cloth they are going to paint with a yellow or green or some other color. This forms a background. Then they draw some very straight lines, without using any instrument and with only their eyes serving as guides. Afterward, between these lines they apply the ends of the canes mentioned above, filling in with colors different from the background. These materials closely resemble the cloth of our Indians and our own colored cotton cloths. The oil with which they are soaked makes them impervious to water. It is said that the natives of Atoüy surpass all the others in the art of cloth-painting.

[5] Huntington adds that this decoration "disfigures them monstrously" (p. 74).

[6] Ross gives a different picture: "The women are handsome in person, engaging in their manners, well featured and have countenances full of joy and tranquility, but chastity is not their virtue." Ross, *First Settlers*, 51. Ross's views appear to be more romantic than Franchère's about all matters concerned with the Hawaiian Islanders. However, Huntington's propensity for moralizing and his obvious puritanism may account for the heavy critical hand he lays upon the aborigines, whether in Hawaii or on the West Coast.

The Sandwich Islanders live in villages or towns of perhaps one or two hundred houses arranged without symmetry—or, rather, grouped in complete disorder. These houses are constructed with posts driven into the ground, bound at the ends and covered with grass, so that they look like our Canadian barns. The size of each house varies with the needs of the people who occupy it. They are not smoky at all, like the wigwams of our Indians on the continent, since fires are always made outside.

Their pirogues or canoes are remarkably well constructed. The wood is light and quite slender. The single canoe has a balancing-pole which is nothing more than two strips of wood, curved and securely tied about a third of the way from the boat's bow so that [the ends] lie even with the water. Another strip, curved and tied to the first two and trailing in the water, keeps the canoe in balance by its weight. Without this [device] the canoe would doubtless capsize. Their paddles, or oars, are long and broad. All these canoes carry a lateen sail which is an exceptionally well-woven matting of grass or leaves.[7]

I did not remain with these people long enough to acquire very extensive and accurate ideas about their religion. I know that they recognize a Supreme Being, whom they call Eatoüa, and a number of subordinate divinities. Each village has one or more morais. These morais are enclosures that serve for cemeteries; in the middle of each one is a temple which only the priests have a right to enter. The temples themselves contain several idols or statues of wood, rudely sculptured. At the feet of these images the offerings of the people are deposited and left to putrefy—dogs, pigs, fowls, vegetables, and so forth. The respect of these savages for their priests amounts almost to adoration. They regard their persons as sacred and feel the greatest scruple against touching the objects or going near the places that the priests have declared taboo or forbidden. The taboo has often been useful to European navigators, by freeing them from the importunities of the crowd.

[7] Huntington's description varies considerably from Bibaud's at this point (p. 76).

In traversing Waikiki, we saw several groups of natives play-ing different games. Checkers appeared to be the most common. The ground itself, squared off with a pointed stick, served as a checkerboard. Little pebbles served as men. Since the games are different from those played in civilized countries, we could not understand them.

Although nature has done nearly everything to bring hap-piness to the inhabitants of the Sandwich Islands, although they enjoy a serene sky, a healthful atmosphere, and although the land requires almost no care in producing all the necessities of life, they cannot, even then, be regarded as a happy people generally.[8] The artisans and farmers, who are called *Toutous*, are much like the Helots among the Lacedemonians, condemned to work al-most continually for their lords, or *Eris*, without hope of com-pensation and restricted even in the choice of their foods.[9]

How can it be that among a still uncivilized people where the intelligence of everyone is about the same, the class which is unquestionably the most numerous voluntarily submits to such a humiliating and oppressive yoke?[10] The Tartars, though in-finitely less numerous, have enslaved the Chinese because the former were warriors and the latter were not. The same thing undoubtedly happened in more ancient times in Sarmatia and in other European and Asian regions. If physical and moral causes are included, the superiority of one caste and the inferi-ority of the other are even more marked. It is common knowl-edge that the natives of the island of Haiti, seeing the Spaniards

8 Ross gives a generalized picture of the lives of the islanders as "all primeval simplicity and happiness." But, he says dismally, "civilized man has now begun to trade on its [Hawaii's] innocent and peaceful soil," thereby offering a view somewhat reminiscent of Herman Melville's in *Omoo* and *Typee*. See Ross, *First Settlers*, 55.

9 Bibaud states in a footnote: "The Toutous and their wives, except for the wives of the king, are condemned eternally to feed themselves on fruits and vege-tables. Dogs and pigs are reserved solely for the mouths of the *Eris*" (p. 58). Hunt-ington reprints this footnote (p. 78).

10 Quaife maintains that the remainder of this chapter was added by Bibaud, but apparently he made no comparison to the Manuscript at this point in order to be certain.

on their shores imitating lightning and thunder with their cannons, took them for beings far superior to themselves.

Assuming that this island had been far removed from any other country and that the Spaniards, after conquering it, had not communicated with any civilized nation, at the end of a century or two the language and the customs would become nearly the same [among them]. Still, there would be two classes, one of lords enjoying all the advantages, the other of serfs, charged with all the burdens. This theory seems to have been recognized in ancient Hindustan.

But if one can accept the legend of the Sandwich Islanders, their country was peopled originally by a man and woman who arrived in Hawaii in a canoe. Thus, unless they mean that this man and woman came with their slaves and that the *Eris* are descended from the first [couple] and the *Toutous* from the last [slaves], they ought to regard themselves as all of the same origin —as equals and even as brothers, in the manner of thinking among savages. The reason for the slavery of women, common among most uncivilized peoples, is easily explained. Men have subjugated them by virtue of greater strength when ignorance and superstition have not already caused them to look upon women as being by nature inferior, created to be their servants rather than their companions.[11]

CHAPTER 6

We stocked a hundred pigs, some goats, two sheep, a quantity of poultry, two boat-loads of sugar cane as food for the pigs, two boat-loads of yams, taro, and other vegetables; and with all our water casks on board, we raised anchor on February 28, sixteen days after we arrived at Kealakekua Bay. As we got under way, Mr. McKay remarked to the captain that we still had an

11 Bibaud adds a footnote: "Some tribes in America think that women have no souls but die altogether like animals. Others assign them a paradise different from that for men" (p. 60) . Huntington extends the footnote by adding: ". . . which indeed they might have reason to prefer for themselves, unless their relative condition were to be ameliorated in the next world" (p. 80n.).

empty water cask and proposed sending it to the watering place and having it filled. The great number of live animals that we had aboard required a large amount of fresh water.[1]

The captain feared that some of his crew would desert if he sent them ashore. He told this to Mr. McKay, who thereupon proposed sending me, in a pirogue which was alongside the ship, with the cask in question. The captain agreed to this arrangement, and I set off for the watering place. After I had filled the cask—not without difficulty—the islanders sought to detain me; and having noticed that they had given me some gourds filled with salt water, I asked for a double pirogue in order to go aboard again.

The ship was under way and already in the offing. As the natives did not hurry to respond to my request, I thought it necessary to go myself—and I went, in fact—to the king. Aware of the captain's temperament, I began to fear that he had planned to leave me on the island. My fears, however, were groundless.

[1] Apparently further to discredit Captain Thorn, Huntington added the following passage to the 1854 edition: "We left another man (Edward Aymes) at Owahou. He belonged to a boat's crew which was sent ashore for a load of sugar canes. By the time the boat was loaded by the natives the ebb of the tide had left her aground, and Aymes asked leave of the coxswain to take a stroll, engaging to be back for the flood. Leave was granted him, but during his absence, the tide having come in sufficiently to float the boat, James Thorn, the coxswain, did not wait for the young sailor, who was thus left behind. The captain immediately missed the man, and on being informed that he had strolled away from the boat on leave, flew into a violent passion. Aymes soon made his appearance alongside, having hired some natives to take him on board; on perceiving him, the Captain ordered him to stay in the long-boat, then lashed to the side with its load of sugar cane. The Captain then himself got into the boat, and, taking one of the canes, beat the poor fellow most unmercifully with it; after which, not satisfied with this act of brutality, he seized his victim and threw him overboard! Aymes, however, being an excellent swimmer, made for the nearest native canoe, of which there were, as usual, a great number around the ship. The Islanders, more humane than our Captain, took in the poor fellow, who, in spite of his entreaties to be received on board, could only succeed in getting his clothes, which were thrown into the canoe. At parting, he told Captain Thorn that he knew enough of the laws of his country to obtain redress, should they ever meet in the territory of the American Union" (pp. 81–83).

Alexander Ross calls the man Emms and gives an even harsher portrait of the Captain. Moreover, he portrays the first mate, Ebenezer D. Fox, as a humane man who attempted to intervene. Fox helped Emms by surreptitiously throwing the poor chap his clothes and "protection papers" and signalling the natives to get him ashore. See Ross, *First Settlers*, 46–47.

The ship turned landward, to my great relief, and a double pirogue was sent to me so that I could return aboard with the water cask.[2]

Our deck was now as much encumbered as when we left New York. We had been obliged to place our live animals at the gangways, where we had shelters, and we had to go around these shelters in order to maneuver the ship. The number of men had also been augmented, for we had employed some islanders for the service of our trading post. Their term of engagement was three years, during which time we were to feed and clothe them, and at its expiration they were to receive a hundred dollars in merchandise. The captain had engaged about a dozen to serve on board.

These men, who make good sailors, seemed very eager to serve us, and we could have taken on a much greater number.

We had contrary winds until March 2. Then, doubling the western extremity of the island, we sailed northward and lost sight of these smiling and temperate countries to enter, very soon, a colder region and one less worthy of being inhabited.

The winds were variable and nothing eventful happened until the sixteenth when, at 35° 11″ North Latitude and 138° 16″ West Longitude, the wind shifted suddenly to SSW and blew so violently that we had to haul in topgallant and topsails and run before the gale with our foresail, which had scarcely six feet out to the wind. The rolling of the ship was far greater than in all the preceding storms. However, we made good headway; and as we were approaching the continent, the captain, by way of precaution, lay to for two nights successively. At last, on the morning of the twenty-second, we saw land. Although we had not been able to take any observations for several days, nevertheless, by the appearance of the coast, we saw that we were near the mouth of the Columbia River and not more than three miles from land. The breakers formed by the bar at the entrance to the river, which we could distinguish from the ship, left us no room to doubt that we had arrived, finally, at the end of our voyage.

2 Huntington varies the text slightly without, it seems to me, improving it.

The wind was blowing in great blasts and the sea ran very high. In spite of that, the captain had a boat lowered, and taking some provisions and firearms Mr. Fox (first mate), Basile Lepensée, Ignace Lapensée, Joseph Nadeau, and John Martin got into her, with orders to sound the channel. The boat was not even supplied with a good sail, but one of our gentlemen offered a bed sheet to serve instead. Messrs. McKay and McDougall could not help remonstrating with the captain on the foolhardiness of sending the boat ashore in such weather, but they could not move his obstinacy. The boat pulled away from the ship. Alas! We were never to see it again, and we already had forebodings about it.[3] The next day the wind seemed to moderate and we approached quite near to the coast.

The entrance to the river, which we easily distinguished, appeared but a confused and agitated sea. The waves, impelled by a wind from the offing, broke upon the bar, and left no perceptible passage. We saw no sign of our men's boat and toward evening we hauled off to sea. All countenances were extremely sad, not excepting that of the captain who appeared to me as much afflicted as the rest, and who had reason to be so. During the night the wind fell, the clouds dispersed, and the sky became serene. On the morning of the twenty-fourth we found that the current had carried us near the coast again, and we anchored in fourteen fathoms of water, north of Cape Disappointment. The general aspect is not nearly as pleasant at this spot as in the Sandwich Islands. The coast offers little but a range of high mountains covered with snow.

Although it was calm, the sea between Cape Disappointment and Point Adams continued to break violently over the bar. We sent Mr. Mumford (the second mate) to take a sounding, but he found the breakers too heavy and returned on board about midday. Messrs. Alexander McKay and David Stuart offered to go

[3] Ross gives a far more detailed description of the action here, is severely critical of Captain Thorn, and has Mr. Fox say to the Canadians, when he is about to be lowered to take soundings: "My uncle was drowned here not many years ago, and now I am going to lay my bones with his," a statement all too prophetic. Ross, *First Settlers*, 60.

ashore to search for our men who had left on the twenty-second, but they could not find a place to land. They saw Indians who made signs to them to pull around the Cape, but they deemed it wiser to return to the ship. Soon afterward, a gentle breeze sprang up from the northwest, we raised anchor, and approached the river entrance. Mr. Aitken then embarked in the pinnace, accompanied by John Coles, Stephen Weeks, and two Sandwich Islanders, and we followed under light sail. Another boat had been sent out before this one, but the captain judged that she bore too far south and signalled her to return. Mr. Aitken found no less than four fathoms. We followed him and advanced between the breakers with a favorable wind, and passed the boat on our starboard, within pistol shot.

We signaled her to return but she could not manage to do so. The rapid current carried her with such great speed that in a few minutes we had lost sight of her.[4] It was near nightfall, the wind began to fall off, and the water was so low with the ebb that we struck six or seven times. The breakers swept over the ship and threatened to submerge her. At last we passed from two and three-quarter fathoms of water to seven, where we were obliged to drop anchor, for the wind had entirely failed us. We were, however, far from being out of danger, and darkness came to add to the horror of our situation. Our ship, though at anchor, threatened to be carried away by the tide every moment and we worked part of the night to prepare anchor and mooring.[5]

However, Providence came to our rescue. The flood succeeded the ebb; and when the wind rose out of the offing we weighed anchor, in spite of the obscurity of the night. Finally we succeeded in reaching a little bay, called Baker's Bay, formed at the entrance of the river by Cape Disappointment. Here we found a good anchorage. It was nearly midnight, and all retired to take

4 Huntington interpolates: ". . . amidst the tremendous breakers that surrounded us" (p. 89). Here is an addition typical of a great number made by Huntington. I shall not cite each one separately.

5 Again, typically, Huntington varies by adding: ". . . the best bower was to let go, and it kept two men at the wheel to hold her head in the right direction" (pp. 89–90).

a little rest. The crew, above all, had need of it. We were fortunate to be in a place of safety, for the wind rose higher and higher during the remainder of the night and on the morning of the twenty-fifth allowed us to see that this ocean is not always pacific.

Some natives visited us this day, with beaver skins; but the uneasiness caused in our minds by the loss of our men, for whom we wished to make a search, did not permit us to think of traffic. We tried with signs to make the savages comprehend that we had sent a boat ashore three days previously, and that we had no news of her; but they seemed not to understand us. The captain and our gentlemen debarked and set themselves to search for our missing people in the woods along the seashore. Soon we saw the captain returning with Stephen Weeks, one of those on the last boat sent out.[6] He gave us an account of his almost miraculous escape from the waves on the preceding night, in nearly the following words:

"After you had passed our boat," he said, "the breakers caused by the meeting of the wind-roll and ebb-tide became a great deal heavier than when we entered the river. The boat, for lack of rudder, became very hard to manage. We let her drift at the mercy of the tide until, after we had escaped several surges, one wave struck midship and capsized us. I lost sight of Mr. Aitken and John Coles, but the two islanders were close by me. I saw them stripping off their clothes. I did the same, and seeing the pinnace within my reach, keel upward, I seized it. The two natives came to my assistance, we righted her, and by pushing her from behind we threw out so much of the water that she would hold a man. One of the natives jumped in, bailed with his two hands, and succeeded in a short time in emptying her. The other native found the oars and about dark we were all three embarked.

6 Again, Ross's story is somewhat different. Ross maintains that he was on the search party, and that Weeks accused them all of passing up the sounding boat intentionally. Ross also dramatizes Thorn's efforts to get the *Tonquin* over the bar and into safe harbor at the mouth of the Columbia. See Ross, *First Settlers*, 66–68. One gets the impression that Franchère was everywhere much more restrained and possibly more objective than Ross, but a comparison of the two is interesting despite the fact that the Ross account was not published until 1849.

"The tide now carried us outside the breakers. I endeavored to persuade my companions in misfortune to row, but they were so benumbed with cold that they absolutely refused. I well knew that without clothing and exposed to the rigor of the air, I needed to keep exercising. Besides, night was coming; and without any resource but the little strength left me, I set to work sculling, and pushed off the bar, but so as not to be carried too far out to sea. About midnight, one of my companions died. The other threw himself upon the body of his comrade, and I could not persuade him to abandon it. Daylight appeared at last; and, as we were near land, I headed for the beach where I arrived on a stretch of sand, thank God, safe and sound. I helped the islander, who still showed some signs of life, out of the boat, and I made my way with him to the woods. But as he was not able to follow me, I left him to his bad fortune. Then, following a beaten path that I perceived, in a few hours I found myself, to my great astonishment, near the ship."

The gentlemen who went ashore with the captain divided themselves into three parties to search for the native whom Weeks had left at the entrance of the forest. But after scouring the woods and the point of the Cape all day, they came on board in the evening without having found him.

PART II

𒀭𒀭𒀭𒀭𒀭𒀭𒀭𒀭𒀭𒀭𒀭𒀭𒀭𒀭𒀭𒀭𒀭𒀭𒀭𒀭𒀭𒀭𒀭𒀭𒀭𒀭𒀭𒀭𒀭𒀭𒀭𒀭𒀭𒀭𒀭𒀭𒀭𒀭

Astoria Enterprise

CHAPTER 7

STEPHEN WEEKS' story told us of the death of three of our companions, and we could not doubt that the five others had met a similar fate. This loss of eight of our number in two days, before we had set foot on shore, was a bad augury, and we felt it very keenly. In the course of so long a voyage, the habit of seeing each other every day, living in the same quarters, busy with the same duties, and facing the same dangers, had formed among all the passengers a connection that could not be broken—above all in a manner so sad and so unexpected. We felt a void like that experienced in a strongly united family when it is suddenly deprived by death of one of its members. We had left New York for the greater part strangers to one another; but by the time we arrived at the Columbia River, we were all friends and regarded each other almost as brothers.

We especially regretted the loss of the two Lapensées and Joseph Nadeau. At their departure from Montreal, these young men had been entrusted by their parents to the particular care of Mr. McKay, and by their good conduct they had acquired the esteem of the captain, the crew, and all the passengers. The brothers Lapensée were second to none of their companions in action, in courage, and in their good will.[1] Messrs. Ebenezer D.

[1] Huntington varies the statement by saying that the brothers Lapensée "were courageous and willing, never flinching in the hour of danger, and had become as good seamen as any on board" (p. 95).

Fox and Job Aitken were both highly regarded by all. The loss of Mr. Fox, particularly, would have been regretted at any time, but it was doubly so in the present situation.[2] For this gentleman, who had already made a journey to the Northwest, could have rendered important services to the captain and to the company. The preceding days had been times of apprehension and uneasiness; this was one of sorrow and mourning.

Early on the following day, the same gentlemen who had searched in vain for the missing islander resumed their labors, and very soon we saw a great fire kindled not far from the ship. I was sent in a boat and arrived at the fire. It was our gentlemen, who had kindled it to revive the islander whom they had at last found under the rocks, half-dead with cold and fatigue, his legs swollen and his feet bleeding. We clothed him and brought him on board, where, with much care, we succeeded in restoring him to life.

Toward evening, a number of Sandwich Islanders, provided with the necessary implements and offerings consisting of biscuit, lard, and tobacco, went ashore to pay last homage to their compatriot who died in Mr. Aitken's boat during the night of the twenty-fourth. Mr. Pillet and I followed them and witnessed the obsequies which took place somewhat after the following manner: Arrived at the place where the body had been hung from a tree, the islanders set about digging a grave of suitable proportions in the sand. Then they took the body from the tree, put the biscuit under one of the arms, the lard under the chin, and the tobacco under the genitals. The body, thus prepared for the journey into another world, was laid into the grave and covered with sand and stones.

[2] Huntington adds words praising Ebenezer Fox as a man "who was endeared to everyone by his gentlemanly behavior and affability" (p. 95). These additions do not, in my opinion, improve the 1854 edition. In fact, to some readers the earlier version is more direct and forceful. Alexander Ross, however, adds reality by having his characters speak, as on a stage, and so has a more dramatic effect—although as to his accuracy one may have some doubts. It should be kept in mind that when he published his book, Ross was thirty-eight years removed from the time when the action took place; by 1854, when his second edition was published, Franchère was even farther away.

43

The compatriots of the dead man afterward knelt along the grave in a double row, faces turned to the east—with the exception of one among them who officiated as a priest. This latter went to get water in his hat, sprinkled the two rows of islanders and recited a kind of prayer to which the others responded somewhat after the manner in which we respond in the litanies in our churches at home. When the prayer was finished they got up and returned to the ship without once looking back. As each of them appeared, in fact, in a role that he played, it is very likely that they observed, so far as circumstances permitted, the ceremonies practiced in their own country on such occasions. Toward dusk, we went on board again.

The next day, the twenty-seventh, we unloaded the remaining animals and put them in the charge of one of the men.[3]

On the thirtieth, the longboat was armed, and the captain, Messrs. McKay and David Stuart, and a few of the clerks boarded her to go upriver and choose a spot suitable for the construction of a trading post. At the same time, Messrs. Alexander Ross and Benjamin Pillet left to survey the coast southward, trying to find out whether or not anyone in Mr. Fox's party might have escaped the shipwreck. We [on board] were ourselves occupied during this time in trading with the Indians who came to the ship every day with beaver, otter, sea otter skins, and so forth. Messrs. Ross and Pillet returned on board on April 1, without having learned anything about Mr. Fox and his party. They did not see any vestiges of the boat along the beach, but the natives who occupy Point Adams, who are called Clatsops, received our young gentlemen very amicably and hospitably. The captain and his companions also returned on the fourth, without having decided where to establish the post. They had not found a place that seemed propitious for this trading structure.

We therefore resolved to explore the south bank; and Messrs. Duncan McDougall and David Stuart departed on that expedi-

[3] Huntington varies by saying, "The next day, the 27th, desirous of clearing the gangways of the live stock, we sent some men on shore to construct a pen, and soon after landed about fifty hogs, committing them to the care of one of the hands" (p. 98).

44

tion the next day, promising to return by the seventh. But that day came and these gentlemen did not return. It rained almost all day. On the eighth, some natives came on board and reported that Messrs. McDougall and Stuart had capsized the evening before, while crossing the bay. This news at first alarmed us, and if it had been verified, it would have completely discouraged us. However, since the weather was extremely bad and since we did not have complete confidence in the story the natives told us (whom, besides, we may not have understood perfectly), we lived in suspense until the tenth. On the morning of that day, we were planning to send some of the people in search of our gentlemen when we saw two large canoes coming toward the ship. They were natives of the Chinook tribe living to the north, and they were bringing back Messrs. McDougall and Stuart.

We told these gentlemen the report we had heard from the Indians, and they informed us that it had been, in fact, well-founded. On the seventh, desirous of reaching the ship as they had promised, they had left Chinook Point, in spite of the remonstrances of the chief, Concomly, who sought to detain them by warning them of the danger to which they would expose themselves by crossing the bay in such a great wind as then blew in. They had made scarcely more than half a mile before a wave broke over their boat and capsized it. The Indians, aware of the danger, had followed, and but for them, Mr. McDougall, who could not swim, would surely have drowned. After the Chinooks had kindled a large fire and dried their clothes, they led them back to the village. The principal chief received them with all possible hospitality, regaling them with the best he could offer. In fact, if they had got back safe and sound to the ship, they owed it to the timely aid and humane care of the Indians whom we saw before us. We liberally rewarded these generous children of nature, and they returned home well satisfied. Thus the expedition of Messrs. McDougall and Stuart to find an advantageous site to build upon was unsuccessful.

Nevertheless, we resolved to establish ourselves on Point George, about twelve or fourteen miles from Cape Disappointment, because the captain wished to take advantage of the fine season to pursue his traffic with the natives along the coast. Accordingly, on the twelfth a dozen of us embarked in a longboat, furnished with tools and with provisions for a week. We landed at the bottom of a small bay, where we formed a sort of encampment. Springtime, usually so tardy in this latitude, was already far advanced. Leaves were beginning to appear and the earth was clothing itself with verdure. The weather was superb and all nature smiled. We imagined ourselves to be in an earthly paradise—the forests looked like pleasant groves, the leaves like brilliant flowers. Without doubt, the pleasure of knowing that we had reached the end of our voyage, free from the ship, made things appear even more beautiful than they really were.

However that may be, we set ourselves to work with enthusiasm and in a few days cleared a point of land covered by underbrush and half-burned tree trunks. The ship came to anchor near our encampment and the trade went on. The natives visited us constantly and in great numbers, some to trade, others out of pure curiosity or to purloin some little articles when they found an opportunity. We landed the frame timbers that we had brought, ready cut, in the ship. By the end of the month we had laid the keel of a coasting-schooner of about thirty tons.[4]

4 Huntington says: ". . . by the end of April, with the aid of the ship carpenters, John Weeks and Johann Koaster . . ." (p. 103). It is of interest to note that Ross expands upon the building of this thirty-ton schooner and takes occasion to comment: "It would have made a cynic smile to see this pioneer corps, composed of traders, shopkeepers, voyageurs, and Owhyhees [Hawaiians], all ignorant alike in this new walk of life, and the most ignorant of all, the leader [McDougall]. Many of the party had never handled an axe before and but few of them knew how to use a gun, but necessity, the mother of invention, soon taught us both." Ross, *First Settlers,* 78–79. Ross's strong antipathy toward McDougall may have been the result of his not rising to a full partnership in later years. But he was stretching a point to say that so many of these men, some of them experienced men of the woods and trails, were innocent of the uses of ax or gun. That it would require *voyageurs,* for example, two days to fell a tree seems to be something of an exaggeration. Ross mentions the death of three men in the expedition, the wounding of two others by falling trees, and the loss still another suffered when his hand was blown off by gunpowder. See Ross, *First Settlers,* 80–81. Franchère says nothing of any of these losses or accidents.

Ross also mentions McDougall's ineptness in the handling of his men, the internal conflicts in the trading party, and the lack of any kind of medical assist-

CHAPTER 8

The Indians informed us that above certain rapids there was an establishment of white men. We had no doubt that it was a trading post of the North West Company. Finally, to make sure, we procured a large canoe and a guide, and set out on May 2— Messrs. Alexander McKay, Robert Stuart, Ovide Montigny, and I—with a sufficient number of men. We first passed a point of land that we named Tongue Point.[1] At this spot the river is about ten miles in width. On the left bank, where we were, there are some little low islands, and we camped at an early hour at the village of Wakaicum, the native village of our guide. We continued our journey on the third. The river narrows considerably about thirty miles from its mouth and is obstructed with islands covered with willows, poplars, alders, and ash. Without exception, these islands are uninhabited and uninhabitable, for they are only swamps and are inundated during the months of June and July. So said our guide, Coalpo, who seemed to be an intelligent man.

As we advanced, we saw high mountains, which offer a stern aspect from the river mouth, recede, and give place to a low and level terrain rising on either bank of the stream.[2] We passed a large village, called Kreluit, and encamped for the night on a low point at the foot of an isolated rock about one hundred and fifty feet high. This rock seemed to me remarkable because of its situation. Its base rests upon a low and marshy terrain and ap-

ance for the sick or wounded. He indicates that threats of desertion were made and in some instances carried out, though the deserters were brought back (pp. 82-83). Franchère reports nothing of McDougall's ineptness and makes no complaint about the care of the men. He does tell about one or two attempts at desertion, and seems to hold the deserters culpable.

1 Huntington interpolates: "a lofty headland, that seemed at a distance to be detached from the main, and to which we gave the name *Tongue Point*" (p. 104).

2 Huntington varies and adds to this passage: "In proportion as we advanced, we saw the high mountains capped with snow, which form the chief and majestic feature, though a stern one, of the banks of the Columbia for some distance from its mouth, recede, and give place to a country of moderate elevation, and rising amphitheatrically from the margin of the stream. The river narrows to a mile or thereabouts; the forest is less dense, and patches of green prairie are seen" (p. 105).

pears to have no relationship at all to the neighboring mountains.[3] It is on this rock that most of the Indians in the surrounding area come to bury their dead. It is the same rock to which Lieutenant Broughton gave the name Mount Coffin.

On the morning of the fourth we arrived at a large village of [people of] the same name as those we had passed the evening before, and we landed to obtain information about a little river that empties into the Columbia here.[4] It comes from the north and is called the Cowlitz by the natives. Mr. McKay embarked with Mr. Montigny and two Indians to examine the course of this river a certain distance upstream. On entering it, they saw a great number of birds that they thought at first were turkeys, which they resembled, but which were only a kind of eagles commonly called turkey-buzzards. We were astonished to see Mr. Montigny return on foot and alone. He informed us that after ascending the Cowlitz about a mile and a half, on rounding a bend of the stream they suddenly came in sight of about twenty canoes full of Indians who made a rush upon them with the most frightful cries and screams.

The two natives and the guide who conducted their little canoe retreated as quickly as possible, but seeing that they would be overtaken, they stopped short and begged Mr. McKay to fire upon these savages. He had no wish to do that; but putting into land, he made signs to the Indians to come to him and they did so.

Mr. McKay had sent Mr. Montigny to find some tobacco and a pipe in order to strike a peace with these barbarians. The latter then returned to Mr. McKay with the necessary articles, and in the evening the party came back to the camp we had set up between the two villages. We were then informed that the Indians Mr. McKay had met were at war with the Kreluit villagers. It was impossible to close our eyes all night. The natives passed and repassed continually from one village to another, making fearful cries and coming every minute to beg us to dis-

[3] Following this, the next sentence in Huntington begins: "On a cornice or shelving projection about thirty feet from its base . . ." (p. 106).
[4] Huntington varies this passage slightly, but adds nothing to its effect.

charge our firearms–all to frighten their enemies and show that they were on their guard.

We paid a visit to the hostile camp on the morning of the fifth; and those savages who had never seen white men regarded us with astonishment and curiosity, lifting our trousers and opening our shirts to see if the skin of our bodies resembled that of our faces and hands. We remained with them for some time, to make proposals of peace, and we assured ourselves that they were disposed to a peaceful settlement.[5] Then, giving them some looking-glasses, knives, tobacco, and other trifles, we departed.

We passed a deserted village and several islands, and to the north saw a high mountain covered with snow—probably the same one that was seen by Broughton and named by him Mount St. Helens.[6] Our guide directed us into a little river and on the bank we found a good camping place, under a grove of oaks and in the midst of sweet-smelling wild flowers. There we passed a night more tranquil than the one which had preceded it.

On the morning of the sixth we continued up this little river and soon arrived at a large village called Kalama, the chief of which was a young man called Keasseno, a relative of our guide.[7] The site of this village could not be more charming. It bordered the little river we had ascended that here is only a clear and winding brook in a verdant plain, decked with fragrant flowers of all colors and surrounded by superb oak groves.[8]

The freshness and beauty of this spot, which nature seemed to have adorned and enriched with her most precious gifts, con-

[5] Huntington varies and adds: ". . . and having ascertained that this warlike demonstration originated in a trifling offense on the part of the Kreluits, we found them well disposed to arrange matters in an amicable fashion" (p. 109).

[6] This mountain is about fifty airline miles north and somewhat to the east of Portland, Oregon and, like Mt. Hood, is clearly visible from the Columbia River. Huntington adds and varies: "about twenty miles distant, all covered with snow, contrasting remarkably with the dark foliage at its base . . ." (p. 109). Actually, the base of the mountain cannot be seen from the river. Its peak rises 9,671 feet above sea level.

[7] Huntington adds that he was a handsome man (p. 110).

[8] The "winding brook" becomes, in Huntington, "here but a torrent with numerous cascades leaping from rock to rock in their descent to the deep, limpid water . . ." a bit of overfine writing on Huntington's part (p. 110).

49

trasted strikingly with the indigence and uncleanliness of its inhabitants. I regretted that it had not fallen to the lot of civilized men, but doubtless I was wrong. Those who are most favored by their common mother are less inclined to pervert her gifts or to prefer the artificial and often the very trivial.

With regret we left this beautiful place and proceeded to another large village that our guide told us was called Katlapoutle. It was situated at the mouth of a small river that seemed to flow down from a snow-covered mountain we had seen the day before. This river was called the Cowiltk [Lewis River]. We coasted by a pretty wooded island that was high enough not to be inundated by the floods and came to two villages called Multnomah.

We then passed the entrance of the Willamette River, above which the tide ceases to be felt. Our guide informed us that up this river about a day's journey there was a large waterfall and beyond it the country abounded in beaver, otter, deer, and other wild animals. Here, where we were, the rows of oaks and poplars lining both banks of the river, the green and flower-covered prairies glimpsed through the trees, and the mountains seen in the distance presented a smiling and enchanting prospect to the observer who loved the beauties of simple nature. We encamped for the night on the edge of one of these beautiful prairies.

On the seventh we passed several low islands and soon discovered Mount Hood, a high mountain capped with snow, so named by Lieutenant Broughton.[9] The view that he had before his eyes appeared to him so charming that, landing upon a point to take possession of the country, he named it Point Bellevue. At two o'clock we passed Point Vancouver, the terminal point of Broughton's journey. The width of the river diminishes considerably at this point and we soon began to notice shoals that

[9] Huntington adds: "and Mount Washington, another snowy summit, so called by Lewis and Clark" (p. 112). Manifestly, this name was inserted in the 1854 edition. Quaife says that Mt. Washington is not mentioned in the Manuscript (see Quaife, p. 76n.). It does not appear, moreover, in Bibaud. Possibly, though unlikely, the mountain described is Mt. Jefferson (10,495 feet) to the south of Mt. Hood; it may have been Mt. Adams (13,307 feet) east of Mt. St. Helens. Mt. Washington is a small (7,800 feet) peak about a hundred miles south of Hood River and can not be seen from the Columbia.

made us realize we could not be far from some falls. We camped that night under a rock escarpment.

The next day, the eighth, we had not proceeded far before we encountered a very rapid current. Soon afterward, we saw the hut of some Indian fishermen and we stopped for breakfast. Here we found an old, blind man who gave us a cordial reception. Our guide said that he was a white man and that he was called Soto. We learned from the old man himself that he was the son of a Spaniard who had been wrecked at the mouth of the river; that some of the crew on this occasion got safely to land, but they had all been massacred by the Clatsops with the exception of four who were spared and who married native women. Disgusted with the savage life, the four Spaniards, of whom the father of this man was one, had attempted, overland, to reach a settlement of white men, but had never been heard of again. When his father and companions left the country, Soto was quite young.[10]

After these good Indians had fed us royally with fresh salmon, we left them and very soon arrived at a rapids opposite what, in 1806, Captains Lewis and Clark called Strawberry Island. We left our men near a large village, to take care of the baggage. Then, following our guide and walking about two hours in a beaten path, we came to the foot of the falls, where we amused ourselves for some time shooting the seals that were here in abundance. The Indians were catching salmon below the narrows.[11] A chief, a fine handsome young man, came to us, followed by some twenty other Indians, and invited us to his wigwam. We accompanied him there, had supper, and spent the night with him.

The next morning we learned that there was no trading post near The Falls [The Dalles]; and Coalpo, our guide, stubbornly refused to proceed further, maintaining that the natives of the

[10] Bibaud adds a footnote: "These facts, were they verified, would prove that the Spaniards were the first to discover the mouth of the Columbia. Certainly a long time before the voyages of Captains Gray and Vancouver, they knew a part at least of the course of this river, which they called the Oregon" (p. 86).
[11] From here to the end of the chapter, Huntington adds a few phrases or clauses, *passim;* but the substance is not altered nor is the text improved.

villages beyond were his enemies and would not fail to kill him if they had him in their power. Thus we decided to return to our establishment. We distributed some presents to our host (I mean the young chief with whom we had supped and lodged) and to some of his followers. Then we re-embarked and reached camp on the fourteenth, without accidents or incidents worth relating.

CHAPTER 9

We had built a warehouse to put under cover the articles we were to receive from the ship, and we were busily engaged from the sixteenth to the thirtieth in stowing away the goods and other effects intended for the establishment.

The ship, having been detained by circumstances much longer than anticipated, left her anchorage at last on June 1 and dropped down to Baker's Bay, waiting there for a favorable wind to get out of the river. She was to coast along northward and enter all the harbors, procure as many furs as possible and touch at the Columbia River on her return, so it was unanimously agreed that Mr. McKay should join the cruise, as much to help the captain as to obtain correct information about the kinds of trade with the natives along that coast. Mr. McKay chose James Lewis and Ovide Montigny to accompany him, but the latter insisted that he got seasick and so was left at the establishment. Mr. McKay took instead a young man by the name of Louis Bruslé, to serve him as a domestic. I had the good fortune not to be chosen for this disastrous voyage, thanks to my having made myself useful at the establishment. Mr. Mumford[1] (second mate) owed the same good luck to the incompatability of his disposition with that of the

---

[1] Quaife maintains in a footnote (p. 8on.) that the statement concerning Mr. Mumford does not appear in either the Manuscript or the Bibaud edition. Actually, it is printed in Bibaud's edition of 1820, and I have translated it here verbatim. The Manuscript has the name of J. D. Mumford interpolated in the text. Edith G. Firth, Head of the Canadian History and Manuscript Division of the Toronto Public Library, writes: "This passage is as close to the 1820 edition as most of the manuscript" (Letter to me on March 10, 1964). The Manuscript reads as follows: *"Un des officiers du vaisseau* [J. D. Mumford interpolated] *ayant en querrelle avec le Capt. demanda permission de rester à l'Établissement ce qui lui fut accordé."*

captain. He got permission to remain, and engaged with the company as a coaster.[2]

On June 5, the ship got out to sea with a good wind. We continued in the meantime to work without interruption, completing the storehouse and erecting a dwelling and a powder magazine. The storehouse, which was framed by hewn logs, was covered with cedar bark because of the lack of planks. The natives, both men and women, visited us very often and formed a fairly large camp near the establishment.

On the fifteenth, some natives from up the river brought us two strange Indians, a man and a woman. These Indians were not dressed like those in our neighborhood. They wore long robes of deerskin, trimmed in the fashion of the tribes to the east of the Rocky Mountains. We questioned them in various Indian tongues, but they did not understand. They showed us a letter addressed to "Mr. John Stuart, Fort Estekatadene, New Caledonia." Mr. Pillet then talked to them in the Kristeneau language, and they answered, although they appeared not to understand it perfectly. We learned from them that they had been sent by a Mr. Finan McDonald, a clerk in the service of the North West Company, who had a post on a river they called the Spokane. Having lost their way, they had followed the course of the Tacoutche-Tesse (the Indian name for the Columbia River), and when they arrived at the Falls the natives made them understand that there were white men at the river's mouth.[3] They believed that the person to whom the letter was addressed would be found there, and had come to deliver it.

We kept these messengers for several days and derived from

2 Huntington varies: ". . . he had permission to remain, and engaged with the company in place of Mr. Aiken as a coaster, and in command of the schooner" (p. 117). There follows this footnote: "This schooner [the Dolly] was found too small for the purpose. Mr. Astor had no idea of the dangers to be met at the mouth of the Columbia or he would have ordered the frame of a vessel of at least one hundred tons. The frames shipped in New York were used in construction of this one only, which was employed solely in the river trade" (pp. 117–18).

3 Quaife notes: "In the 1820 edition of Franchere's narrative this name is spelled 'Tacousah-Tesse.' It does not appear in the Manuscript at all" (p. 81n.). In Bibaud the spelling is exactly as I have used it here.

them some important information about the interior of the country. We decided to send an expedition there, under the command of Mr. David Stuart, and July 15 was fixed for its departure.

In fact, all was ready on the date planned and we were about to load the canoes when, toward midday, we saw a large canoe, carrying a flag, rounding what we called Tongue Point. We did not know who it could be; for we did not yet expect our own men, who (as the reader will remember) were to cross the continent by the route which Captains Lewis and Clark had followed in 1805, and who were wintering on the banks of the Missouri. We were soon relieved of our uncertainty by the arrival of the canoe, which landed near a little wharf that we had built to facilitate the unloading of supplies from a ship.

The flag she bore was the British, and her crew was composed of nine boatmen in all. A well-dressed man, who appeared to be the commander, was the first to leap ashore; and addressing us without ceremony, he said that his name was David Thompson, and that he was one of the partners of the North West Company. We invited him to our quarters at one end of the storehouse. Our dwelling-house had not yet been completed. After the usual civilities, Mr. Thompson said that he had crossed the continent during the preceding season, but that the desertion of some of his men had forced him to winter at the base of the Rocky Mountains, near the source of the Columbia. In the spring he had built a canoe and had come down the river to our establishment.[4] He added that the wintering partners had resolved to abandon all their trading posts west of the mountains and enter into an agreement with us on the condition that we promise not to meddle in their trade to the east. To support what he said, he let us read a letter to this effect addressed to Mr. William McGillivray (chief of the North West Company in Canada).

Mr. Thompson had kept a regular journal and had traveled, it seemed to me, more like a geographer than a fur trader. He

[4] Huntington interpolates: ". . . the materials for which he had brought with him across the mountains . . ." (p. 121).

54

was provided with a sextant, and during the week's sojourn that he made at our place had an opportunity to make several astronomical observations. He recognized the two Indians who had brought the letter addressed to Mr. John Stuart, and told us that they were two women, one of whom had dressed herself as a man in order to travel with greater security. The description this gentleman gave of the interior of the country was not calculated to leave with us a very favorable impression, and did not perfectly accord with that of our two Indian guests.[5] However, we persevered in our resolution to send an expedition into the interior. On the twenty-third, Mr. David Stuart set out, accompanied by Messrs. Benjamin Pillet, Alexander Ross, Donald McLennan, and Ovide Montigny, with four Canadian *voyageurs* and the two Indian women, in company with Mr. Thompson and his crew. The wind was favorable and they were soon out of our sight.

The natives, who until then had surrounded us in great numbers, began to depart and soon we saw no more of them. At first we attributed their retreat to the lack of furs to trade with; but we soon learned that they acted, in that matter, from another motive. According to the advice of one of them who had formed a friendship for Mr. Robert Stuart, seeing us reduced in number, they had made some plans to surprise us.[6] We has-

[5] The Huntington edition has the following footnote about David Thompson: "Mr. Thompson had no doubt been sent by the agents of the Northwest Company to take possession of an eligible spot at the mouth of the Columbia, with a view to forestalling the plan of Mr. Astor. He would then have been there before us, no doubt, but for the desertion of his men. The consequence of this step would have been his taking possession of the country and displaying the British flag, as an emblem of that possession and a guarantee of protection thereafter. He found himself too late, however, and the stars and stripes floating over Astoria. This note is not intended by the author as an afterthought: as the opinion it conveys was that which we all entertained at the time of that gentleman's visit" (pp. 122–23).

It is possible, nevertheless, that David Thompson knew before he set out for the river mouth that the Astor party had established itself there. He was probably driven by his great curiosity to explore the Columbia River area.

Quaife says that this footnote "is not found in Franchère's Manuscript nor in the 1820 edition, edited by Bibaud. Although it purports to be the commentary of Franchère, it was evidently written by Huntington" (p. 85n.). Quaife offers no evidence, however, to support his contention.

[6] Huntington adds: ". . . to take our lives and plunder the post" (p. 123).

tened, therefore, to put ourselves in the best possible state of defense. The dwelling-house was raised, parallel to the warehouse. We cut a great number of pickets and formed a square, with palisades of about ninety feet flanked by two bastions on which we put four small cannons.[7] The whole had an aspect sufficiently formidable to make the Indians fearful, and for greater security we kept guard day and night.

Toward the end of the month, a large assembly of Indians from the neighborhood of the Strait of Juan de Fuca and Gray's Harbor formed a huge camp on Baker's Bay to fish for sturgeon. The rumor circulated among these Indians that the *Tonquin* had been destroyed on the coast and Mr. McKay (or the chief trader, as they called him) and all the crew massacred by the natives. We did not believe a word of this rumor. Some days later, other Indians from Gray's Harbor, called Chehalis, confirmed what the first had told, and even gave us, as far as we could judge by the little we knew of their language, a very detailed account of the affair. This second report, while not entirely convincing, left us uneasy.[8] We redoubled our efforts and our vigilance, and even had drills from time to time to accustom ourselves to the use of arms.[9]

To the need for protecting ourselves against an attack by the natives was added the need of obtaining provisions for the winter. Those that we had procured from the ship were very quickly exhausted, and from July 1 we were forced to accustom ourselves to a diet of fish. Not having brought hunters with us, for our venison we had to rely on the undependable hunting of

---

This may easily have been exactly the situation as it appeared to the men at the establishment.

[7] Huntington interpolates: ". . . with palisades in front and rear, of about 90 feet by 120; the warehouse built on the edge of a ravine, formed one flank, the dwelling-house and shops the other . . ." (p. 123). Certainly this addition gives a more nearly complete description of the structures on the post site.

[8] Huntington adds: ". . . did not fail to make a painful impression on our minds, and keep us in an excited state of feeling as to the truth of the report. The Indians of the Bay looked fiercer and more warlike than those of our neighborhood" (pp. 124–25).

[9] Huntington says "regular daily drill . . ." (p. 125).

Gabriel Franchère, fils, *at the height of his career as a fur dealer. This is a reproduction of an oil painting by his nephew, Joseph-Charles Franchère.*

John Jacob Astor about the time of the Astorian venture. From a portrait by Alonzo Chappel.

The Tonquin *entering the Columbia River, March 25, 1811.
Three men sent by Captain Thorn to take soundings near a bar
at the mouth of the river were drowned in these violent waters.
From Franchère's* Narrative of a Voyage to the Northeast Coast
of America *(1854).*

Astoria (later Fort George) as it looked in 1813. Only the site is remembered in the modern coastal city of Astoria. From Franchère's Narrative of a Voyage to the Northeast Coast of America *(1854).*

Fort Okanogan, from a painting by John Mix Stanley. Franchère's fellow Astorians Alexander Ross and Ross Cox both managed the post shown here. It was situated a short distance from the confluence of the Okanogan and Columbia rivers.

"Indians taking salmon at the falls of the Willamette, June, 1851." From a drawing by George Gibbs. Franchère found this area a virtual paradise. It abounded in fur-bearing animals and served as wintering quarters for a number of Astorians.

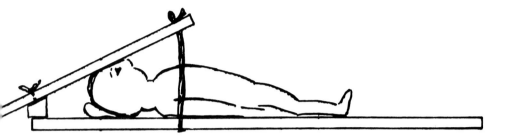

Cradle, board type. After Meriwether Lewis and William Clark. Redrawn for Chinook Ethnographic Notes, *Vol. VII, No. 2, from an illustration in* Original Journals of Lewis and Clark Expedition, 1804–1806, *edited by Reuben G. Thwaites.*

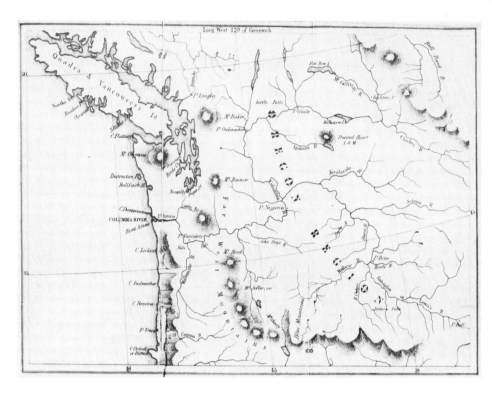

Map of Columbia River region. From Adventures of the First Settlers on the Oregon, *by Alexander Ross (Londan, Smith, Elder & Co., 1849).*

one of the natives who had not abandoned us when all the other Indians left. From time to time this man brought us a very lean and very dry doe, for which we nevertheless had to pay a high price. The ordinary cost of a stag was a blanket, a knife, some tobacco, a little powder, and some balls.[10] In a word, we certainly had no royal banquet. Those who best accommodated themselves to our nourishment were the Sandwich Islanders. Salmon and elk were delicacies to them.

On August 11 a large number of Chinooks brought us a strange Indian who had, they said, something of interest to tell us. This savage told us, in effect, that he and ten of his tribe had been led off by a Captain Ayres to hunt seals on the islands of Sir Francis Drake's Bay, where these animals are quite numerous, with the promise that they would be returned home and paid for their services. The Captain had left them on the islands in order to go south, he said, to buy provisions on the California coast. When he did not return, they concluded that he had been shipwrecked, and embarked in a canoe he had left with them and reached the mainland, which was not far away. But as they approached the shore, their canoe was broken into pieces and they saved themselves by swimming. Thinking they were a short distance from the Columbia, they had followed the strand. They lived along the way on shellfish and frogs. Eventually they arrived at the villages of some strange Indians who—far from receiving them well—killed eight of their number and took the others prisoner. However, the Kilinoux, neighbors of the Clatsops, heard that these men were captives and ransomed them.

These events must have occurred in March or April, 1811. The Indian who told us the story appeared to be endowed with a good deal of intelligence and knew several English words. He told us also that he had been at the Russian trading post at Chitka, on the California coast, in the Sandwich Islands, and in China.

10 Huntington adds: ". . . besides supplying our hunter with a musket" (p. 125). Then he adds further: "This dry meat, and smoke-dried fish, constituted our daily food, and that in very insufficient quantity for hardworking men. We had no bread, and vegetables, of course, were quite out of the question" (pp. 125–26).

Meanwhile, Chief Concomly asked Mr. Stuart and me to cure him of a sore throat which, he said, made him suffer greatly. As it was late in the day, we postponed going to cure the chief of the Chinooks until the next day. It was well that we did, for the same evening the sister of the Indian who had accompanied us on our journey to the Falls warned us that Concomly was perfectly well and that he had asked for us only in order to take us prisoners. Her advice ended the venture completely.

CHAPTER 10

On September 26 our house was finished, and we moved into it. The masonry had at first caused us some difficulty, but finally, unable to make lime because there was no limestone, we used native clay as mortar. This structure was large enough to hold us all, and we had planned it in the most suitable manner possible.[1] We also built a workshop for the blacksmith, who until then had worked in the open air.

The construction of the schooner had necessarily been delayed because the carpenter had had no help from the cooper. It was finally launched on October 2, and named the *Dolly,* with the ceremonies usual in such a case. I was then at Young's Bay, where I saw the ruins of the buildings that Captains Lewis and Clark had built in the autumn of 1805.[2]

On the evening of October 5, Mr. Pillet and Mr. McLennan arrived in a canoe sent from Mr. David Stuart and paddled by two of his men. As passengers they brought an Iroquois family and Mr. Régis Bruguier, whom I had known in Canada.[3]

[1] Huntington inserts the following: "It comprised a sitting, a dining room, some lodging or sleeping rooms, and an apartment for the men and artificers, all under the same roof" (p. 129).

[2] Huntington adds: "They were but piles of rough, unhewn logs, overgrown with parasite creepers" (p. 130). Quaife says that it is not in Bibaud, nor in the Manuscript. (p. 91n.).

Fort Clatsop, built by Lewis and Clark, was not on Young's Bay. It was located on the Lewis and Clark River which flows into the Bay. The site is now a national monument.

[3] Huntington interpolates: ". . . as a respectable country merchant . . ." (p. 130). Bibaud names Pillet and McLellan. I have corrected this error and used the name McLennan. See Part I, Chapter 1, n. 2.

Mr. Bruguier came to hunt beaver and was supplied with traps and other necessary equipment.[4] The report these gentlemen gave us about the interior of the country was most satisfactory. They had found the climate healthful and they had been well received by the natives. These Indians owned a large number of horses and Mr. Stuart had bought several at a bargain. While going upstream they had come upon a pretty little river the natives called the Okanogan. Mr. Stuart had decided to build his trading post on the bank of this stream; and after he had constructed a house, he thought it best to send the above-named persons back to the establishment, satisfied to keep only Mr. Ross, Mr. Montigny, and two other men with him for the winter.[5]

Meanwhile, the season had come when the Indians left the seashore and retired into the woods to establish their winter quarters along the brooks and rivers. We were able to get almost no food at all from them, and we found ourselves short of provisions. We therefore agreed that Mr. Robert Stuart should set out in the schooner with Mr. Mumford, for the threefold object of obtaining all the provisions they could, cutting oak staves for the use of the cooper, and trading with the Indians. They left for this purpose on the twelfth. After five days Mr. Mumford returned in an Indian canoe. This man wanted to assume command and give orders (after the manner of Captain Thorn) to the one who had engaged him for service. Consequently, he had been sent back to the establishment.

On November 10 we discovered that Paul D. Jeremie and the two Belleaux had deserted.[6] Mr. Matthews and I procured a large canoe and embarked to go after them, with orders to pro-

[4] Huntington inserts: "had been a trader among the Indians on the Saskatchewine river, where he had lost his outfit: he had since turned trapper . . ." (p. 130).

[5] Bibaud adds the following footnote: "One of these men had been left with him by Mr. Thompson in place of a Sandwich Islander [Hawaiian] whom that gentleman planned to take to Canada" (p. 100). Huntington adds: ". . . and thence to England" (p. 131).

[6] Huntington adds by way of explanation: "They had leave to go out shooting for two days, and carried off with them firearms and ammunition, and a handsome light Indian canoe" (p. 132).

ceed as far as the Falls, if necessary. On the 11th, on our way
upriver to a place called Oak Point, we overtook the schooner
that Mr. Stuart was loading with wood.[7] Mr. Russel Farnham
and one other man joined us, and we went on our way.[8] We came
to the end of our planned journey without having learned anything satisfactory about our deserters; and because we were short
of provisions, we turned back, arriving at Oak Point on the sixteenth and finding Mr. Stuart ready to depart.

However, the natives of the vicinity told us they had seen
the marks of shoes on the sand in that neighborhood, so we got
some small canoes and scoured the area during a part of the
day of November 17. We went up a small stream as far as some
mountains that are visible from Oak Point and are about six miles
distant from it. The area that lies between the river and these
mountains is low and marshy and is intersected by an infinite
number of channels. Toward evening we returned on our path to
regain the schooner, but night was coming on and we got lost.[9]
Our situation became more and more disagreeable. We were unable to find a landing place, so we were forced to continue paddling, or rather turning around, in this species of labryinth, constantly kneeling in our little barks that would have upset at the
slightest movement.

It rained torrents and was dark as pitch. At last, after we
had wandered about during a part of the night, we managed
to reach the edge of a forest. There we left our canoes and strug-
gled through the trees in the darkness, tearing ourselves on the
brush. At about two o'clock in the morning we reached the
schooner, half-frozen and exhausted.

[7] Oak Point is west of, and across Bradbury Slough from the west end of
Crims Island. It should not be confused with the point near St. Helens, Oregon,
named Oak Point by Lieutenant Broughton, who sailed up the Columbia in 1792.
See Lewis A. McArthur, *Oregon Geographic Names* (Portland, Oregon, Binfords
and Mort, 1952, third edition), 453–54.

[8] Huntington adds: "journeying day and night, and stopping at every Indian village, to make inquiries and offer a reward for the apprehension of our
runaways" (p. 153).

[9] Huntington adds and explains: ". . . but instead of taking the circuitous
way of the river, by which we had come, we made for Oak Point by the most direct
route, through these channels" (p. 134).

On the eighteenth we unloaded the small vessel and the next morning we hoisted anchor. As we went up the river, the natives of the Kreluit village came to us and offered to help us search for our deserters. Mr. Stuart put me ashore at this village and Mr. Farnham joined me. We spent that day drying our clothes, and the next day we embarked in a canoe with two men and a squaw and again paddled upriver. We soon met a canoe of natives who told us that the runaways had been taken prisoner by the chief of a tribe dwelling upon the banks of the Willamette River, whom they called Cathlamets.

We kept on our way and encamped on a sand beach opposite Deer Island.[10] There we passed a night almost as disagreeable as that of the seventeenth and eighteenth. We had lighted a fire and contrived a shelter of mats, but soon a violent wind arose, accompanied by a heavy rain. Our fire was put out and our mats were blown away. We could neither rekindle the one nor find the others, so we had to remain all night exposed to the fury of the storm. As soon as it was day, we re-embarked and set ourselves to paddling with all our might to get warm. In the evening we drew near the village where our deserters were captives, and we saw one of them on the outskirts. We proceeded to the hut of the chief, where we found that all three were more inclined to follow us than to remain slaves to these barbarians. We spent the night in this place, though not without some fears and not without taking some precautions. The chief had the reputation of being malicious—capable of violating any laws of civilized people. He was tall, handsome, and exceedingly proud, as we discovered by the cold and haughty manner in which he received us.[11] The natives chanted and made good medicine nearly the whole night through, all over a dying man.

I had an opportunity to see the sick man make his last

10 In Columbia County, named by Lewis and Clark on November 5, 1805. The town is named for the island. See McArthur, *Oregon Geographic*, 177.

11 Huntington adds: "Farnham and I agreed to keep watch alternately, but this arrangement was superfluous, as neither of us could sleep a wink for the infernal thumping and singing made by the medicine men all night long, by a dying native" (p. 136).

testament. He had brought to him his most precious possessions —his bracelets of copper, his glass beads, his bow and arrow with their quiver, his fishhooks and fishing lines, and his pipe. These he distributed among his best friends, with a promise on their part to restore them to him if he recovered.

On the twenty-second, after a great deal of difficulty and quibbling on the part of the chief, we bargained with him for the ransom of our men.[12] We gave him all our blankets, a copper kettle, a hatchet, an ugly-looking little pistol, a powder horn, and some balls.[13] He returned our deserters with the arms he had taken from them and their canoe that he had hidden in the wood. We then set out and camped that night near the Cowlitz River.

Upon our departure the following day, the wind sprang up. We split open a double rush mat, and having cut a branch of a tree, we made a mast and sail for the canoe. Soon enough we arrived in sight of Gray's Bay, about fifteen or sixteen miles from our establishment. We had to make a long crossing, however, for the river forms a kind of lake there. The wind was favorable and we sailed out in order to make the crossing about sunset, leaving a little island where we had amused ourselves by hunting.

It was not long before we repented our temerity, for soon the sky became overcast and the wind blew against the tide. Waves rose to a prodigious height and spilled over into our frail canoe. We lightened it as much as we could by bailing out water and jettisoning some of the baggage we still had with us. Finally, after having been for three hours the plaything of the raging

[12] Here Huntington draws a quite different picture from the simple situation described in Bibaud's edition: "I had visited every lodge in the village and found but few of the young men, the greater part having gone on a fishing excursion; knowing, therefore, that the chief could not be supported by his warriors, I was resolved not to be imposed upon, and as I knew where the firearms of the fugitives had been deposited, I would have them at all hazards" (p. 137).

[13] Huntington continues: ". . . with these articles placed in a pile before him, we demanded the men's clothing, the three fowling pieces, and their canoe . . . Nothing but our firmness compelled him to accept the articles offered in exchange; but at last, with great reluctance, he closed the bargain . . ." (pp. 137–38). The situation is obviously more dramatic in the Huntington version.

waves, menaced every moment with being swallowed up, we had the unexpected luck of landing in a place of safety. Our first care was to thank the Supreme Being for delivering us from so imminent a danger. Then, with some tree branches, we made a shelter against the wind, which continued to blow violently, and we built a fire to warm ourselves and dry our clothing. All that did not prevent us from shivering the rest of the night, even while congratulating ourselves on our luck in setting foot on land at the very moment we began to despair completely of saving ourselves.

The morning of the twenty-fourth brought a clear sky; and although the wind was still very strong, we again embarked and arrived with our deserters at the establishment, where they never expected to see us again. Some Indians who had followed us in a canoe, up to the moment when we undertook the passage across the evening before, had followed the river banks and happily arrived at Astoria. These natives, believing us to be lost, so reported us to Mr. McDougall, who was overcome with joy and surprise at seeing us once more.[14]

CHAPTER 11

The natives informed us that the beaver was very abundant in the country where the Willamette flowed. Mr. Robert Stuart hired a guide and set out on December 5, accompanied by Messrs. Benjamin Pillet and Donald McGillis and a few of the men, to go up the Willamette and determine whether or not the establishment of a trading post on its banks would be advantageous. Mr. R. Bruguier went with them as hunter.

The season during which we expected the return of the *Tonquin* had passed, and we began to believe as quite probable the report of the Indians at Gray's Harbor. We still indulged ourselves, however, with the hope that perhaps the ship had sailed for the East Indies without touching at Astoria. But this was a conjecture at most.

14 The concluding sentence in the chapter varies from the Bibaud text but does not improve it.

Christmas Day passed very agreeably. We treated our men with the best the establishment afforded. Although that was not much, they seemed well satisfied, for during the preceding two months they had been restricted to a very meager diet, living, one might say, only on smoked fish. On the twenty-seventh, when the schooner returned from her second voyage up the river, we dismantled her and laid her up for the winter at the entrance to a small creek.

It had been raining almost without interruption since the beginning of October, but on the evening of December 31 the weather cleared and on January 1 [1812] the sky became serene. We celebrated the New Year with a discharge of artillery. A small allowance of liquor was served to the men and the day passed in gaiety, every one amusing himself as much as possible.

The holiday over, our men went back to their daily chores. While some cut timber for building, others made charcoal for the blacksmith. The carpenter constructed a barge, and the cooper made barrels for the trading posts that we proposed to establish in the interior. On the evening of the eighteenth, two canoes filled with white men arrived at Astoria. Since Mr. Mc-Dougall, who was in command, had been confined to his room because of illness, I was delegated to receive these strangers. I was greatly surprised to recognize among them Mr. Donald McKenzie, the very one who had left Montreal in July, 1810, with Mr. Wilson P. Hunt. He was accompanied by Mr. Mc-Clellan,[1] one of the owners, Mr. Reed, a clerk, and eight boatmen. After a short rest, these gentlemen told us the story of their journey, which was, in effect, as follows:

In the autumn of 1810, Mr. Wilson P. Hunt and Mr. Mc-Kenzie set out on the Missouri, wintering at a place called Nod-

---

[1] Robert McClellan, who came to Astoria with the overland party, was one of the earliest of the American fur traders. It is highly probable that he joined the Astor expedition at the instigation of Ramsay Crooks, with whom he had engaged in a trade. As noted also, Franchère mistakenly put his name in the *Tonquin's* list, but corrected his error in the 1854 edition. I have followed the correction throughout this book.

away, on the banks of the river.[2] They were joined there by Mr. Robert McClellan, a Mr. Ramsay Crooks, and a Mr. Joseph Miller, traders from the South who had business relations with Mr. Astor.[3] In the spring of 1811, having secured two large barges, or boats, they went up the Missouri as far as the country of the Arikaras, or Ris [Rees Indians].[4] There they disposed of their barges and a good part of their equipment to Mr. Manuel Lisa, a Spaniard trader.[5] Then, at the beginning of August, following a purchase of about 130 horses from the Rees Indians, they betook themselves and sixty-odd other men over the mountains to the Columbia River.

Wishing to avoid a meeting with the Blackfoot Indians, a warlike and ferocious tribe who killed every stranger who fell into their hands, they followed a southerly course until they reached the fortieth degree of latitude. Then they turned again toward the northwest and came upon an old fort, or trading post, on the banks of a little river. They learned later that this post, which was then abandoned, had been built by an American trader named Andrew Henry. Our gentlemen had no doubt that this river would take them to the Columbia, and they constructed canoes to make the descent. They left some hunters near the old fort with Mr. Miller, who was dissatisfied with his bargain and was returning to the United States. Our gentlemen

---

2 Quaife is correct in saying that the name "Nadaoi" appears in the 1820 edition, but maintains that it is not in the Manuscript. It is just possible that he overlooked it, for Bibaud would have no reason to be acquainted with this place name; otherwise, Franchère may have recalled it during the process of the publication of the 1820 edition.

3 Ross credits Miller with being chiefly responsible for organizing the overland party when Wilson Hunt ran into difficulties with the Canadians. See Ross, *First Settlers*, 189–91.

4 "The Aricaras, commonly called Rees by the traders, were one of the principal divisions of the Caddoan family whose pristine habitat seems to have been in the vicinity of the Red River of the Natchitoches. . . . At the time of the voyage of Lewis and Clark they probably numbered 3,600 souls." H. M. Chittenden, *The American Fur Trade of the Far West* (2 vols., Stanford, Academic Reprints, 1954.), II, 861–62.

The French version of the abbreviation of the name Aricaras, or Arikaras, was *Ris*.

5 See Chittenden, *American Fur Trade*, I, 125–36, for a good brief account of Manuel Lisa.

embarked upon the river, but they soon encountered too many falls, and when they lost a man, as well as a part of their baggage, they decided to abandon their canoes and proceed on foot.

Considering the few provisions they had left, the enterprise was difficult. Nevertheless, since they had no time to lose in deliberating, after they had cached the superfluous part of their supplies they divided themselves into four troops, under the commands of Mr. McKenzie, Mr. Hunt, Mr. McClellan, and Mr. Crooks, and proceeded along the banks of the river which, because of the insurmountable difficulties it presented, they called the Mad River.[6] Messrs. McKenzie and McClellan followed the right bank, Messrs. Hunt and Crooks the left. They hoped to reach the Columbia quickly, but they followed the course of the Mad River for twenty days, finding nothing at all to eat and suffering horribly from thirst. The rocks between which this river flows are so precipitous that they could not get down to the water to quench their thirst, and they suffered something like the torments of Tantalus—with this difference: he could not reach the water that was above his head, while our travelers had it below their feet. Several men, in order not to die from thirst, drank their own urine. All of them, to appease the hunger that tormented them, ate beaver skins roasted over their fires. They came, finally, to the extremity of eating even their shoes.

However, those who skirted the left bank suffered less than the others because from time to time they encountered Indians, who fled at their approach, taking their horses with them. To all appearances, these savages had never seen white men. When our travelers came into sight of one of these wandering tribes they approached it with as much precaution as they would have approached a herd of wild animals. Firing upon their horses, they would kill some, but were careful to leave some trinkets to

6 Ramsay Crooks was only twenty-four or twenty-five years old at this time, but had already made something of a name for himself in the Indian trade. He was to take over Astor's American Fur Company in 1834 and become its president. His later associations with Franchère were close and, by all the records in their correspondence, entirely warm and cordial. See Franchère's Letter Books, the American Fur Company Papers, in the Clarke Historical Collection.

repay the owners for what they had thus, in effect, stolen from them.[7]

Mr. McKenzie overtook Mr. McClellan, who had gone ahead, and their two troops proceeded together. Soon they had an opportunity to come near enough to Mr. Hunt (who, as I have said, was on the other side of the river) to speak to him and tell him of the suffering they had experienced. Mr. Hunt had a canoe constructed of horse skins, though, as one might well imagine, it was not very large. Nevertheless, they succeeded by this means in transporting a little horseflesh to the men on the north bank. They even tried to pass the men across, one by one (for they could not take more than one at a time), to the South bank. Unhappily, the river was quite violent, a canoe capsized, one man was drowned, and the two parties lost hope of joining forces. Thus they went on their way, each party on its own side of the river.

Before long, those on the north bank came to a river of considerable size and they followed along its banks. Most fortunately, moreover, they met some Indians who sold them a number of horses. In this area they also came upon a young American who was deranged, but who had some lucid moments. The young man told them, during one of his clearer intervals, that he was from Connecticut and that his name was Archibald Petton [Pelton].[8] He said that he had come up the Missouri with Mr. Henry and that the people at the trader's post had been massacred. He alone had escaped and had wandered for three years among the Indians.

Our travelers took this young man with them. When they arrived at the confluence of the Columbia and the river they had been following, they realized that in 1805 the latter had been named the Lewis River by an American of the same name. Finally, after exchanging their remaining horses for canoes, they

---

[7] Huntington adds: "This resource prevented the party from perishing of hunger" (p. 148).

[8] Ross Cox was in error, calling this man Petton; but he confirms Franchère's story and expands it somewhat to show Pelton the victim of a kind of melancholia. Cox, *Columbia River*, 60–61.

arrived at the establishment [Astoria], safe and sound, it is true, but in a pitiable state, their clothes but tattered rags.

The story of these gentlemen interested us greatly. They went on to say that since their separation from Messrs. Hunt and Crooks they had not seen them again and believed it unlikely they would reach Astoria before spring. However, they were mistaken. Mr. Hunt arrived on February 15, with thirty men, one woman, and two children. He had left Mr. Crooks and five men with the Snakes.[9] They might have arrived almost as soon as Mr. McKenzie; but they had spent eight or ten days in the middle of a plain among some friendly Indians, both to revive themselves from their fatigue and to search for one of their men who had been lost in the woods.[10] Failing to find him, they resumed their journey and arrived at the banks of the Columbia somewhat below the mouth of the Lewis River where Mr. McKenzie had emerged.

The arrival of so great a number of people would have embarrassed us had it taken place a month earlier. Happily, the natives now brought us fresh fish in abundance. Until March 30 we were occupied in preparing triplicates of letters and other necessary papers in order to send to New York the news of our arrival and of the reunion of the two expeditions. The letters were entrusted to Mr. John Reed, who left Astoria (thus we had named our establishment) in the company of Mr. McClellan and Mr. Robert Stuart, the latter conveying an assortment of goods from the establishment to his uncle on the Okanogan.[11] Messrs. Farnham and McGillis set out at the same time, with a guide, to search for the equipment that Mr. Hunt had put in a cache near old Fort Henry, on the banks of the Mad River.[12] I

[9] Bibaud adds a footnote: "A savage tribe that lives west of the Rocky Mountains, between 43° and 44° latitude" (p. 114n.).

[10] Unaccountably, Huntington says that the search was made for "two of the party" (p. 151).

[11] The parenthetical statement appears in Bibaud. Quaife says that it is also in the Manuscript, and adds that "This is the first time the name is mentioned in Franchere" (p. 111n.).

[12] Huntington himself adds a long footnote, utilizing a Lewis and Clark description of a cache (See the 1854 edition, p. 152n.).

made use of this opportunity to write my family. Two days afterward, Messrs. McKenzie and Matthews set out with five or six men to make an excursion up the Williamette River.

CHAPTER 12

After the departure of Mr. Donald McKenzie, nothing unusual took place at Astoria until May 9. On that day, to our great surprise and joy, we discovered a sail in the offing, not far from the mouth of the river. Immediately Mr. McDougall embarked in a small boat and rounded the Cape [Disappointment] to make the signals. The next morning, since the weather was fine and the sea quiet, the boat pushed out and arrived safely alongside the ship. Soon after, the wind sprang up and the ship made sail and entered the river, where she dropped anchor at about 2 P.M. Toward evening the small boat returned to the Fort with the following passengers: Messrs. John Clarke of Canada (a partner), Alfred Seton and George Ehninger, clerks, the latter a nephew of Mr. Astor, and two other men. We learned from these gentlemen that the ship was the *Beaver*, under Captain Cornelius Sowles, and was consigned to us. She had left New York on October 10, 1811, and had touched, in the passage, at Massa Fuero and at the Sandwich Isles. Mr. Clarke handed me letters from my father and from several of my friends; I thus learned of the death of a beloved sister.

On the morning of the eleventh we were strangely surprised by the return of Messrs. David Stuart, Robert Stuart, McClellan, Crooks, Reed, and Farnham. This return, sudden and unexpected, was brought about because of an unfortunate adventure that had befallen the party while ascending the river. When they reached the Falls, where the portage is very long, some natives came with their horses to offer aid in transporting the goods above the portage. Mr. Robert Stuart, not suspecting them, put in their care several bales of merchandise, which they packed on their horses. But, in getting under way, they darted up a narrow path among the rocks and fled at full gallop before it was possible for anyone to overtake them. Mr. Stuart had several shots fired over their heads to frighten them, but they succeeded in escaping with the merchandise. Our gentlemen continued to carry the remainder of their goods. As there were among the party a great number of natives whom the success and impunity of the thieves had emboldened, Mr. Stuart thought it best to keep watch over the goods at the upper end of the portage, while Messrs. McClellan and Reed served as the rear guard.

Mr. Reed, who carried on his back a tin box containing the papers given him to take to New York, found himself some distance from McClellan; and the Indians thought it a favorable opportunity to attack him and carry off his box, the brightness of which no doubt had tempted them. They attacked him so suddenly that he had no time to defend himself. After a few moments of resistance, he received a blow on the head from a war club. He fell to the ground and the Indians seized his goods. McClellan witnessed what had been done, fired his *carabine* at one of the robbers and killed him; the rest took flight but carried off what they had stolen, even so. McClellan immediately ran up to Reed, but finding him motionless and bathed in blood believed him to be dead and so rejoined Stuart, urging him to get away from these robbers and murderers.

Mr. Stuart had no wish to continue his journey without making sure that Mr. Reed was actually dead.[1] He went back, despite the urgings of Mr. McClellan, toward the spot where the latter had left his companion. He had gone scarcely two hundred paces when he met Mr. Reed coming toward them, holding his head with both hands.[2]

[1] Huntington adds: ". . . or, if he were, without carrying off his body" (p. 157).

[2] Quaife says that "The Manuscript states at this point: 'We were informed of this unfortunate affair by natives from up the river on the 15th of April'"; and that Bibaud had added "but disbelieved it." The French in Bibaud can be more aptly translated: "The news of this unfortunate encounter had been told us by some natives from up river on April 15, but we had not given credit to the story *(La nouvelle de cette rencontre fâcheuse nous avait été annoncée par des naturels du haut de le rivière, vers le 15 d'Avril; mais nous n'y avions pas ajouté foi.)*" (See Bibaud, p. 119). Huntington himself makes an extended comment about the lack of "military sagacity and precaution which characterized the operations of these traders. . . ." (p. 158).

The object of Mr. Reed's journey was defeated by the loss of his papers, and he returned with the other gentlemen to Mr. David Stuart's trading post, whence they all set out, at the beginning of May, to travel to Astoria. Coming downriver, they met Mr. Ramsay Crooks and a man named Day [John Day]. The reader may recall from the preceding chapter that Mr. Crooks and five other men had remained [in the Snake country] among some so-called friendly Indians. This gentleman and his companion were the only members of the party who ever reached the establishment, and they, too, arrived in a most pitiable state. The savages had stripped them of all their clothes, leaving them only some pieces of deerskin to cover their nakedness.[3]

On 12 May, the schooner that had been sent to the ship [the *Beaver*] returned with a cargo and the following passengers: Messrs. B. Clapp, J. C. Halsey, C. A. Nichols, and Ross Cox, clerks; five Canadians; seven Americans, all tradesmen; and a dozen Sandwich Islanders for service at Astoria. The captain sounded the channel for several days; but he failed to find water deep enough and was unwilling to bring her up to Astoria. It was necessary, consequently, to unload the ship with the schooner, and this operation occupied us during the greater part of the month of June.

Captain Sowles and Mr. Clarke confirmed the report of the destruction of the *Tonquin*; they had learned about it at Hawaii, through a letter which a certain Captain Ebbets, in the employ of Mr. Astor, had left there. It was thereupon agreed that Mr. Hunt should board the *Beaver*, make a careful survey of the commerce along the coast, and touch at the Russian posts in Chitka Sound [Sitka].

[3] Ross gives a rather long account of what happened to Ramsay Crooks and John Day. See Ross, *First Settler*, 202–207. Curiously enough, Franchère does not mention the fact that Day, a tall, straight Virginian whom Hunt had employed for the overland journey, was with Robert Stuart, Crooks, and McClellan when they started on their return trip to St. Louis in June, 1812; nor does he say anything about Day's being returned to the fort, quite insane, or about Day's death not many months later. Although now, in Oregon, Day's name is known especially for its association with gold-mining operations carried on in the central part of the state years after Day died, the name of John Day has been given to a river, a town, and, in recent years, to a great dam in the Oregon watershed.

The necessary papers were prepared once again. They were entrusted to Mr. R. Stuart, who was to cross the continent in the company of Mr. Crooks and Mr. McClellan, partners dissatisfied [with the Astor enterprise] who planned to return to the United States. At the same time, Mr. Clarke prepared to leave with a considerable assortment of merchandise, accompanied by Benjamin Pillet, McLennan, Farnham, and Cox, to form a new establishment on the Spokane River. [Clarke River?] Mr. McKenzie, in turn, prepared to survey the wonders of the Lewis River with Mr. Seton, while Messrs. D. Stuart, Matthews, and McGillis explored the land to the north.[4] These gentlemen numbering sixty-two in all left us on June 30, in the evening. The following pages will reveal the results of their several enterprises.

During the whole month of July the natives were so openly hostile that we were forced to be constantly on our guard. We constructed covered ways inside our palisades and raised our bastions another story. The alarm became so serious toward the end of the month that we kept sentries continually at the doors, and night and day watches in the high bastions.[5]

At the end of June, the *Beaver* was ready to depart on her coasting voyage, and on July 1 Mr. Hunt went on board. But westerly winds prevailed during the entire month and it was not until August 4 that she hoisted sail and got out of the river, due to return at the end of October.[6]

We spent August and September finishing a house forty-five by thirty feet. This building, which was covered with shingles, came to serve as a hospital for the men at the establishment and as a lodging for the mechanics.

Experience had taught us that from the beginning of Oc-

4 Huntington varies this passage and adds: ". . . while Mr. Stuart, reinforced by Messrs. Matthews and McGillis, was to explore the region lying north of his post at Okanogan. All these outfits being ready, with the canoes, boatmen, and hunters, the flotilla quitted Astoria on the 30th of June, in the afternoon, having on board sixty-two persons" (pp. 160–61).

5 Huntington adds: ". . . and never allowed more than two or three Indians at a time within our gates" (p. 161).

6 Huntington explains: ". . . to leave her surplus goods and take in our furs for market" (p. 161).

tober to the end of January, the natives would bring provisions in very small quantity. It was thought best that I, accompanied by Mr. Clapp, should take the schooner to look for a cargo of dried fish. We left Astoria on October 1 with a small packet of merchandise. The trip was highly successful. We found the game very abundant, killed a great quantity of swans, plovers, ducks, and so forth, and returned to Astoria on the twentieth with a part of our venison, 750 smoked salmon, and 450 beaver skins.[7]

A few days later, this time alone, I left again with the same objective. But this second voyage was not in the least agreeable. I experienced continual rains, and the game was much less plentiful. I managed, nevertheless, to exchange my goods for furs and dried fish, and on November 15 I returned to Astoria, where the need for fresh provisions was beginning to be felt so severely that several of the men were attacked with scurvy.

On the twenty-third, Messrs. Halsey and Wallace were sent with fourteen men to establish a winter trading post on the Willamette; and as Mr. McDougall was still confined to his room by sickness, Mr. Clapp and I were left with the entire charge of the post at Astoria and were each other's only resource for companionship. Happily, Mr. Clapp was a man of amiable character, of a lively disposition, and agreeable conversation. In the intervals between our daily duties we enjoyed music and reading, having some instruments and a good library.[8] Otherwise we should have passed our time rather sadly during this rainy season, in the midst of the deep mud that surrounded us and made the pleasure of a stroll impossible.

CHAPTER 13

The months of October, November, and December passed without our having any news of the *Beaver*, and we feared that

---

7 Huntington further interpolates: ". . . a quantity of the Wapto root (so called by the natives), which is found a good substitute for potatoes" (p. 162).

8 On the invoice of merchandise shipped by John Jacob Astor on board the *Beaver* and consigned to the establishment at Astoria is a long list of books that, apparently, became the "library" that Franchère mentions. Such volumes as Carr's *Scotland,* Pindar's *Works,* Burns's *Poems* (2 vols.), and a *History of Chile* were included. For the complete list see Porter, *John J. Astor,* I, 500–501.

there had happened to her, as to the *Tonquin*, some disastrous accident. It will be revealed in the following chapter why this ship did not return to Astoria in the autumn of 1812. However, on January 15, 1813, Mr. McKenzie arrived from his post in the interior—which he had abandoned after storing a part of his stock of goods in a cache.[1] He came to tell us that war had been declared between Great Britain and the United States. The information had been brought to his post by a gentleman of the North West Company, who had given him a letter containing the proclamation of the President to that effect.

Upon learning this news, all of us at Astoria who were British subjects and Canadians wished ourselves in Canada. But we could not permit even the thought of going there—at least not immediately. We were separated from our country by an immense space, and the difficulties of the journey at this season were insurmountable. We therefore held a sort of council of war, weighing our situation maturely.[2] We considered seriously the fact that nearly all of us were British subjects, yet we were trading under the American flag. And as we could not expect to receive further supplies from the American ports, all of which probably were blockaded, we decided to abandon the establishment the following spring, or, at the latest, in the beginning of summer. We did not communicate these resolutions to our men, lest they should, in consequence, abandon their work. But from that moment we discontinued our trade with the natives—except for provisions—not only because we no longer had a large stock of goods on hand, but also because we already had more furs than we could carry away.

As long as we had expected the return of the ship, we had served out a regular supply of bread to the men. Upon the arrival

1 Huntington adds: "Before his departure he paid a visit to Mr. Clark on the Spokane, and while there had learned the news, which he came to announce to us . . ." (pp. 165–66). This addition explains how McKenzie came by his information, an explanation lacking in the Bibaud text.

2 At this point Huntington interpolates: ". . . to which the clerks of the factory were invited *pro forma,* as they had no voice in the deliberations . . ." (p. 166).

of Mr. McKenzie and his men, we found ourselves very short of food. With this increase in the number of mouths to feed, we were forced to reduce the ration of each man to four ounces of flour and one and a half pounds of dried fish a day, and even to send a number of the men to spend the rest of the winter with Messrs. Wallace and Halsey, on the Willamette.

Meanwhile, the sturgeon began to enter the river, and on February 13 I left to fish for them. On the fifteenth I sent the first boat-load to the establishment. This proved a very timely relief to the men, who for several days had broken off work from want of sufficient food. I formed a big camp near Oak Point, and Mr. McDougall sent to me all the men who were sick with scurvy, for the restoration of their health.[3]

On March 20, Messrs. Reed and Seton, who had led part of our men to the post on the Willamette, to feed them, returned to Astoria. These gentlemen described the country of the Willamette as charming and abounding in beaver and deer, and they told us that Messrs. Wallace and Halsey had built a trading house on a great prairie about 150 miles from the mouth of that river [that is, at the confluence of the Willamette and the Columbia]. Mr. McKenzie and his party left us again on the thirty-first, to tell the gentlemen who were wintering in the interior the decisions that had been made at Astoria.

On April 11, two birch-bark canoes bearing the British flag arrived at Astoria. They were commanded by Messrs. John G. McTavish and Joseph Laroque, who had nineteen Canadian *voyageurs* under them. They made camp on a point of land beneath the guns of the Fort. We invited these gentlemen to our quarters, and learned from them the object of their visit. They had come to await the arrival of the ship *Isaac Todd*, which had left Canada in October, 1811, and England in March, 1812, with a cargo for the North West Company.[4] They had orders to wait at the mouth of the Columbia until July and thereafter to return if the ship did not make her appearance by then. They also in-

[3] Huntington interpolates: . . . whence I continued to despatch canoe after canoe of fine fresh fish to Astoria . . ." (p. 168).

formed us that the natives of the interior had shown them fowling pieces, shot, and powder; and that they had communicated this news to Mr. McKenzie, presuming that the Indians had discovered and plundered his cache. *That* we found to be exactly the case.

During the month of May we prepared for our departure. On the twenty-fifth, Messrs. Wallace and Halsey returned from their winter quarters with seventeen packets of skins and thirty-two bales of dried meat. The latter articles were welcomed with much pleasure, for otherwise it would have been necessary for us to exist on the journey with only that food which we had on hand. Mr. Clarke, Mr. David Stuart, and Mr. McKenzie also arrived, at the beginning of June, with 140 packets of furs, a collection from two years in the trading post at Okanogan and one at the Spokane post.[5]

The wintering partners did not agree that we should abandon the country as soon as we intended, believing that the idea was impracticable because of our lack of provisions for the journey and of horses to transport the goods. The project was thus deferred until the following April.[6] These gentlemen, after getting a new supply of merchandise, set out again for their trading posts on July 7. Mr. McKenzie, whose goods had been pillaged by the natives, remained at Astoria and occupied himself in carefully collecting as great a quantity of dried salmon as possible. To this end he made seven or eight jaunts upriver, while at the Fort we were busy, baling the beaver and other skins.[7]

4 Unaccountably Huntington alters this clause to read, ". . . with a cargo of suitable merchandise for the Indian trade" (p. 169).

5 Bibaud adds a footnote: "The profits of the latter post were not large, because those who were engaged there had to live on horseflesh; and they ate ninety of them [horses] during the winter" (p. 128).

6 Quaife states that the Manuscript continues: ". . . for we had decided to follow the route of Lewis and Clark and to descend the Missouri" (p. 126n.).

7 Huntington adds: "Mr. Reed, in the meantime, was sent to the mountain passes where Mr. Miller had been left with the trappers, to winter there, and to procure as many horses as he could from the natives for our use in the contemplated journey. He was furnished for this expedition with three Canadians, and a half-breed named Daion [this was Pierre Dorion, whose fate is described in Part IV, Chapter 22], the latter accompanied by his wife and two children. This man came from the lower Missouri with Mr. Hunt in 1811–12" (pp. 171–72). One may

Our object, before leaving the country, was to provide ourselves with the food and horses necessary for the journey. In order
to avoid all opposition on the part of the North West Company,
we entered into an agreement with Mr. McTavish.[8] That gentleman explained to us that he was altogether lacking the supplies
to procure food for the trip homeward. Therefore we outfitted
him from our warehouse and had his promise that he would repay us the following spring, either in furs or in bills of exchange
on the North West Company in Montreal.

CHAPTER 14

On August 4, contrary to all expectations, we saw a sail at
the mouth of the river. One of our gentlemen immediately got
into the barge to reconnoiter. But before he had crossed the river,
we saw the ship pass the bar and direct her course toward Astoria.[1]
I had stayed at the Fort with Mr. Clapp and four other men. As
soon as we had recognized the American flag, not doubting any
longer that it was a ship destined for the establishment, we saluted
her with three guns. She came to anchor opposite the Fort, but on
the other side of the river, and returned our salute. Shortly afterward we saw, or rather heard (for it was already night), the oars
of a boat coming toward us. We awaited her approach, impatient
to know who the stranger was and what she brought us. Soon we
were relieved of our uncertainty by the appearance of Mr. Hunt,
who informed us that the ship was called the *Albatross* and was
commanded by Captain Smith.

It will be recalled that Mr. Hunt had left [Astoria] on board
the *Beaver* on August 4 of the preceding year, and should have
returned with that ship in October of the same year. We told him

conjecture that Franchère kept the notes of his diary and did not include these
data when writing his *Journal* for Bibaud to publish. Otherwise his recall of
specific information is remarkable.

[8] At this point, Quaife maintains, the Manuscript reads: "One of our young
men, Rossenberg Cox, preferred to engage in the service of the [North West] Company rather than cross the Continent with us" (p. 127n.). Where Franchère
acquired the first name, Rossenberg, for this "little Irishman," is not known.

[1] Huntington adds: ". . . as if she were commanded by a Captain to whom
the intricacies of the channel were familiar" (p. 173).

of our surprise that he had not returned at the expected time, and expressed the fears that we had, not only for him but also for the *Beaver*. In reply, he explained the reasons why neither he nor Captain Sowles could fulfill the promise they had made to us.

After leaving the Columbia River [he said], they had sailed northward before the wind and had put into the Russian trading post at Sitka, Alaska, where they had exchanged a part of their merchandise for furs. With the governor of that establishment, whose name was Baranoff, they had made arrangements by which they agreed to supply him regularly with all the goods he needed, and each year to send him a ship, not only for that purpose but also to transport furs from his post to the East Indies.

After that, they sailed farther north and touched at the islands of St. Peter and St. Paul, near Kamtchatka, where they procured nearly eighty thousand seal skins.[2] These operations had taken a great deal of time. The winter season was already far advanced, they found ice forming around them, and it was not without encountering grave danger that they finally succeeded in getting out of that locality. Having escaped from the icy seas in the north, they set their course for the Sandwich Islands, where they arrived after enduring several severe storms. At these islands Mr. Hunt debarked with the men who had accompanied him and who were not part of the ship's crew, and when the ship had undergone necessary repairs, she left for Canton.

Mr. Hunt had spent nearly six months in Hawaii, expecting a ship from New York and not once imagining that war had been declared. But at last, tired of waiting uselessly, he bought a small schooner from one of the chiefs on the island of Oahu and was preparing to return to the Columbia River when, on the open sea, he perceived four sails that soon came to anchor at Waikiki. Immediately he went on board one of these ships and

---

2 Huntington interpolates the following: ". . . and being there informed that some Kodiak hunters had been left on some adjacent isles, called the islands of St. Peter and St. Paul, and that these hunters had not been visited for three years, they determined to go thither, and having reached those isles, they opened a brisk trade, and secured no less than eighty thousand skins of the South-sea seal" (p. 175).

learned that they had come from the Indies—from which they had departed in great haste in order to avoid the British cruisers. He learned also from Captain Smith that the *Beaver* had arrived in Canton a few days before the news of the declaration of war. Captain Smith carried some merchandise that Mr. Astor's agent ordered for the Astoria post. Mr. Hunt chartered the *Albatross* to carry him and his goods to the Columbia River. That gentleman had not been idle during the time he remained on the Sandwich Islands. He brought us thirty-five barrels of pork or dried beef, nine casks of rice, a large quantity of dried taro, and a good supply of salt.

Because I knew the river channel, I got aboard the ship and piloted her to the [former] moorage of the *Tonquin*, under the guns of the Fort, in order to facilitate unloading the goods.

Captain Smith informed us that in 1810, a year before the founding of our establishment, he had entered the river in this same ship and had gone upstream as far as Oak Point. He had attempted to establish a trading post there, but the site he had chosen for building—and where he had even started a garden—was submerged by high water during the month of July, and he was forced to abandon his enterprise and sail away. We had, in fact, seen some vestiges of that projected trading post at Oak Point.

Captain Smith had rented his ship to a Frenchman by the name of P. Demestre, who was then a passenger on board, to collect a cargo of sandalwood at the Marquesas, where Demestre had left some men the preceding year. As a consequence, he could not grant our request that he spend the summer with us in order to carry our goods and men to the Sandwich Islands.

Mr. Hunt was astonished when we told him of our decision to leave the country. He criticized us severely for acting so precipitously, pointing out to us that the success of the voyage along the coast and the arrangements that he had made with the Russians promised a most advantageous business.[3] Nevertheless, he

___

[3] Huntington adds: ". . . which it was a thousand pities to sacrifice, and lose the fruits of the hardships he had endured and the dangers he had braved, at one fell swoop, by this rash measure" (p. 179).

saw that we had decided to hold firm to our initial resolution; and since he could not by himself fulfill his agreements with Governor Baranoff, he consented to put to sea again in order to find a ship to transport those among us who wished to return home by the sea route. In fact, he sailed away in the *Albatross* at the end of the month. My friend Clapp sailed with him. They planned first of all to range along the California shores in the hope of meeting some American ships, which often frequent these areas to get provisions from the Spaniards.

Some days after the departure of Mr. Hunt, the old Chief Concomly came to tell us that an Indian from Gray's Harbor, who had sailed on the *Tonquin* in 1811, and who was the only one to escape the massacre of the crew of that ship, had returned to his tribe.[4] Since the distance from the Columbia River to Gray's Harbor was not great, we sent for this native. At first he offered considerable resistance to following our people, but was finally persuaded. He arrived at Astoria and related to us the circumstances of that disaster very nearly as follows:[5]

"After I had embarked on the *Tonquin*, he said, "that ship sailed for Nootka.[6] When we arrived opposite a large village

4 Ross quotes the Indian as saying, "My name is Kasiascall, but the Chinooks hereabout call me Lamazu. I belong to the Wickanook tribe of Indians near Nootka Sound . . . ." In fact, Ross's account of the loss of the *Tonquin* differs from Franchère's in a number of details. He has McKay warning the Captain of impending trouble and having some presentiments of disaster, a warning which the Captain dismissed cavalierly. See Ross, *First Settlers*, 172–80.

Cox also tells a somewhat different story of the destruction of the *Tonquin*, but in the essentials he is close to Franchère. Cox, *Columbia River*, 64ff. In all basic elements, Irving follows Franchère. See Irving, *Astoria*, edited by Todd, 108–14.

5 Bibaud's footnote may be translated as follows: "It is to be understood that I gallicize somewhat the language of this barbarian and that I put into words and phrases what he could express only by gestures and signs" (p. 136).

6 Bibaud explains in a footnote that Nootka was "a great colony of Indians, among whom the Spaniards had sent missionaries, under the leadership of Señor Quadra; but from which they [the Spaniards] were chased by Captain Vancouver, in 1792" (p. 136). See also Franchère's Introduction.

It is commonly assumed that the *Tonquin* was destroyed somewhere within Nootka Sound on the west coast of Vancouver Island. Nootka, which had been for almost ten years a post for maritime fur traders, was practically unvisited after 1795. By 1805, however, there were two other trade centers on this northern coast: Kygarney, in the Queen Charlotte Islands, and Newettee, a small inlet on the

called Newity, we dropped anchor. The natives invited Mr. Alexander McKay to land and he did so, and he was received in a most cordial manner. They even kept him several days at their village and made him lie every night on a couch of sea-otter skins. Meanwhile Captain Thorn engaged in trading with the natives who visited his ship. But when he had some trouble with one of the principal chiefs about the price of certain goods, he ended by putting the latter off the ship, and in the act of repelling him struck him on the face with the furs that the native had brought to trade. This act was regarded by the chief and his followers as a most grievous insult and they resolved to take vengeance for it.

"To arrive more surely at the object of their design, they hid their resentment and came, as usual, on board ship. One day, very early in the morning, a large pirogue, containing about a score of natives, came alongside. Each of the savages in the boat held in his hand a packet of furs, and they said that they had come to trade. The watch let them on deck. A little later, a second pirogue arrived carrying about as many men as the first. The sailors believed that these also came to exchange their furs, and allowed them to mount the ship's side like the others. Very

northwestern promontory of Vancouver Island. It is of interest to note that Ross Cox mentions New Whitty, "in the vicinity of Nootka," in his account. Cox, *Columbia River*, 63–64.

According to John D'Wolf, master of the *Juno*, "Newettee was one of the southernmost harbors frequented by American furtraders, being in lat. 51 N and long. 128 W." He said that the Indians had no permanent residence there "but made it merely a place of resort for traffic on the arrival of ships. For this purpose it was considered at certain seasons one of the best harbors on the coast, as there are many large villages in its vicinity." He found the natives "exceedingly sharp in all their intercourse . . . being great beggars, withal. It seemed impossible to satisfy them for their skins, and they were ready to grasp at everything they saw." John D'Wolf, *Voyage to the North Pacific and a Journey Through Siberia More than Half a Century Ago* (Cambridge, 1861), Chapters I and II. D'Wolf offers a thread of evidence with which to tie the *Tonquin* incident to this locality. When he tried to enter Newettee he was rescued from trouble by Captain John Ebbets, master of the ship *Pearl*. Ebbets was an employee of John Jacob Astor, and principal source of the latter's information about trade on the Northwest Coast. Hence it can be argued that Astor had directed Thorn to take the *Tonquin* to Newettee, not to Nootka, and therefore that Newettee Inlet was the site of the *Tonquin* disaster.

soon more pirogues arrived, one after another, and the crew found themselves surrounded by a multitude of savages who came upon the deck from all sides. Alarmed about the situation, they went to warn the captain and Mr. McKay, who hastened onto the deck.

"I was with them," our Indian narrator said, "and because of the great number of Indians that I saw on the bridge and because of the movements of those on shore, who were hurrying to embark in their pirogues to come to the ship, I feared some evil design was being plotted. I communicated my suspicions to Mr. McKay, who himself spoke to the captain.[7] The latter affected an air of security and said that with the firearms on board there was no reason to fear an even greater number of Indians. Meanwhile, these gentlemen had come on deck unarmed, without so much as their daggers.[8] I urged them to put to sea; and, seeing the numbers of savages increase at each moment, the captain at last was persuaded to act. He ordered a part of the crew to raise anchor and the rest to go aloft and unfurl the sails. At the same time he warned the natives to leave, because the ship was putting to sea.[9] But they made a great hue and cry, drew out the knives that they had concealed in their bundles of furs, and fell upon the crew of the ship.

"Mr. McKay was the first victim they sacrificed to their fury. Two Indians from the taffrail of the deck (where I was seated) whom I had seen follow this gentleman step by step, now hurled themselves upon him. They gave him a blow on the back of the head with a potumagan (a kind of sabre about which more will be said later) and felled him to the deck. Then they took him up

[7] Cox indicates that an unreconcilable hostility existed between Thorn and McKay, a hostility that Franchère does not mention. Cox, *Columbia River*, 67.

[8] Huntington adds: "The trade, nevertheless, did not advance; the Indians offered less than was asked, and pressing with their furs close to the Captain, Mr. McKay, and Mr. Lewis, repeated the word Makoke! Makoke! 'Trade! Trade!'" (pp. 182–83).

[9] Huntington adds further: "A fresh breeze was then springing up, and in a few moments more their prey would have escaped them; but immediately upon receiving this notice, by a preconcerted signal, the Indians, with a terrific yell, drew forth the knives and war-bludgeons . . ." (p. 183).

and flung him into the sea, where the women left in the canoes quickly finished him off.[10] Others flung themselves upon the captain, who defended himself for a long time with his knife, but who perished also under the blows of these murderers, overpowered by their number. I next saw (and that was the last thing that I witnessed before quitting the ship) the sailors who were aloft, slip down by the rigging and into the hatchway.[11] One of them in descending received a knife-stab in the back.

"I then jumped overboard to escape a fate similar to that of the captain and Mr. McKay. The women captured me and told me to hide myself quickly in a pirogue under some mats. And that I did. Soon after, I heard the discharge of firearms, and the Indians fled the from the ship and pulled for the shore.[12]

"The next day, having seen four men leave the ship in a small boat, the Indians sent some pirogues in pursuit.[13] I have every reason to believe that these four men were recaptured and massacred, for I never saw any one of them again. Now that they found themselves absolute masters of the *Tonquin,* the savages rushed on board in a crowd to pillage her.

"But shortly, when there were about four or five hundred of them, and as many aboard as round about, the ship blew up with a horrible noise. I was on the beach," said our narrator, "when the explosion occurred and I saw arms, legs, heads, fly in the air on all sides. This tribe lost nearly two hundred of their people on that occasion. As for me, I remained their prisoner and have been their slave for two years."[14]

10 Cox varies the story by saying that McKay, after being thrown overboard, was taken into a canoe by the Indian women, who intended to hold him for ransom. But the spirit of revenge prevailed with the Indians and they battered his brains out as his head hung over the side of the canoe. Cox, *Columbia River,* 65.

11 Huntington adds: "They were five, I think, in number, and one of them . . . (p. 184).

12 Huntington builds upon the story by adding: ". . . nor did they venture to go alongside the ship again the whole of that day" (pp. 184–85).

13 Huntington says ". . . but whether these men were overtaken and murdered, or gained the open sea and perished there, I never could learn." In the 1820 version, Franchère seemed certain that they had been massacred.

14 Huntington adds further to the Indian's account: "It is but now that I have been ransomed by my friends. I have told you the truth, and hope that you

When our Indian finished his discourse, we made him some presents proportionate to the courtesy he had shown us and the trouble he had taken. He returned to his tribe, apparently well satisfied with our liberality.

According to the Indian's account, Captain Thorn was, by his brusk manner and hotheadedness, the primary cause of his own death and the deaths of all his crew. What appears certain, at least, is that he was guilty of unpardonable negligence and imprudence in not rigging the boarding nets, as do all the explorers who frequent this coast, and in allowing too many Indians to come aboard his ship at one time.

Captain Smith (of the *Albatross*), who had seen the wreck of the *Tonquin* and who also spoke of this disastrous event, attributed the blame to Captain Ayres, of Boston. As has been noted earlier, this navigator had taken ten of twelve Indians from Newity as hunters, with the promise that he would bring them home; but he had inhumanly abandoned them on some deserted islands. The fellow tribesmen of these unfortunate men, outraged by the conduct of the American captain, had sworn to avenge themselves on the first white men who appeared in their harbor. Mere chance decreed that our ship would be the first to sail into that bay, and the natives subjected our men to the full fury of their vengeance.

Whatever may have been the first and principal cause of this disaster (for it must be supposed that there were other blunders), seventeen white men on the ship were massacred.[15] No one, except the Indian of Gray's Harbor, escaped the butchery to bring us the news of it. The slaughter of our people was avenged, it is true, by the destruction of ten times the number of their murderers; but this circumstance, that could perhaps gladden the heart of a savage, was little, if any, consolation for civilized men.

---

will acquit me of having in any way participated in that bloody affair"—all of which seems to be an unlikely bit of Indian sign language! (p. 186).

15 Huntington adds: ". . . and twelve Sandwich Islanders . . ." (p. 188). In view of the concluding sentence in this chapter, the statement seems almost contradictory.

The death of Mr. Alexander McKay was an irreparable loss to the company, which would probably have been dissolved then but for the arrival of Mr. Hunt. As interesting as the recital of the Indian of Gray's Harbor was to us, when he came to the unhappy death of that truly estimable man, marks of regret were visibly painted on the faces of all who listened.

At the beginning of September, Mr. McKenzie set off with Mr. Wallace and Mr. Seton to take supplies to the gentlemen in the interior (as well as to inform them about the arrangements made with Mr. Hunt) and to ask them to send all their furs and all the Sandwich Islanders to the Fort, so that the latter could be returned to their country.[16]

CHAPTER 15

A few days after Mr. McKenzie's departure we were greatly surprised to see, rounding Tongue Point, two canoes bearing the British flag, with a third between them carrying a flag of the United States. It was none other than Mr. McKenzie himself, who was returning with Mr. John G. McTavish and Mr. Angus Bethune of the North West Company. Mr. McKenzie had met these gentlemen near the first falls and had come back to the establishment with them because of the information they gave him. They were in express canoes, having left Mr. John Stuart and Mr. McMillan behind them with a flotilla of eight canoes loaded with furs.

Mr. McTavish came to our quarters at the factory and

[16] The 1854 edition appends the following "Note" at the end of the chapter: "It will never be known how or by whom the *Tonquin* was blown up. Some pretend to say that it was the work of James Lewis, but that is impossible, for it appears from the narrative of the Indian that he was one of the first persons murdered. It will be recollected that five men got between decks from aloft, during the affray, and only four were seen to quit the ship afterward in the boat. The presumption was that the missing man must have done it, and in further conversation with the Gray's Harbor Indian, he inclined to that opinion, and even affirmed that the individual was the ship's armorer, Weeks. It might also have been accidental. There was a large quantity of powder in the run immediately under the cabin, and it is not impossible that while the Indians were intent on plunder, in opening some of the kegs they may have set fire to the contents. Or again, the men, before quitting the ship, may have lighted a slow train, which is the most likely supposition of all" (p. 189).

showed us a letter from Mr. Angus Shaw, one of the partners of the North West Company. Mr. Shaw informed him that the ship *Isaac Todd* had sailed from London in March, in company with the frigate *Phoebe,* which came with orders from the government to seize our fort, represented to the Lords of the Admiralty as being an important colony founded by the American government.

The eight canoes left behind now came up to join the others. They formed a camp of about seventy-five men at the lower end of a little bay near our quarters. Because they had no provisions, we supplied them. We kept ourselves on guard, however, fearing a possible surprise by them, since we had the smaller force on our side.[1]

As the season advanced and their ship did not arrive, the Northwesters found themselves in a very disagreeable situation, without food and without merchandise with which to bargain with the natives. The Indians, in turn, regarded them with distrust. They had good hunters but lacked ammunition; and, finally, disgusted at having to ask us constantly for food, they proposed that they buy our establishment and its contents.

Situated as we were, expecting from day to day the arrival of an English man-of-war to seize all we possessed, we listened to their proposition. We held several consultations, and the negotiations between us extended over a long period.[2] At length the price of the goods and furs in the establishment was agreed upon, and the bargain was signed by both parties on October 23, 1813.[3]

Thus the gentlemen of the North West Company took over Astoria, agreeing to pay the employees of the Pacific Fur Com-

1 Huntington alters this passage to say, ". . . but Messrs. McDougall and McKenzie affecting to dread a surprise from this British force under our guns, we kept strictly on our guard. . . ." And he appends at the conclusion," . . . although our position was exceedingly advantageous" (pp. 191–92).

2 Huntington adds: ". . . by the hope of one party that the long-expected armed force would arrive, to render the purchase unnecessary, and were urged forward by the other in order to conclude the affair before that occurrence should intervene . . ." (p. 193).

3 Franchère was wrong about the date of the signing of this agreement. The documents show October 16, 1813. Alexander Ross confirms the latter date. Ross, *Fur Hunters,* 4. Quaife makes no mention of it in his 1954 edition.

pany (the name that had been chosen by Mr. Astor) the sum of their wages–to be deducted from the price of the goods that we delivered to them—to supply them with provisions, and to give a free passage to those who wished to return to Canada.[4]

It was in this way that, after having sailed the seas and having suffered all sorts of fatigue and privation, I lost in a moment all my hopes of fortune. I could not help remarking that we had no right to expect such treatment from the British government, after the assurance we had received from His Majesty's chargé d'affaires before we left New York. But as I have just said, the importance of the Fort had been exaggerated in the eyes of the British Ministry; if the latter had known about its true condition, they surely would never have taken umbrage at it, or, at least, they would never have considered it worthy of a maritime expedition.[5]

Most of the employees of the Pacific Fur Company entered the service of the North West Company. The others preferred to return to their country, and I was among them. However, Mr. McTavish told me that he needed me at the establishment.[6] Con-

---

[4] Huntington adds at this point: "The American colors were hauled down from the factory, and the British run up, to the no small chagrin and mortification of those who were American citizens" (p. 193). This sentence is not in Bibaud, and Quaife maintains that it is not in the Manuscript. See Quaife (p. 143n.).

[5] Huntington interpolates: ". . . a mere trading post—and that nothing but the rivalry of the fur-traders of the Northwest Company was interested in its destruction. . . . The sequel will show that I was not mistaken in this opinion" (p. 194).

[6] Huntington explains in greater detail: ". . . after many ineffectual attempts to persuade me to remain with them, having intimated that the establishment could not dispense with my services, as I was the only person who could assist them in their trade, especially for provisions, of which they would soon be in the greatest need, I agreed with them. . . ." (pp. 194–95).

Ross Cox states that "From this gentleman's [Franchère's] knowledge of the Chinook language Mr. McTavish made him handsome offers to join the North-West Company, which he refused. He however remained until the following spring." Cox, *Columbia River*, 120n. Franchère's statement derived neither from pride nor from an attitude of defense. The Northwesters had only a handful on whom they could rely for help in the Astoria enterprise. Quite apart from his knowledge of the Chinook language, Franchère also knew the sources of food and pelt supply upriver and, in fact, much that the Northwesters had yet to learn.

John George McTavish was at Grand Portage with the North West Company in 1802 and in the Athabasca District for the company in 1808. In company with John McDonald, of Garth, he went west to the relief of David Thompson in 1811,

sequently I engaged myself with them for a period of five months
—that is, until the departure of the group that was to go upriver
in the springtime and return to Canada by way of the Rocky
Mountains and the interior rivers.[7] Messrs. John Stuart and Mc-
Kenzie left toward the end of the month, McKenzie to hand over
to Stuart the trading posts that had been established by the afore-
mentioned company.

On November 15, Mr. Alexander Stewart and Mr. Alexander Henry, both partners of the North West Company, arrived
at Astoria in two bark canoes manned by sixteen *voyageurs*.[8]
These gentlemen had left Fort William, on Lake Superior, in
July. They told us the news from Canada, by which we learned
that the British had been successful in the war. They also confirmed the report that an English frigate should have arrived to
take over our establishment, and were quite surprised not to
see the *Isaac Todd* lying at anchor.

---

and he was on the Columbia to receive the surrender of Fort Astoria in 1813. In
that same year he became a partner in the North West Company. He was arrested
by the Hudson's Bay Company in 1819 in connection with the Selkirk troubles,
and was released from the charges made against him following a trial in London
in 1821. Thereafter he served in a number of the fur-trading posts, ending his
career by working as factor of the Lake of the Two Mountains agency from 1836
until 1847. He died on July 20, 1847. See *Dictionary of Canadian Biography*. He
should not be confused with Donald McTavish, who sailed from London on the
Isaac Todd in 1813, in command of the expedition to Astoria. Donald McTavish
was drowned near the mouth of the Columbia on May 23, 1814. Nor should he be
confused with Alexander McTavish, who also was aboard the *Isaac Todd*, a clerk
for the North West Company who remained in the fur trade until his death in 1832.

7 Alexander Ross says that Franchère "was the only clerk in the American
service who showed a wish to join the newcomers." Ross, *First Settlers*, 275. All
the evidence points to the contrary. Franchère remained only until the spring of
1814, according to his contract, and in subsequent years he became an American
citizen. Ross, on the other hand, remained with the North West Company and
always retained his British citizenship.

8 Huntington was in error in his use of the name Alexander Stuart, an
error repeated by Quaife in his 1954 edition. Franchère correctly spelled the name
Stewart in the 1820 text. See also Ross Cox, *Columbia River*, p. 148.

Alexander Stewart entered the services of the North West Company in 1796,
and was in the Fort des Prairies and Lesser Slave Lake posts until 1812, when he
was put in charge of the Athabasca River department of the company. He became
a partner in 1813, was transferred to the Columbia, and was present at the exchange made at the fort in that year. When North West and Hudson's Bay merged,
he was made chief factor at Fort William (1821–23) and, later, at other posts. He
died in May, 1840. See *Dictionary of Canadian Biography*.

On the morning of the thirtieth we discovered a ship doubling round Cape Disappointment and soon afterward dropping anchor in Baker's Bay. As we did not know whether it was friend or foe, we thought it best to send out Mr. McDougall in a canoe, with those men who had been in the service of the Pacific Fur Company, with orders to call themselves Americans if the ship were American, and British subjects in the contrary case.

Meanwhile, Mr. McTavish embarked with two barges and all the furs which were marked with the name of the North West Company and went upriver as far as Tongue Point, where he was to wait for a given signal. Toward midnight, Mr. Halsey, who accompanied Mr. McDougall to the ship, returned to the Fort and told us that it was the British corvette *Racoon,* with twenty-six guns, 120 sailors, commanded by Captain Black.

Mr. John McDonald, a partner in the North West Company, was a passenger on the *Racoon,* and was accompanied by five *voyageurs.* He had left England on the frigate *Phoebe,* that had sailed as far as Rio de Janeiro with the *Isaac Todd.*

They had joined an English squadron there, and the Admiral had given them the corvettes *Racoon* and *Cherub* as convoys.[9] Thus these four ships sailed in company as far as Cape Horn, where they separated, agreeing upon Juan Fernandez Island as a rendezvous. Three of the warships did effect a meeting, but waited in vain for the *Isaac Todd.* Finally Commodore Hillier, who commanded this little squadron, learned that the American Commodore Porter was playing havoc with British shipping—particularly among the whalers that sailed these seas. Hillier decided to go after Porter and make a fight of it, and he sent Captain Black ahead to destroy the American trading post at the mouth of the Columbia.

For this reason, Mr. McDonald had embarked with his men on board the *Racoon.* This gentleman told us that they had experienced severe weather while doubling Cape Horn.[10] He

9 Huntington makes minor variations of detail in the following passage but no substantive alterations or additions.

10 Huntington adds: ". . . and that he entertained serious apprehensions for the safety of the *Isaac Todd*" (p. 198).

thought that if the *Isaac Todd* had not put into port somewhere during her passage, she should appear in the Columbia in less than two weeks.[11]

At the prearranged signal, Mr. McTavish returned to Astoria with his furs, and was pleased to learn of Mr. McDonald's arrival.

On December 1, the corvette's barge came to the Fort with Mr. McDonald and first lieutenant, Mr. Sheriff.[12] These two men were convalescents, following an accident that had happened to them during the voyage from Juan Fernandez to Astoria. The captain wished to have the cannons cleaned out, and had ordered them all to be fired. During the exercise, one of the guns had a delayed firing; the fire touched off cartridges hanging above the cannon and reached some powder horns strung from a joist. There followed an explosion that struck twenty men. Eight died afterward from their burns, and Mr. McDonald and Mr. Sheriff suffered severely. In fact, it was difficult to get them out of their clothes, and when the lieutenant left the ship he could not use his hands, they were so badly burned. Among those who were victims of this accident was an American by the name of J. Flatt, who was in the service of the North West Company and whose death these gentlemen regretted a great deal.

Since the *Racoon* carried some merchandise destined for the North West Company, a schooner was finally sent to Baker's Bay to bring it to the Fort. But the weather was so bad and the wind so violent that not until the twelfth did it return, bringing Captain Black, a marine officer, four soldiers, and four sailors. We entertained our guests as lavishly as we possibly could. After dinner the captain had guns distributed to the employees of the company and we all gathered, thus armed, on a platform on which a flagstaff had been erected. There the captain took a British flag he had brought for the purpose and had it run up on the staff. Then, taking a bottle of Madeira wine, he broke it across

---

11 Huntington states "in two or three weeks" (p. 198).
12 Huntington adds in parentheses "(surnamed *Bras Croche*, or crooked arm)" (p. 199).

the staff, declaring in a loud voice that he was taking possession of the establishment in the name of His Royal Majesty. And he changed the name of the Fort from Astoria to Fort George. Indian chiefs had been assembled to serve as witnesses to the ceremony, and I explained to them, in their language, what had taken place. Three rounds of artillery and musketry were fired, and the health of the King was drunk, according to the usual custom on such occasions.

Since the ship was detained in the harbor by contrary winds, the captain had some practice bearings made of the river mouth, as well as of the channel between Baker's Bay and Fort George. The officers came to see us, by turns, and to me they seemed generally unhappy with their voyage. They had looked forward to finding several American ships loaded with furs and had counted in advance upon their share in the Astoria prize. They found nothing, and their astonishment reached its peak when they discovered that the establishment had been transferred to the North West Company and was under the British flag. The reactions of Captain Black will be sufficient to show how much they had been deceived about us. The captain landed at night. When, the next morning, we let him see the palisades of the establishment, he asked whether there was another fort. Finding none, he cried out in even greater astonishment: "Why, is this the fort that was represented to me as so great? Good Lord, I could knock it over in two hours with a four-pounder!"[13]

On board the *Racoon* there were two young men from Canada who had been impressed for duty aboard the ship when she had anchored at Quebec some years before her voyage to Astoria. One of them, named Parent, was from Quebec; the other, named McDonald, was from upper Canada. They expressed their desire to remain at Fort George; and as there were among us several men who could have wished nothing better than to sail on the corvette, we suggested an exchange to the captain, but he would not consent to it. An American, John Little, who had been sick

[13] A footnote in Bibaud states in English what I have already translated here in these last utterances of Captain Black (p. 152).

for some time, was sent aboard and put in the care of the ship's surgeon, Mr. O'Brien. He was to debark at the Sandwich Islands. Paul D. Jeremie also went aboard. The ship hoisted sail and left the river on March 31.[14]

<h2>CHAPTER 16</h2>

On January 3, 1814, two canoes loaded with supplies and manned by fifteen *voyageurs* were sent into the interior under the command of Mr. Alexander Stewart and Mr. James Keith.[1] Two of their party were ordered to go east of the Rockies with instructions to get canoes and provisions for the journey the following spring. I took advantage of the opportunity to write Montreal. This was the third time since my arrival at Astoria that I attempted to get news to my family and friends and, again, without success.

On the morning of the sixth, Mr. John Stuart and Mr. Mc-Kenzie, who earlier had been sent to the interior to inform the

[14] The 1820 edition does, in fact, read *"le 31 Mars,"* but manifestly Franchère meant December 31. See Bibaud (p. 152).

The following paragraph appears in Huntington. It does not appear in Bibaud nor, Quaife maintains, in the Manuscript (See Quaife, p. 152n.).

"From the account given in this chapter the reader will see with what facility the establishment of the Pacific Fur Company could have escaped capture by the British force. It was only necessary to get rid of the land party of the Northwest Company—who were completely in our power—then remove our effects up the river upon some small stream, and await the result. The sloop-of-war arrived, it is true; but as, in the case I suppose, she would have found nothing, she would have left, after setting fire to our deserted houses. None of their boats would have dared follow us, even if the Indians had betrayed to them our lurking-place. Those at the head of affairs had their own fortunes to seek, and thought it more for their interest, doubtless, to act as they did, but that will not clear them in the eyes of the world, and the charge of treason to Mr. Astor's interests will always be attached to their characters" (pp. 203–204). Huntington to the contrary notwithstanding, time has pretty well erased the stigma attendant upon the action of the men at Astoria who sold out; and in the strong light cast later upon the entrepreneurs who operated during the Gilded Age following the Civil War, their figures would cast only a faint shadow.

[1] Ross tells a story in no way intimated by Franchère, to the effect that Alexander Stewart and James Keith (Ross also confuses Stewart with Stuart) went to the interior to relate the good news about their acquisition of Fort George to the post at Ft. William, the chief depot of their inland trade on Lake Superior. He says that everyone tried to dissuade them from going on "so perilous an adventure with so few men. . . ." See Ross, *Fur Hunters* 11 ff.

gentlemen there of what had happened at Fort George [Astoria], returned to the Fort. They told us that they had left Mr. David Stuart and Mr. Clarke behind with the loaded canoes, and that they had been attacked by natives near the Falls.

As they were coming down the river, toward evening, between the first and second portages they saw a great number of Indians gathered. This caused them some uneasiness.

Shortly afterward they encamped, and all were asleep but Mr. Stuart, who stood guard. But the savages stole upon the camp and shot several arrows, one of which penetrated the covers of a man who lay near the baggage, piercing one of his ears. Pain made him cry out so loudly that he alarmed the entire camp and caused general confusion. Seeing this, the natives fled, howling and yelling, with a horrible din. At daylight our men picked up eight arrows around the camp. They could still hear the Indians whooping and bellowing in the woods, but they reached the lower end of the portage without being molested.

The boldness these barbarians had shown in attacking a party of forty to forty-five men gave us reason to think that they would be much more likely to attack Mr. Stewart's party, numbering only seventeen. Consequently, I received orders to prepare a canoe and arms at once. Everything was ready within two hours, and I embarked immediately with six men and a guide.[2] Our instructions were to make all possible speed to overtake Mr. Stewart and Mr. Keith and convoy them to the upper end of the last portage, or to return with the goods if we found too much resistance.

We paddled all the day and all the night of the sixth and all of the seventh until evening. Finding that we were a short distance from the Falls, I gave order to halt, so that we could put our firearms in readiness and give the men a little rest. About midnight I had them re-embark and ordered them to sing as they paddled, so that the party we wished to join would be aware of our passing—if by chance they had camped on one of the islands that fill the river in this area.

2 Huntington says "eight" (p. 207).

Soon we heard someone hail us. We stopped paddling and were joined by our own people, all in one canoe headed downriver. They told us that they had been attacked the evening before and that Mr. Stewart had been wounded. We turned about, and in company together took up our route toward the Fort. At daybreak we stopped to eat and Mr. Keith gave me the details of the fray of the night before.

Arriving at the foot of the rapids, they had begun their portage on the north bank of the river, which is studded with rock over which they had to carry their goods. After they had moved two canoes and a part of their supplies, Indians approached in great numbers, seeking stealthily to make off with something. Mr. Stewart was alone at the upper end of the portage, which is about six hundred yards long, and Mr. Keith was at the half-way point.

An Indian seized a sack containing some goods of small value and ran off. Mr. Stewart, seeing him, ran after the thief in order to take the sack away; and after meeting with some resistance, he managed to make the fellow let go of it. At once he saw coming toward him a group of savages armed with bows and arrows. One of them strung his bow and took aim. Mr. Stewart likewise took aim at the Indian, who called out to him not to shoot. At the same moment he got an arrow in his left shoulder. He wanted to return the fire, but because it had rained all day, his fuse failed. Before he could reprime his gun, another arrow, better directed than the first, struck him on the left side between two ribs and near the heart.[3] At that moment his gun fired and the Indian fell dead.

Several other Indians then came up to avenge the death of their compatriot. But two of our men, arriving with their bundles and their guns (for they made these portages with guns in their hands), saw what had happened and one of them threw his packet to the ground, fired at one of the Indians, and brought him

[3] Huntington adds: ". . . and would have proved fatal, no doubt, but for a stone-pipe he had fortunately in his side pocket, and which was broken by the arrow" (p. 210).

down. The savage got up, however, and tried to pick up his weapons; but the other of our men ran to him, wrested his dagger away from him, and finished him off by beating him repeatedly over the head.

Now that the main body of our people had arrived at the scene of combat, the other savages fled across the river. Meanwhile, with the help of one of the men, Mr. Stewart pulled the arrows from his body. Blood flowed profusely from his wounds and he saw that it would be impossible for him to continue the journey. He therefore ordered the canoes and supplies carried to the other end of the portage.

Soon they saw a large number of pirogues filled with warriors coming from the opposite bank of the river. Our men believed that the best thing to do was to get under way as fast as possible. They all got into one canoe, abandoning the other canoe and the goods to the Indians. While the natives were pillaging these effects, more precious to them than the golden apples of the Garden of the Hesperides, our men got away and out of sight. Nevertheless, the retreat was so precipitous that they left stranded one of their own Indians—from the tribe of the Lake of the Two Mountains—who had been engaged by the Company as a hunter. This man had hidden behind some rocks, intending, as he said later, to kill some of the thieves, and he had not returned at the time of the departure.[4] Mr. Keith regretted this very much, believing, with good cause, that he would only be discovered and massacred by the natives.[5]

[4] Bibaud's note about the Indian left at The Dalles appears as follows in the 1820 edition: "Some time after, this Indian returned to the establishment, but in a pitiable condition. When the canoes left, he had hidden behind a rock and so spent the night. At daybreak, fearing to be discovered by the native tribesmen, he took to the woods and set out toward the Fort across mountainous country. He had arrived at the banks of a little river that at first he was unable to cross. Hunger pressed him, however; he could have appeased it, as he had encountered several fallow deer, but unfortunately he had lost the flint of his gun. Finally, he had crossed the river and arrived at a village whose inhabitants disarmed him and made him their prisoner. Our men learned where he was, went out to find him, and gave some blankets for his ransom" (p. 161).

[5] Quaife cites the Manuscript as follows: "Despite the insistence of Mr. Keith the canoe pushed off without taking this man, so precipitate was the retreat" (See Quaife, p. 159n.).

We paddled all day and part of the night of the eighth and arrived at the Fort at sunrise on the ninth. Our first care, after we had announced the disaster overtaking our men, was to attend to Mr. Stewart's wounds, which had been bound with a miserable piece of cotton cloth.

The goods that the party had been forced to abandon were of consequence to the company, inasmuch as they could not be replaced. It was dangerous, moreover, to leave the savages in possession of about fifty guns and a considerable quantity of ammunition that they could use against us. The partners decided, therefore, to set out immediately to punish the thieves, or at least to try to recover the lost supplies. I went, by their order, to the principal chiefs of the neighborhood, explaining what had happened and inviting them to join us—an invitation they accepted very willingly. Then on the tenth, having readied six canoes, we embarked with sixty-two men, armed to the teeth and provided with a small cannon.

In a short time we reached the cascades, but an essential element was lacking to our little army—we were without provisions. Our first need was to find a way to procure them. Approaching a village, we saw on the bank about thirty armed savages who appeared to be waiting steadfastly for us. We had no wish at all to seem warlike, so we put ashore on the opposite side of the river. I then crossed over with five or six men, to parley with them and try to get some supplies. I soon saw that the village had been abandoned; the women and children had taken to the woods, and with them all the food. These Indians offered us some dogs, however, and we bought twenty. Then we went on to a second village, where the natives had been informed of our coming. We bought some more dogs and a horse from them, and afterward crossed the portage and made camp on an island.[6]

Since we had now provided ourselves with enough food for several days, we informed the Indians why we had come and told them that we were determined to kill them and burn their villages if they did not bring back to us, in two days, what they

[6] Huntington says "forty-five" dogs (p. 214).

had stolen on the seventh.[7] We reached a large village on the south bank that was deserted. We made inquiries about the Nipissing Indian who had been left at the portage, but the natives assured us that they had not seen him.

We failed to recover any of the lost goods above the Falls. Since the inhabitants protested that it was not they, but the Indians in the villages below, who had stolen our supplies, we went downriver to camp on Strawberry Island.[8] The partners intended only to intimidate the savages, if possible without shedding blood; and we paraded our numbers and from time to time fired our little cannon in order to let them know that we could reach them from one side of the river to the other.

An Indian and his wife who had accompanied us advised us to make one of the chiefs our prisoner.[9] We soon succeeded in doing so, without running any risk. We invited one of the natives to smoke with us, and he came; a little later, another followed suit. Finally, one of the chiefs came—a man highly regarded among them.[10] Immediately we seized him, pinioned him under a tent, and set over him two guards with drawn swords.

Then we sent the other two natives to their people with the news of the capture of their chief, telling them that if they did not return to us at once the supplies they had taken, we would put him to death. Our stratagem worked. They soon brought us some of the guns, a few brass kettles, and other smaller

[7] Huntington adds and varies: "A party was detached to the rapids, where the attack on Mr. Stewart had taken place. We found the villages all deserted" (p. 214).

[8] The Strawberry Island named by Lewis and Clark is now Hamilton Island. Not having the Lewis and Clark Journals to guide them, the Astorians applied the name to what is now called Bradford Island. See McArthur, *Oregon Geographic*, 67.

[9] According to Huntington this Indian man's name was "Coalpo" (p. 215).

[10] Huntington varies this story, saying ". . . at last, one of the chiefs, and one of the most considered among them, also came. Being notified secretly of his character by Coalpo, who was concealed in the tent, we seized him forthwith, tied him to a stake, and placed a guard over him with a naked sword, as if ready to cut off his head on the least attempt being made by his people for his liberation" (pp. 215–16). This supplement to the original seems to be a deliberate effort to heighten the dramatic effect of the situation.

articles, protesting that this was all they had in their share of the loot. We then went on to other villages and succeeded in recovering all the guns and about a third of the other supplies.

The Indians had, of course, been the aggressors. But since two of their men had been killed, while we had lost no one on our side, we thought it our duty to conform to the custom of the country and give them the remainder of our goods to pay for or, according to their expression, "to cover the bodies" of their two compatriots. Besides, we were beginning to run short of provisions and could not easily have pursued our enemies if they had taken to the woods, as was their habit when they felt themselves to be the weaker party.

We released our prisoner and gave him a flag, telling him that when he presented it to us unfurled, we would regard it as a sign of peace and friendship; but that if, when we made our portages, some natives made the mistake of approaching our baggage, we would kill him at once.

On the morning of the nineteenth we again got under way and on the twenty-second arrived at the establishment, where we made a report on our warlike expedition. We found Mr. Stewart very ill from his wounds, particularly the one in his side, which was so badly inflamed that we had reason to think the arrow had been poisoned.

If we did not do the savages as much harm as we might have done, it was not from timidity but from humanity and in order not to spill human blood uselessly. For after all, what good would have followed the massacre of some of these barbarians, whose crime was not the result of depravity and villany, but an ardent and irresistible desire to better their condition? It was generally understood that the partners opposed too greatly marked acts of hostility on our part. It was a matter of some importance to them not to make irreconcilable enemies of all the people near the portages, since they would have to pass and repass these spots so often in the future.

It was likely, besides, that the natives living along the river and by the ocean could not have looked on with indifference as strangers punished their fellows too openly and rigorously. They would have made common cause with their own against the invaders, and perhaps would have driven them from the country.[11]

CHAPTER 17

The new owners of our establishment were not satisfied with the site we had chosen for the Fort and decided to change it. But after surveying and examining both banks of the river, they found nothing more favorable than the neck, or point, that we called Tongue Point.[1] This point, or perhaps one should better say this cape, extends for about ten or a dozen acres into the river and is abutted by a perpendicular rock, the summit of which must be 250 feet above the river level.[2] This summit is covered by timber and many springs are to be found upon it. One can climb it on a path formed by a gentle slope on its back side, where it is neither high nor broad. On either side is a small bay.[3] In effect, while it is truly a tongue of land, from a distance it looks like an island. When the wind is strong, the natives fear to go around, and instead make a simple portage across it.

Astoria was closer to the river mouth than Tongue Point, but this advantage was offset by greater and more numerous superiorities. In addition to the fact that the ground on the Point is less muddy in the rainy season, one can more easily build shelters there against attacks by the natives, and need have less apprehenion about sea attacks by civilized enemies in time of war.

11 Huntington adds a paragraph at the end of Bibaud's chapter, as follows: "I must not omit to state that all the firearms surrendered by the Indians on this occasion, were found loaded with ball, and primed, with a little piece of cotton laid over the priming to keep the powder dry. This shows how soon they would acquire the use of guns, and how careful traders should be in intercourse with strange Indians, not to teach them their use" (pp. 218–19).

1 The Fort was not moved to Tongue Point, despite the advantages pointed out by Franchère, probably because all hands were needed to bring in food supplies.

2 Huntington adds and varies this passage: ". . . being connected with the main-land by a low, narrow neck, over which the Indians, in stormy weather, haul their canoes in passing up and down the river . . ." (p. 220).

3 Further variations appear in Huntington: ". . . on either side it had a cove to shelter the boats necessary for a trading establishment. This peninsula had truly the appearance of a huge tongue" (p. 221).

The men from the interior returned to the Fort and the food in the sheds was quickly consumed.[4] It was necessary, therefore, that most of those at the Fort should go elsewhere to subsist. I left on February 7, 1814, to take a number of the employees to the Willamette, where there were several hunters under the charge of Mr. William Henry.[5] I found it a superb river as I traveled up it. It is, in fact, one of the most beautiful of all the rivers that flow into the Columbia. From the confluence to a falls of considerable size, the country is, in truth, low and marshy; but at the falls the banks begin to rise on either side, and above it they offer the happiest and most picturesque of views, laid bare of trees in several places and rising gradually in the form of an amphitheater. Deer and elk are to be found there in great number.

The post had been established for the purpose of keeping a number of hunters constantly engaged to provide the Fort with venison. Upon our arrival at Astoria we had expected to find the wintertime as severe as that we were accustomed to in the same latitude in the East. But we soon found that we were mistaken. The mildness of the climate never permitted us to take fresh meat from the Willamette to Astoria [without its spoiling], and the attempts that we made to dry or smoke the venison always failed.

Having put my companions under the charge of Mr. Henry, I took leave of that gentleman and started my return to the Fort. I found Mr. Keith and Mr. Pillet camped at Oak Point, to spend the season fishing for sturgeon. These men informed me that I was to remain with them.[6]

[4] Huntington adds that the small stock of provisions had been given by the Pacific Fur Company men to the people of the North West Company (p. 221).

[5] In the Bibaud edition Franchère correctly used the name William Henry. Huntington names Alexander Henry and is, of course, wrong. Northwester Alexander Henry was a nephew of a man by the same name who was in earlier years a friend, adviser, and partner of Astor in New York, and an employee of the North West Company. Quaife corrects the name but does not mention the fact that Bibaud was altered by Huntington.

These errors, at times, cause some loss of confidence in the 1854 edition. How close an eye Franchère gave the text no one knows, but it appears that he examined Huntington's work only sporadically.

[6] Huntington adds two paragraphs: "Accordingly I remained at Oak Point

But while I was there, a sail appeared at the mouth of the Columbia on February 28. Our gentleman dared for a moment to flatter themselves that this was the ship for which they had waited so long [that is, the *Isaac Todd*]. They were soon disillusioned by a letter from Mr. Hunt that the Indians brought to the Fort from the ship. Mr. Hunt had, during his voyage, bought a brig called the *Pedlar*, that had for its pilot Captain Northrup, former commander of the ship *Lark*.

The *Lark* had been chartered by Mr. Astor and had left New York with provisions for our company [Astor's Pacific Fur Company]. But, unhappily, she had been struck by a furious storm and had capsized at about 16° North Latitude, some three hundred miles from the Sandwich Islands. The first mate, who was sick, drowned in his cabin and four other members of the crew perished at the same time. The captain immediately had the masts and rigging cut away; and this action righted the ship, though it was full of water.

One of the sailors dived into the cabin of the sail-maker and brought up a small sail that was attached to the bowsprit. He dived again and brought up a case containing a dozen bottles of wine. For thirteen days they had no other nourishment than a piece of shark meat they had the good luck to catch, and which they ate raw, and a gill of wine a day for each man to drink.

the rest of the winter, occupied in trading with the Indians spread all along the river for some 30 or 40 miles above, in order to supply the factory with provisions. I used to take a boat with four or five men, visit every fishing station, trade for as much fish as would load the boat, and send her down to the fort. The surplus fish traded in the interval between the departure and return of the boat, was cut up, salted and barrelled for future use. The salt had been recently obtained from a quarter to be presently mentioned.

"About the middle of March Messrs. Keith and Pillet both left me and returned to the fort. Being now alone, I began seriously to reflect on my position, and it was in this interval that I positively decided to return to Canada. I made inquiries of the men sent up with the boats for fish, concerning the preparations for departure, but whether they had been enjoined to secrecy, or were unwilling to communicate, I could learn nothing of what was doing below" (pp. 223–24).

Perhaps Franchère had had some misgivings about his rejection of the lavish offers made him by McTavish, rued the loss of the fortune that he had come to the West Coast to make, and pondered what his condition might be if he remained. If so, he finally kept to his original decision to return to Canada.

Finally, the trade winds brought them to the Island of Tahoura-ha [Kauai?], where the ship broke up on the rocks. The islanders saved the crew, and plundered all the goods that floated on the water. Mr. Hunt was then at Oahu. Some islanders from Molokai told him that there were some shipwrecked Americans at Kauai. Mr. Hunt went at once to get them, and gave over the command of his ship [the *Pedlar*] to Captain Northrup.

One can imagine Mr. Hunt's surprise when he saw Astoria under the British flag and passed into strange hands. Nevertheless, the misfortune was without remedy for him, and he could content himself only by taking on board his ship all the Americans who were at the establishment but not employed by the North West Company. Messrs. Halsey, Seton, and Farnham were among those who embarked.[7] I shall have occasion to inform the reader of the results of their voyage.

I spent the rest of the winter securing provisions for the men at the Fort. It was during this time that I determined to return to Canada. Realizing that the canoes would set out at the beginning of April, I raised camp at Oak Point and arrived at the Fort on the second of the month. The brig *Pedlar* left the river on the same day, after several futile attempts, in one of which she was almost broken on the rocks.[8]

Upon my arrival I found everything ready for the departure of the canoes, which had been set for April 4. I packed up the few effects that I possessed; and despite the quite advantageous offers of the gentlemen of the North West Company and their repeated pleas that I stay in the country for at least one more year, I remained firm in my first resolution.

[7] In their *Empire of the Columbia* (New York, Harper and Brothers, 1957), Professors Johansen and Gates note that Russell Farnham left Astoria with Wilson Price Hunt aboard the *Pedlar*, proceeding with him to Sitka, Alaska. There Farnham transferred to the *Forester*; thence he was taken to the coast of Kamshatka. Finally, in 1816, after having made an arduous trek across Siberia to St. Petersburg and Copenhagen, he arrived in New York City. On the way he negotiated the bills of exchange, representing approximately $40,000, the purchase price that the North West Company had paid for Astor's furs, and a figure quite to his employer's advantage.

[8] Huntington adds: "I would gladly have gone in her, had I arrived but a day sooner" (p. 227).

The voyage that I was about to make was a long one; it would be accompanied by extreme fatigue and severe privation and even some danger. But I was used to both privation and fatigue, and I had faced perils of more than one kind. Yet even if this had not been so, the desire to see my country again, my parents, and my friends—the hope of finding myself in a few months once more in their midst—would have outweighed every other consideration.

Thus I leave the banks of the Columbia and conduct the reader across the mountains, the plains, the forests, and the lakes of North America. But before doing so, I must give him at least an idea of the customs and traditions of the natives, as well as the principal products of the country that I leave behind after a stay of three years. That is what I shall try to do in the following chapters.[9]

[9] Bibaud adds the following footnote: "Some readers might, without doubt, wish that I give them some scientific details on the flora and fauna and the natural history of the country. That is what might be expected of a man who had traveled for pleasure or to make such discoveries. But the object of my travels was not such at all. My business had no connection with science; and, as I said in my preface, I was not, and am not now, either a naturalist or a botanist" (p. 171).

Quaife states that the last two paragraphs of this chapter were written by Bibaud and that the next three chapters, 18, 19, and 20, Part III, were transferred by him to their present position from an earlier position that they occupy in the Manuscript. In the latter, says, Quaife, "the opening sentence of Chapter 21 follows at this point" (p. 171n.). As I pointed out in my Introduction to this book, however, the head of the Canadian History and Manuscript Section of the Toronto Public Library maintains that these chapters are not in the manuscript at all.

🔳🔳🔳🔳🔳🔳🔳🔳🔳🔳🔳🔳🔳🔳🔳🔳🔳🔳🔳🔳🔳🔳🔳🔳🔳🔳🔳🔳🔳🔳🔳🔳🔳🔳🔳🔳🔳

PART III

Columbia Country

CHAPTER 18

THE MOUTH of the Columbia River is situated at 46° 19″—20″ North Latitude, and between 125° and 126° Longitude west of the meridian of Greenwich. The tide rises to nine feet at the river entrance, and is felt for about seventy-five or eighty miles upstream from this entrance.

During the three years that I spent there, the temperature almost never fell to the freezing point, and I do not believe that it was ever hotter than 75° or 76°. The west wind prevails in the spring and part of the summer; it usually rises with the tide and tempers the heat of the day. Northwesterly winds prevail almost continually during the remainder of the summer and into the autumn. Then a southwesterly wind blows almost without ceasing from the beginning of October to the end of December or early January. This is the rainy season, the most disagreeable of the year.[1]

The surface of the soil in the valleys consists of a layer of black and vegetable earth five or six inches thick, at most. This layer covers another of extremely cold gray earth. Below the second stratum is a bed of sand and gravel over rock. On high land

1 Huntington adds: "Fogs (so thick that sometimes for days no object is discernible for five or six hundred yards from the beach) are also very prevalent" (p. 230). In some seasons, weather conditions of this nature still prevail far to the south and to the north along the shores of the Pacific.

a very thin layer of black earth covers stones or quarries of building stone. Along the seashore, south of Point Adams, we found a bank of earth white as chalk.[2] The Indians also brought us—but from far to the south—samples of red, green, and yellow earth, and a species of glistening earth resembling lead ore. We constructed several kilns, but futilely, for we found no limestone.

We had taken pains to bring with us on the *Tonquin* all kinds of vegetable seeds, and we planted them in the month of May.[3] The garden had a beautiful appearance in August; but even though these vegetables remained in the ground until the end of December, except for the radishes, turnips, and potatoes, they failed to mature. The turnips were of prodigious size. One of the largest, that we had the curiosity to measure, was thirty-three inches in circumference and weighed fifteen and a half pounds. They were still in blossom at the end of December, and we left them in the ground. But the seeds were all destroyed by the mice that infested our garden and hid under the stumps we had not uprooted. From the dozen potatoes that we had been able to keep sound, we grew ninety plants. These were nurtured carefully, in order to use them as seed in the following spring. But our pains were unavailing, for during the second year the ground was colder than the first, and all came to absolutely nothing.[4]

It would follow from these facts that the soil is scarcely proper for cultivation along the Columbia River, or at least that the vegetation is slow and late in maturing. It could be, however,

2 Huntington adds: ". . . which we used for whitewashing our walls" (p. 230).

3 Huntington adds further: ". . . on a rich piece of land laid out for the purpose on a sloping ground in front of our establishment" (p. 231).

4 Inexplicably, the 1854 text reads: "Nevertheless, we raised one hundred and ninety potatoes the first season and after sparing a few plants for our inland traders we placed about fifty or sixty hills, which produced five bushels the second year; about two of these were planted, and gave us a welcome crop of fifty bushels in the year 1813" (p. 232).

It is possible, of course, that some potatoes were saved for seed and used by the men farther upriver, where a likely crop might have been expected. Perhaps Franchère confused the two locations; otherwise the contradiction between the readings of the 1820 and 1854 editions can hardly be explained.

that the soil is not everywhere the same and that some spots are more suitable for gardening than the one we chose. This supposition becomes the more likely when one considers that the vegetable crops of any country are different upriver from what they are downriver.

The most common varieties of trees at the river mouth and near our establishment are cedar, spruce, white spruce, and alder.[5] The cedars are from twenty-four to thirty feet in circumference. The alders are also of great size, being from twelve to twenty-one inches in diameter. But the most extraordinarily large tree that I saw in the country was a white spruce. This tree, that had been topped and its upper branches destroyed by a stroke of lightning, was no more than a straight trunk, eighty to a hundred feet high and resembling a tall column. It stood on the slope of a hill behind our establishment. Seven of us stood around its trunk and by extending our arms and touching only the ends of our fingers, we still could not embrace it. Later we measured it in the regular manner and found its circumference to be forty-two feet.[6] We planned to build a stairway around it and construct a platform at the top as an observatory and lookout, but more pressing business forced us to abandon the project.

Some miles upriver the ash and the oak are common enough. The latter is neither very large nor very majestic.

From mid-June until mid-October we constantly had wild fruit in abundance—at first the white strawberries, small, but delectable; after that the red and orange raspberries. These raspberries grow on a bush twelve to fifteen feet high, in wet and shady terrain. They are more unfailing than those in Canada.

The months of July and August furnish an acid fruit that is very agreeable. It is blue and a bit larger than the cherry, and

[5] Huntington makes minor variations and additions in this paragraph. The substance, however, is unchanged.

[6] Bibaud adds the following footnote that is not reprinted in the 1854 edition: "Every time that I have mentioned this fact here at home, I have found some people incredulous; but there are presently among us some worthy people of honor who could attest to it" (p. 175).

grows on a medium-size bush with little round leaves. Some are also red in color, but they are smaller.[7]

August brings still another fruit that grows in bunches on a shrub the size of a red-currant bush or garden-currant tree. Its leaves resemble those of the bay tree and are always green. The fruit is oblong and grows in two rows on the cluster; the upper end opens in four parts and allows one to see the inside of the fruit. This fruit does not have a very good flavor, but it is wholesome and one can eat a quantity of it without being uncomfortable. The natives make great use of it; they prepare it for winter, crushing it and molding it into small loaves which they dry over a fire on screens.

We also found some bluebottles (cornflowers), choke-cherries, currants, wild pear, and some little wild apples of a species called in England the crabapple. These last grow in clusters and are much too tart to eat unless boiled. The upper part of the river furnishes wild mulberries, hazelnuts, and acorns in abundance. The country likewise grows a great variety of roots. The Indians make particularly good use of those having the power to cure or prevent scurvy. We ate a good quantity of them ourselves, for the same reason and with the same success.

One of these roots that looks very much like a young onion serves the Indians in the place of wheat.[8] Gathering a sufficient amount, they bake them on red-hot stones from the fire, after which they knead them until they are reduced to a paste, and then form them into loaves of five or six pounds each. This "bread" tastes something like licorice. At the time of our first journey to the Falls, the Indians upriver gave us some well-worked biscuits, square in form and decorated with diverse figures. They make the biscuits from a white root which they press

[7] Huntington adds: ". . . that have not pits, or stones in them, but seeds, such as are to be seen in currants" (p. 235).

Huntington also adds that cranberries grow in abundance and are used as an antiscorbutic.

[8] Huntington mistranslated Franchère's word "froment," as "cheese." The word means "wheat," as indicated here, and is in proper context. See Bibaud (p. 178).

and reduce to a paste, dry, and then mold and fashion on clay in the heat of the sun.

But the chief food of the Columbia River Indians is fish. Salmon fishing begins in July. This fish has a delicate flavor; but it is extremely fat and oily, a fact that makes it unwholesome for those who are not accustomed to it and who eat a large amount of it. Several of our men were attacked by diarrhea a few days after we made it a part of our regular diet. But they found an effective remedy in the wild raspberries, which have an astringent property.

The months of August and September bring excellent sturgeon, a fish that varies greatly in size. There are some almost eleven feet long, and we caught one that weighed 390 pounds, even after the eggs and intestines had been drawn.[9] The sturgeon does not come into the river in as great numbers as the salmon.

In the months of October and November we had still more salmon, but of a different species from the one in July. The later one is very lean and dry, with a whitish color and an insipid flavor. It also differs from the other in its shape, having very long teeth and a hooked nose like the beak of a parrot. In derision, our men gave it the name of the fish with seven barks, as they found in it so little substance.

February brings a little fish, somewhat longer and broader than the sardine, that we took at first to be a smelt. It has a delicate flavor and is abundant, but the season for catching it lasts only a short time.

The principal quadrupeds are the elk, the black-tailed deer, the red deer, and four species of bear, distinguished especially by the color of their fur—to wit: black, brown, gray, and white. The gray bear is extremely ferocious and is flesh-eating; the white bear lives along the seashore to the north. The wolf, panther, lynx, a species of marmot, prairie dog, wood rat, mink, beaver, otter, and sea-otter are also to be found.[10] The sea-otter furnishes the most

9 Huntington inserts the sentence: "We took out nine gallons of Roe" (p. 237).

10 Bibaud has the following footnote that is not reprinted in the 1854 edition: "Horses are quite abundant up river, but these animals are not native to the country; I shall say more about them later" (p. 180).

beautiful fur known, surpassing that of the beaver both in grandeur and in fineness. It is sought everywhere, but especially in China, where it brings a good price.

The most remarkable birds are the eagle-nun—so called by the *voyageurs* as much because of the color of its head, which is white, as because the rest of the plumage is pitch black—the black eagle, the stink-bird (another species of eagle), the hawk, pelican, cormorant, swan, heron, crane, bustard, several species of geese, several of ducks, and so forth.[11]

CHAPTER 19

The natives of the Columbia River area from the mouth to the falls, a distance of about 240 miles west to east, are, generally speaking, rather small in stature, the tallest about five feet and some scarcely more than four. They pluck out nearly all the beard, in the same manner as other savages in America. Only a few old men allow it to grow. Upon arriving among them, we were surprised to see that most of them had flat heads. This is not at all a natural deformity, but in fact one wrought by artifice.[1] As soon as the child is born, he is placed in a cradle which is nothing but a trough on an oblong plank. One of the ends of this plank is raised higher than the other and little trusses are placed carefully on each side. A child's head rests on the raised end, and a pad of cedar bark is put on his forehead; and by means of a cord slipped into the trusses, the pads are pressed against the head. In time, this arrangement gives the head the flat form that is extremely shocking to strangers, particularly at first sight.

However, among these barbarians, the flat head is an indispensable ornament, and when we said that this fashion seemed to us to violate nature and good taste, they answered that it was only the slave who did not have a flat head. Slaves do, in fact, have round heads, and are never permitted to flatten those of their in-

[11] Huntington also mentions pigeon, woodcock, and pheasant that are found in the forests of Oregon, much as they are in the forests of Canada.

The reader will find some interest in comparing chapters 18, 19, and 20 of Alexander Ross's *First Settlers* with the same-numbered chapters in this text.

[1] The following two sentences describing the process of effecting the flat head in infants are not reprinted in the 1854 edition.

fants, destined to bear the chains of their fathers. The natives get their slaves from neighboring tribes and from the interior, giving beads, beaver skins, and other things in exchange. They treat them well enough as long as their services are useful; when old and unable to work, they are neglected and left to die in misery. When they die they are thrown, without ceremony, under tree trunks or at the edge of the woods.

The Indians on the Columbia are active and are, above all, good swimmers. They are addicted to thieving—or rather, when they find an opportunity, they have no scruples about robbing strangers of whatever takes their fancy. Merchandise and supplies of European manufacture are often of such great value in the eyes of these savages that they rarely can resist the temptation of stealing them.

They are not addicted to strong liquor, and are in this respect different from the greater part of the other Indians in America—unless it be the Patagonians who, like them, regard intoxicating liquors as poisons and drunkenness as a mark of dishonor. I can tell a story about this: When a son of Chief Concomly came one day to the establishment, one of our gentlemen amused himself by giving the young man some wine, and he was soon drunk. He became ill and remained in a stupor for two days. The old Chief came to reproach us, saying that we had degraded his son and exposed him to the ridicule of his slaves. He begged us not to give him strong drink in the future.

The Indian men go entirely naked, not concealing any part of their bodies, not even the genitals. Only in the wintertime do they throw around their shoulders a panther skin or some kind of cape made from the skins of wood rats sewn together.[2] Besides the cape, women wear a kind of skirt or petticoat, made of cedar bark which they hang around their waists and which comes to the middle of their thighs. This skirt is somewhat longer in back than in front and is made in the following manner: they tear off

2 Huntington adds: "In rainy weather I have seen them wear a mantle of rush mats, like a Roman toga, or the vestment which a priest wears in celebrating mass; thus equipped, and furnished with a conical hat made from fibrous roots and impermeable, they may call themselves rain-proof" (p. 243).

the fine bark of cedar, soak it as one soaks hemp, and lay it out in fringes. Then, taking a cord of the same material they divide the fringes around and tie them down firmly. With such a wretched garment they manage to hide the private parts.[3]

Cleanliness is not a virtue among these women, and in this respect they are like other Indian women of North America. They apply to both body and hair a fish oil that has little resemblance to perfume.[4] Sometimes, too, in imitation of the men, they paint their bodies with a red clay mixed in oil. Their ornaments consist of brass bracelets, which they wear indiscriminately on wrist or ankle; glass beads, preferably blue ones; and white shells called *haiqua* in the native language, which are a kind of coin of the Indian realm. These shells are found beyond the Strait of Juan de Fuca and are four inches long and about an inch in diameter. They are a little curved and naturally perforated; the longest ones are the most highly valued. The price of all Indian goods is reckoned in terms of these shells, and a six-foot string is ordinarily worth ten beaver skins.

Though a little less slaves (as I have observed) than among most Indians in America, the Columbia River women are burdened with the hardest labor. They fetch water and wood; they carry supplies whenever they move their homes; they clean the fish and cut it into small slices for drying; they prepare the food; they cook the fruits in season. Among their primary duties is the making of cane mats, baskets for the gathering of roots, and hats of very ingenious design. Since they find little necessity for clothing, they sew very little, and more often the men take the needle in hand.

The men are not lazy, particularly in the fishing season. Since they are not hunters and consequently eat little meat (al-

[3] Huntington adds: ". . . when they stand it drapes them fairly enough; and when they squat down in their manner, it falls between their legs, leaving nothing exposed but the bare knees and thighs. Some of the younger women twist the fibres of bark into small cords, knotted at the ends, and so form the petticoat, disposed in a fringe, like the first, but more easily kept clean and of better appearance" (pp. 243–44).

[4] Huntington adds that women, like the men, have jet-black hair which they part in the middle and smear with fish oil (p. 244).

though they like the taste of it), fish, as I have already said, becomes their principal food. They take advantage, therefore, of the seasons in which it can be caught, and catch all they can, realizing that the periods between seasons will be for them times of scarcity and fasting if they do not provide enough.[5]

This is the manner in which they catch the different varieties of fish that periodically enter their river: They catch salmon with net or darts. Their nets are made of nettle fibers and are from eighty to one hundred fathoms long. Their darts, or harpoons, are made of two pieces of curved bone, in the middle of which they bind a small iron point about half an inch long. The bone pieces are tied firmly together and are separated at the top to hold the shaft, which is a long pole with two forks. When these hit a fish, the two darts penetrate the flesh; and lest the shock given it and with which the fish feels itself struck break the shaft, which is very slender because of its length, the Indians draw it back and allow the fish to swim until it is exhausted, holding onto the fish, however, by a line attached to the darts.

The sturgeon is taken with a hook or a net. The hooks are ingeniously made of iron and bound by a strong cord of nettle so that they do not break. They are spaced about twelve feet apart on a line made of tree bark. Having attached a rock weighing fifteen or sixteen pounds to the end of the line, they throw it crosswise over the river, careful to place the buoy at the other end. For bait they use a little fish, called mullet, passing the hook through the gills and sliding the fish along the cord that holds it to the line. As the cord glides up and down, the little fish gives the appearance of being alive; the sturgeon, deceived, swallows the bait and is caught. Although this fish grows very large, he offers almost no fight at all. The Indians catch about ten or twelve a night in this manner.

The nets which they use to take this fish are also made of

[5] The following five paragraphs are in Bibaud, as I have translated them here, but are not in the 1854 edition. Quaife makes no comment about this omission and follows Huntington in his own rendering.

nettle fibers, in the shape of a funnel five or six feet wide and ten to twelve feet long. At the extremity that ends in a point, the Indians attach a small piece of white shell. The entrance of the net funnel opens and closes at will by means of a cord, on the end of which is hung a stone that weighs seven or eight pounds. Another cord is tied to a piece of wood in such a manner that when the cord attached to the stone is pulled, the sack closes, and when slackened it opens.

When the net is thus readied, two men embark in a small canoe and, each taking an end of the cord, they drop it on the bottom and draw it along as they drift. The sturgeon searching for food sees the white object at the end of the net; he swims in and, pushing against the sides, he moves it. This movement warns the fishermen, who quickly close the net.

The small fish that we call the smelt and that the Indians call *outhelekane* (candlefish) is caught with a rake. The rake is nothing more than a long pole, on the end of which some small pointed pegs are fixed. Passing this back and forth in the water, the fisherman hooks the fish on the pegs and soon has enough to fill a canoe. The Indian women dry them and string them in a double row on lines about six feet long. Smelt is the chief nourishment for the natives during the months of April, May, and June. Those who live up the river buy them from the others, because the fish does not run farther upriver than to the villages of the Kreluits, about forty-five or fifty miles from the seaboard.[6]

Their canoes, or pirogues, are all made of cedar and are all of one piece. We have seen some that were five feet wide and thirty feet long. These are the largest, and they often carry twenty-five or thirty men. The smallest carry only two. The sharply-pointed bow extends four or five feet. It thus serves to break the waves that otherwise would swamp the canoe when the water on the river is rough. Their oars, or paddles, are of ash and are about

6 Franchère was wrong about the smelt—unless, that is, these fish have altered their habits from that day to this; for they are taken today in great quantity even in the tributaries of the Willamette River.

five feet long; the top end has a grip very much like the top of a crutch. The blade is cut in a half-moon shape, having two sharp points.[7]

The native houses, built of cedar, are remarkable for their form and, above all, for their size. They are nearly a hundred feet long and thirty to forty feet wide. They are constructed in the following manner: The Indians sink some posts into the earth about seven or eight feet apart, between which they set some planks that they tie at the top with strong cords. At each end of the building they place a pole about fifteen to twenty feet in height. These have notches at the top to hold the ridge pole. The rafters, attached two by two, are placed below the ridge pole and hang down across the edges of the planks which, in turn, rise to about five feet from the ground. The roof is made of planks laid across, and attached to, the rafters. Fires are made in the middle of the house and smoke escapes through a hole in the roof. Several families, separated from each other by partitions, live in one of these large buildings. The doors, raised well above the ground level, are oval and very small.[8]

Kitchen utensils consist of hewn-ash trays and square cedar kettles. With only these the Indians succeed in cooking their fish and meat in less time than we take with our pots and saucepans. This is the way they do it: First, they heat a number of stones red hot; then, one by one, they drop these into the kettle that will hold the food. As soon as the water boils they put the fish or meat into it, and cover it with small rush mats to hold the steam. Left thus, the food is soon properly cooked.

One might ask, no doubt, what tools these savages use in the building of their canoes and their houses. In order to appreciate their patience and their industry as much as they deserve, the reader needs only to know that we found not one ax among them.

[7] Huntington explains that the paddle is so devised as to permit its being swept through the water noiselessly when the Indians hunt the sea-otter. He adds that their canoes are painted red and are "fancifully decorated" (p. 247).

[8] With reference to the Indian dwellings, Huntington varies the passage: "The door is low, of an oval shape, and is provided with a ladder, cut out of a log, to descend into the lodge. The entrance is generally effected stern-foremost" (p. 248).

They use a two-inch chisel, usually made from an old file, and a hammer that is nothing but an oblong stone. With these wretched instruments and some wedges made of hemlock knots, oiled and hardened by firing, they cut down cedars twenty-four to thirty feet in circumference, dig them out, and fashion them into canoes; or they split and transform them into beams and planks for their houses.[9]

CHAPTER 20

Among the Columbia River natives, the political structure is reduced to its simplest form. Each village has its chief, but he does not appear to exercise great authority over his fellow citizens. However, at his death they render him great honors. They practice a kind of mourning and chant his funeral song for almost a month. These chiefs are honored in proportion to their wealth; the one who has many wives, slaves, strings of beads, and so forth, is a great chief. In this respect, the savages follow the patterns of civilized peoples among whom a man is esteemed according to the money he possesses.

Since all the villages form so many little sovereignties, differences often arise among them, whether among chiefs or among the peoples. These disputes usually are resolved by payments equivalent to the injuries. However, when the offense is grave, as in the case of murder (which is pretty rare), or the stealing of a woman (and this is common enough), the injured parties, assured of the help of a number of young men, prepare for war.

But before initiating any warlike action, they warn the enemy of the day on which they will attack their village. In this procedure they do not follow the custom of nearly all the other American Indians, who seize upon their enemies without warning and kill or capture men, women, and children. To the contrary, these people embark in their canoes, which on such occasions are paddled by women, approach the enemy village, enter into parley, and do all that they can to settle their differences

9 Sometimes Huntington's additions are merely gratuitous, as is the case with the last sentence in this chapter to be found in the 1854 edition: "Such achievements with such means, are a marvel of ingenuity and patience" (p. 249).

amicably. Sometimes a third party, observing a strict neutrality as mediator, attempts to negotiate an agreement between the two warring tribes. If those who demand justice do not obtain it to their liking they retire a little distance, and combat begins and continues for some time, with fury on both sides. But as soon as one or two men are killed, the army that has lost them acknowledges itself defeated and the battle stops. If it is the party of the village attacked who are the losers, the attackers do not leave until they have received some presents.

If, however, the war is to be continued on the following day (for they conduct their wars only in daylight, as if to make nature witness to their exploits), both sides carry on all night with hideous whooping, each defying the other—at least when they are near enough to each other to be heard—with menacing cries, taunts, and sarcastic remarks, somewhat like the heroes of Homer and Virgil. The women and children always leave the village before combat begins.

Their wars are nearly all maritime affairs. Ordinarily they fight from their canoes, which they take care to careen so as to present a broadside to the enemy and in which they keep themselves half-hidden. In this way they avoid most of the enemy's arrows.[1]

Their weapons are bow and arrow and a sort of broadsword, the blade of which has two cutting edges about two and a half feet long and six inches wide. But they rarely fight close enough to use them. For defensive armor they wear a cassock, reaching from shoulder to ankle, made of two thicknesses of elkskin, with holes for their arms. Arrows will not penetrate it, and since their heads are also covered, by a kind of helmet, the neck is almost the only part of the body in which they can be wounded.

They have another kind of armor that is a corset made of rounded lengths of a very hard wood, interlaced with twine. The warrior who puts on this corset does not wear the elkskin cassock.

---

1 Huntington adds: "But the chief reason of the bloodlessness of their combats is the inefficiency of their offensive weapons, and the excellence of their defensive armor" (pp. 252–53).

He is somewhat less protected but has much greater freedom of movement, since the cassock is very heavy and very stiff.

We found the natives in possession of some firearms, but without powder they could not make use of them. And to tell the truth, only a small number of them knew how to use these weapons.[2]

Needless to say, in their warlike expeditions they daub their bodies and faces with paints, and usually in a most bizarre manner. I recall having seen the chief of the Cathlamets come to the aid of the Kalamas against the Tillamooks with exactly half his face painted white and half painted black.

Their marriages are held with much ceremony. When a young man seeks the hand of a girl, his parents make the proposal to the girl's parents. And when agreement is reached as to what presents the bridegroom is to give his bride, both parties meet in the latter's lodge, where all the neighbors are invited to witness the agreement. The presents, which consist of slaves, strings of beads, copper bracelets, shells, and so forth, are distributed by the young man, who, on his part, receives from the bride's parents as much and sometimes more, according to their means or their generosity. The bride is then led in by the village matrons and presented to the young man, who takes her for his wife. All then retire to their own quarters.

The men are not very scrupulous about their choice of wives, and seldom inquire how the young woman has behaved before the marriage. It must be admitted that few marriages would occur if the young men wished to marry only chaste young women, for the girls have no qualms as to their conduct and their parents give them complete liberty in that respect. But when a marriage has been contracted, the spouses observe an absolute fidelity toward one another. Adultery is almost unknown among them, and the wife who is guilty of it would be punished by death. However, the husband can repudiate his wife, in which event she can marry another man. Polygamy is customary among

[2] This paragraph is in Bibaud but is not translated for the 1854 edition; nor does Huntington name the tribes in the following paragraph, possibly because he could not identify them from Franchère's spellings.

these savages. Some men have as many as four or five wives; and although it often happens that the husband loves one more than the others, they never display jealousy, and live together in perfect harmony.[3]

There are charlatans everywhere, but they are more numerous among the savages than elsewhere because among these ignorant and superstitious people the craft is more profitable and less dangerous. When a native of the Columbia is indisposed, no matter what the illness, they send for a medicine man, who begins his ministrations in this fashion: The sick man is put on his back; his parents and friends are arranged about him, each holding a long stick in one hand and a shorter one in the other. The medicine man chants a lugubrious song, joined by those present, who beat time with their sticks. Sometimes they make a slave sit on the roof of the house, where he strikes responding blows on the planks, chanting like those inside.

During this time the medicine man works to heal the sick man, kneeling before him and, with all his strength, pushing his two fists into the patient's stomach. This violent action causes the sick man to cry out with piercing yells. But the doctor only sings more loudly, and the others follow his example. Thus the voice of the poor victim is drowned out. At the end of each stanza, or couplet, in the song, the medicine man joins his two hands, brings them to his lips, and blows on them. This operation he repeats until finally he brings from his mouth a little white stone that he has put there beforehand. With an air of triumph, he shows this immediately to those interested in the health of the sick man, telling them that the illness has been extracted and that he cannot fail to recover. I have seen some who [pretend to] wrap the source of the malady in a piece of bark, throwing that into the fire and blowing on it.[4]

[3] Huntington moralizes in a footnote (pp. 255–56), complaining against the degradation of the Indian women. His comment seems inordinately naïve to a modern reader.

[4] This paragraph and the paragraph following, in which the medicine man's practice are described, are in Bibaud but do not appear in the 1854 edition. Quaife did not note the omission and followed Huntington's rendering.

Thus these tricksters impose upon simple and credulous children of nature. It often happens that a sick person who might have been saved by a bleeding or a simple purge is carried off by sudden death. But whether the sick one lives or dies, the charlatan is always, as among us, equally well paid. Some of the wiser natives doubtless are aware of the quackery of these tricksters, but for fear of displeasing the superstitious multitude, they remain silent.

The Indians put their dead in canoes, on rocks high enough so that the spring floods will not wash over them. By the side of the dead man they put his bow and arrows and some of his tools. His wives, his parents, and his slaves cut their hair, as a sign of mourning; and for several days, at sunset and at some distance from the village, they sing a funeral song.

These Indians have not, properly speaking, a public worship.[5] During my stay with them I never once saw them worshipping an idol. They had some small sculptured figures, but they seemed not to value them greatly and offered them to us in exchange for trifles.

Having traveled with a son of the Chinook chieftain Concomly, an intelligent and communicative young man, I asked him several questions about their religious beliefs and here is the substance of what he told me: Men were created by a divinity whom they call Etalapass, but they were imperfectly made. They had mouths that were not slit to open; eyes that were closed; hands and feet that could not move. They were more like fleshly statues than true men. A second divinity, whom they call Ecannum, less powerful but more benign than the first, seeing men in their imperfect state, took a sharp stone and opened both mouths and eyes and gave motion to their hands and feet. This compassionate divinity was not content with these first benefits. He taught men how to make canoes, paddles, nets, and all the tools which they use. He did even more. He threw rocks into the river to obstruct

[5] Again Huntington moralizes, quoting Coleridge's comment that every tribe is barbarous "which has no public worship or cult . . ." (p. 257).

the fish and make them gather together so that men could catch as many as they needed.

The natives of the Columbia believe that men who have been good citizens—good fathers, good husbands, and good fishermen—who have not committed murder and other evils, will be perfectly happy after death in a country where they will find fish, fruit, and good things in abundance; and that, contrariwise, those who have lived bad lives will find themselves in a country of fasting, with only bitter roots to eat and salt water to drink.

If these ideas about the origin and future destiny of man do not conform exactly to sound reason, one must admit, at least, that one does not find in them those absurdities that form the myths of nearly all the ancient peoples of Asia and Europe.[6] The Indians' belief that skill in fishing is a virtue worthy of reward in the next world does not distort the salutary and consoling dogma of immortality of the soul and future punishments and rewards as much as one at first might think. For, reflecting a little, one perceives that the good fisherman, while working for himself, works also for society. He is a useful citizen who does as much as he can to banish the scourge of famine from his fellow creatures. He is a religious man who honors the divinity by making use of his benefits.[7]

One should not expect these altogether ignorant men to be free from superstitions. Among the most ridiculous is their mode of preparing and eating fish. In the month of July, 1811, they brought us at first a very small number of salmon at a time, fear-

6 Specific mention of Asia and Europe is not repeated in the 1854 edition, but Huntington once more takes occasion to moralize gratuitously upon Indian mythology (p. 259).

7 Huntington adds: "Surely a great deal of the theology of a future life prevalent among civilized men, does not excel in this profundity" (p. 260).

Perhaps Mr. Huntington's concern with moral and religious problems can best be explained by the fact that he gave up a career in medicine to enter the Episcopal ministry. After 1838, when he made something of a reputation for his "Coronation Sonnets" (Blackwoods Edinburgh Review, September, 1838), he became involved in the Oxford Movement then flourishing in England. He appears to have become unsettled in his creed, and finally became a convert to Roman Catholicism. It is quite possible that Franchère and Huntington met in church circles, probably in New York City. See Dictionary of American Biography.

ing that we would cut them crosswise and believing that if we did so, the river would be obstructed and fishing useless. After we approached the chiefs on this subject, they brought us a large-enough quantity, but all baked; and in order not to displease them, we had to eat it before sunset. Reassured at last by our solemn promises not to cut the salmon crosswise, they supplied us abundantly during the entire fishing season.

In spite of the vices with which one can reproach the Columbia River people, I believe them closer to a civilized state than any of the tribes living east of the Rocky Mountains. They did not seem to me so bound by their customs that they could not easily adopt those of civilized men. They would willingly dress after the European fashion if they had the means to buy the goods. In order to encourage this taste among them, we gave pants to those chiefs who wanted to come into our houses and never permitted them to visit us naked. They possess to an eminent degree those qualities opposite to idleness, improvidence, and stupidity. The chiefs, in particular, distinguish themselves by their good judgment and their intelligence. Generally speaking, they have quick minds and tenacious memories. I had occasion to note this last quality especially in Concomly. That old chief, having been on the *Albatross*, immediately recognized her captain, Captain Smith, whom he had seen in 1810. He even remembered the first mate, although it had been sixteen years since the mate had come to the Columbia River area. Upon meeting him, Concomly said to him in his own language, "Ship Bowles," wishing the man to know that he had seen him in former times on a ship commanded by Captain Bowles. This, the mate told us, was true.[8]

It remains for me to say something about the Chinook language, which is spoken by all the native tribes from the river's mouth to the rapids. It is a hard language and difficult for strangers to pronounce, filled as it is with gutterals like those of the

8 These last two sentences are not to be found in the 1854 edition. Quaife does not mention their not appearing in the Manuscript, and follows Huntington's text.

Scottish Highlanders. The Chinooks have no consonants "f," "v," and so forth. They do not even have our "r," but a strongly articulated gutteral that is somewhat like this letter pronounced as a uvular, as in "Kreluit," or perhaps better, "Hreluit." The combinations "thl" or "tl" and "lt" are as frequent in Chinook as they are in Mexican [Spanish].[9] To conform to recognized custom, I shall list some words of this language for the reader, although I am aware of the uselessness of such a nomenclature.

Etalapass	God, or the Supreme Being
Ekannum	The Good Spirit of the Waters
Tilikum	Men
Chouttilikum	some men
Papische aiyouks	Europeans
Koutane	horse
Kamoux	dog
Moulak	deer
Equannet	salmon
Flaighte	slave
Tanasse	child
Olik	girl
Ibikats	the nose
Tlaoltk	blood
Outlah	the sun

[9] The Huntington edition ends at this point and Huntington made no effort to translate Franchère's list of Chinook words. He did add a footnote that today seems curiously arbitrary: "There can not be a doubt that the existing tribes on the N. W. coast, have reached that country from the South and not from the North. They are the *débris* of the civilization of Central America, expelled by a defecating process that is going on in all human societies, and so have sunk into barbarism" (p. 262).

Huntington appears to have come under the influence of the German Diffusionists of the 19th Century, who did not hold with the theory of cultural evolution. These scholars sought to establish the idea that the culture of Central America derived from the Old World—from Europe or from the Middle East, for example—that the coastal Indians had come from Central America and had no independent cultural development. Today, cultural anthropologists believe that the coastal Indians probably came from northeast Asia and that they did, in fact, have an independent cultural growth which may have reached its height during the latter 18th Century. The latter theory is, I believe, questioned, to some extent, by linguistic scholars.

Ocoutlamaine	the moon
Ilekai	the earth
Icanneve	canoe
Issik	paddle
Thlipaight	cord
Olo	hunger
Potlatch	a present
Ste Kech	I love you
Kakhpah emoreya?	Where do you go?
Kantchik euskoya?	When will you return?
Nixt nothlitkal	You do not understand.
Mitlaight o kok	Sit down there.
Tane tse koulama	Show me your pipe.
Potlatch nain maika	Do you wish to give it to me?
or	Will you give it to me?
Ikta mika makoumak?	What do you want to eat?
Thlounasse otile?	Perhaps some fruits?
Nix, quatiasse moulak thlousk	No, give me some meat.
Passischqua	cover
Kaienoulk	tobacco
Sakquallal	gun
Chalaks	anger
Icht	one, an
Makust	two
Thloun	three
Lakut	four
Quannum	five
Takut	six
Sinebakust	seven
Nix or Nixt	no, not
Passiche	cloth
Pousk	ship
Ouapto	potatoes
Naika	mine
Stoutekane	eight
Quainst	nine

Itallilum	ten
Ekoun-icht	eleven
Ekoun-makust	twelve, and so forth
Makust Thlalt	twenty
Kantchick?	When?
Ouinapi	Soon

✖✖✖

PART IV

The Journey Home

CHAPTER 21

We LEFT FORT GEORGE on Monday morning, April 4, [1814], in ten canoes, five of which were of bark and five of cedar. Each carried seven crewmen and two passengers, all well armed. Messrs. McTavish, D. Stuart, J. Clarke, B. Pillet, W. Wallace, D. McGillis, and D. McKenzie were in the party.

Nothing unusual happened as far as the first falls, where we arrived on the tenth, and we camped on an island for the night.[1] Our great numbers had put most of the natives to flight, and those who remained in their villages displayed only the most peaceful intentions. They sold us four horses and thirty dogs [for food].

Early on the morning of the eleventh we resumed our journey. The wind was favorable, but blew violently. Toward evening, the canoe in which Mr. McTavish was a passenger, doubling a point of rock, overturned and sank. Fortunately, the river was not deep at this juncture; no one was drowned and we managed to save all the baggage. This accident forced us to camp at an early hour.

On the twelfth we came to a rapids called The Dalles.[2] This

1 Franchère used interchangeably the terms *rapide* and *chute* for rapids and falls. Here these terms are applied in line with present usage.

2 In his *Oregon Geographic Names*, McArthur writes: "As far as the compiler knows, the first use of the name Dalles in Oregon is in Franchere's *Narrative*, on April 12, 1814, where it is used to describe the Long Narrows" (p. 594).

In current French usage, the term *dalles* means "slabs," or "flagstones."

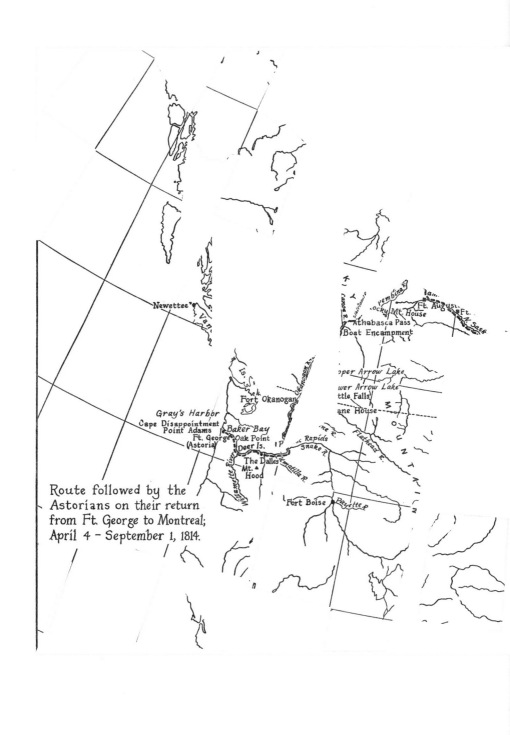

Newettee

Ft. Augus·Ft.
·ocky Mt. House ⌐N Sask
Athabasca Pass
Boat Encampment

·pper Arrow Lake
·wer Arrow Lake
·ttle Falls
·ane House

Fort Okanogan

Gray's Harbor
Cape Disappointment
Point Adams   Baker Bay
Ft. George Oak Point
(Astoria)   Deer Is.
Rapids
Snake R.
The Dalles
Mt. ▲
Hood

Route followed by the
Astorians on their return
from Ft. George to Montreal;
April 4 – September 1, 1814.

Fort Boise   Payette R.

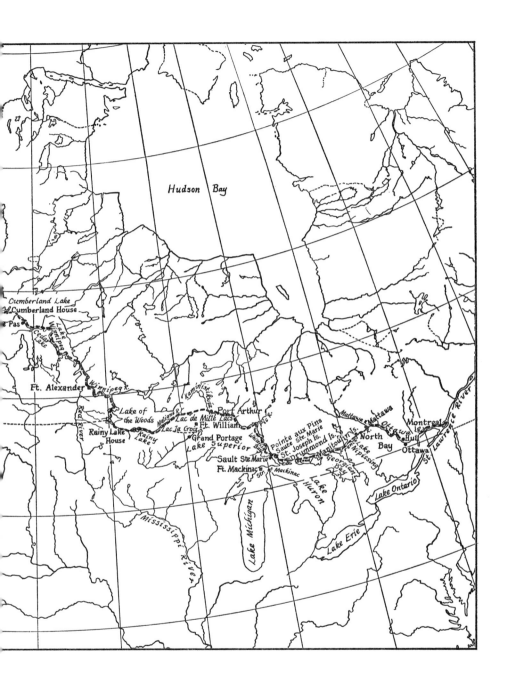

Hudson Bay

Cumberland Lake
Cumberland House
Pas
Lake Winnipeg
Cedar Lake

Ft. Alexander
Winnipeg R.
Red River

Lake of
the Woods
Rainy Lake
House
Rainy Lake
Maligne R.
Lac Ja Croix
Lac de Mille Lacs
Kaministikwia R.
Port Arthur
Ft. William
Grand Portage
Lake Superior
Pic R.

Mississippi River

Lake Michigan

Pointe aux Pins
Sault Ste Marie
St. Joseph Is.
Sault Ste. Marie
Ft. Mackinac
Str. of Mackinac
Drummond Is.
Manitoulin Is.
Georgian Bay
Lake Huron
Lake Erie

Mattawa R.
Mattawa
Ottawa R.
Lake
Nipissing
North
Bay
Montreal
Hull
Ottawa
St. Lawrence River
Lake Ontario

is a channel cut by nature through the rocks which nearly every-where are sliced perpendicularly. The channel is from three to four hundred feet wide and about two miles long.[3] The portage occupied us until dusk. Although during the day we had not seen a single Indian, we kept a watch all night; for it was there that Mr. Stewart and Mr. Reed had been attacked by the natives.

On the thirteenth we made two portages and met some In-dians from whom we bought some horses and some wood. We camped early on the sandy plain, where we spent a bad night. The wind, which blew furiously, raised little tornadoes of dust that annoyed us greatly and spoiled our food.

On the fourteenth and fifteenth we passed what are called the Columbia Plains. From the upper end of the first rapids the aspect of the country becomes more and more dreary and dis-agreeable. At first one sees only barren slopes that offer a few lonely pines, one a great distance from another. After that the stripped terrain affords not even a single shrub. The little grass that grows in this arid soil appears burned by the harshness of the climate. The Indians who frequent the river banks to catch salmon have no other wood but driftwood. We passed several rapids and came to a river called the Umatilla, that flows from the southeast.

On the sixteenth we found the river narrower, the banks rising on either side, but still barren of trees. We came to the Walla Walla River, which flows to the southeast. It is narrow at its confluence and is not navigable for any great distance. About forty-five to sixty miles to the southeast, a range of mountains can be seen. Behind these the country again becomes flat and sandy, and is inhabited by Indians called the Snakes. On the left bank of the Walla Walla we found an Indian camp consisting of about twenty lodges. The natives here sold us six dogs and eight horses, for the most part very lean, and we killed two of the latter. Then I mounted one of the remaining animals, Mr. Ross

---

[3] Huntington says 150 to 300 feet wide, and he adds: "The whole body of the river rushes through it, with great violence, and renders navigation imprac-ticable" (p. 264).

got on another, and we drove the other four ahead of us. Toward evening we passed the Snake River, called the *Chahaptin* in the language of the country. It flows from the southeast and is the same river that Lewis and Clark descended in 1805. The Snake seemed shallow to me and appeared to be about twelve hundred feet wide at its mouth.

The country through which we were passing is made up of small hills, precipitous rocks, and valleys covered with wormwood, the stems of which are nearly six inches in diameter and might serve as fuel. We killed six rattlesnakes on the fifteenth, and on the sixteenth saw a good many more among the rocks. These dangerous reptiles seem to abound in great numbers in this part of the country. The plains are also inhabited by a small quadruped only eight or nine inches long and much like a dog in form. These animals have a coat of dull red hair, and strong forepaws provided with long claws that serve to dig out their underground burrows. They are quite curious. The moment they hear a noise, they come out of their holes and bark. They are not vicious, however, and can be tamed easily.

The natives of the upper Columbia River, commencing at the falls, differ fundamentally in language, customs, and habits from those who have been discussed in preceding chapters. In this area they do not live in villages at all but are nomadic, like the Tartars and the Arabs of the desert lands. Their women are more industrious and the girls more reserved than those of the natives downriver. They do not go naked, but wear deerskin habits, which they take care to rub with chalk in order to keep them clean. Nearly always they can be seen on horseback, and they are, as a rule, good horsemen. They hunt deer and range [into the interior] as far as Missouri to kill buffalo, the flesh of which they dry and carry back on their horses, to provide their principal food during the winter.

These journeys are not without perils for them, for they have much to fear from their enemies, the Blackfeet. Since this tribe is powerful and ferocious, the Snakes, the Nez-Percés, or Chahaptins [Shahaptians], and the Flatheads make common cause, joining forces against them when hunting east of the Rockies. They travel with their families and often their cavalcade grows to include two thousand horses. When they have the good luck not to meet their enemy, hunting is usually good; they load some of their horses with venison and return home to spend the winter peacefully. Sometimes, on the other hand, they are so harassed by the Blackfeet, who pounce upon them at night and steal their horses, that they are forced to return home without hunting. In this case they have only roots to eat during the whole winter.

These Indians are passionately fond of horse racing. The bets they make on these occasions sometimes strip them of all that they possess. Women ride like the men. For a bridle, they use a rope made of horsehair, which they fasten in the horse's mouth.[4] The saddle is a cushion, quite appropriate for the use to which it is put, rarely chafing the horse or tiring the rider as do our European saddles. The stirrups are made of hardwood, igeniously wrought, wound, and of the same structure as those used in civilized countries. They are covered by a piece of deerskin which is applied wet and which, when drying, tightens and becomes hard and firm.

They get their horses from the wild herds that sometimes number from a thousand to fifteen hundred. These wild horses come from New Mexico and are of a Spanish breed. We saw some that had even been branded by the Spaniards. Some of our men who had been in the southlands told me they had seen bridles with the bits made of what appeared to be silver. The form of the saddles that the women use prove that they have imitated the Spanish saddles destined for the same use. One of the partners of the North West Company (Mr. J. G. McTavish) said that among the Spokanes he had met an old woman who told him that she had seen white men plowing. She told him also that she had seen churches, demonstrating the fact by imitating the sound of a church bell swung by a bell-rope. And she further

4 Huntington adds: ". . . with that he is easily checked, and by laying the hand on his neck, is made to wheel to this side or that" (p. 269).

confirmed her story by showing him the sign of the cross. Mr. McTavish concluded that she had been taken prisoner and sold to the Spaniards who lived on the upper banks of the Del Norte River [Río Grande].[5] The source of this river must be found south of a range of mountains seen distinctly by Mr. Hunt and Mr. McKenzie when they crossed the continent to reach the Columbia River.[6]

As the manner of capturing wild horses cannot be known to my readers generally, I shall tell about it here, briefly. The Indian who wants to take some of these horses first mounts one of his best steeds, supplied with a long horsehair rope, one end of which has a slip-knot. When he comes upon a herd [of wild animals], he runs into their midst, and throwing his rope, passes it skillfully over the head of a horse that he wishes to capture. Then quickly turning his own mount, he pulls the rope after him. The wild horse, feeling itself strangled, offers little resistance. The Indian then approaches the beast, binds the forefeet together, and leaves him until he has captured, in this way, as many as he wishes to take home. He then drives them home before him and breaks them in as they are needed.

CHAPTER 22

On the seventeenth, the fatigue that I had experienced on the preceding day, riding horseback, forced me to return to my canoe. About eight o'clock we passed a little river flowing from the northwest. Soon afterward we noticed some canoes, paddling hard to overtake us. As we still went along our course we heard a child's voice cry out in French *"Arretez donc, arretez donc"* ["Stop, stop"]. We landed and the canoes joined us. In one of them we recognized the wife and children of a man named Pierre Dorion, a hunter who had been sent with a party of eight men, under the leadership of Mr. J. Reed, to get some provisions from the Snakes.[1]

5 Huntington interpolates: ". . . but I think it more probable it was nearer, in North California, at the Mission of San Carlos or San Francisco" (p. 271).

6 This sentence does not appear in the 1854 edition.

1 Chittenden says that Pierre Dorion was "a half-breed, and son of the Dorion

The wife told us of the disastrous end of all those who made up the hunters' party. She said that during the month of January when the hunters had spread out, here and there, to set traps for the beaver, Jacob Reznor,[2] Giles Leclerc, and Pierre Dorion, her husband, had been attacked by the Indians. Leclerc, who was wounded mortally, returned to her tent where he died a few minutes after reporting to her that her husband had been killed. She immediately took two horses that were tethered near her lodging, mounted her two children on one of them, and fled in haste to Mr. Reed's post, which was about a five-day journey from the area where her husband had been killed. Her shock and anxiety was extreme when she found the post deserted and found also some traces of blood. She did not doubt that Mr. Reed had been massacred, and she fled without hesitation toward the mountains south of the Walla Walla River, where she spent the winter, killing the two horses to provide food for herself and her children.

Finally, her food supply exhausted, she decided to cross the mountains and reach the banks of the Columbia in the hope of meeting some more humane Indians, who would let her live among them while awaiting the arrival of the canoes that she knew would come upriver in the spring. The Walla Walla Indians had, in fact, received this woman with open hospitality. They were the ones who brought her to us. We gave them some

---

who accompanied Lewis and Clark on a portion of their expedition across the continent. He was hired by Hunt as an interpreter and joined the overland expedition with his Indian wife and two children. He figures frequently in Irving's account of the expedition and generally in an interesting way." Chittenden, *American Fur Trade*, II, 906.

2 Franchère used the spelling Reznor in the Bibaud edition. The Huntington text printed the name as Regner.

Ross Cox's *The Columbia River* contains the following interesting note about the name: "This name is spelled in a variety of ways, including Rizner, Reznor, and Regner. He was a Kentuckian who had been with Andrew Henry. On his way back to St. Louis with several companions, he met the Hunt party and proceeded to join it. Along with four or five others he was left in the mountains to trap. They met Robert Stuart's party of returning Astorians and accompanied them for a short distance, but they subsequently left and returned to the Snake River country. In 1813, he and his companions joined Reed's party and were killed with them" (p. 152).

See also Irving's *Astoria* for many references concerning the life and activities of this man.

presents to repay them for their care and trouble, and they returned home well satisfied.

The people who died in this unhappy wintering party were Mr. John Reed (clerk), Jacob Reznor, John Hobhough, Pierre Dorion (hunters and trappers), Giles Leclerc, Francois Landry, J. Baptiste Turcot, André Lachapelle, and Pierre Delaunay.[3] We had no doubt that this butchery was only a vengeance wrought on us by the natives over the death of one of their tribe whom the men of Mr. Clarke's party had hanged for theft during the preceding spring.[4] This event,[5] the massacre of the *Tonquin's* crew, the disastrous end of Captain Cook, and many other similar instances demonstrate how those Europeans who have relations with barbaric people must refrain from treating them on the basis of a too marked inequality, or to punish them for their misdeeds, according to the customs and codes where often there is an enormous disproportion between the crimes and the punishments. If these punishments, pretended as exemplary, seem to have a good effect, they are nearly always followed by terrible consequences.

On the eighteenth we passed Priest Rapids, so named by Mr. Stuart and his men who saw near this spot in 1811 a number of Indians, one of whom made use of sprinkling and other rites that had the aspect of being a crude imitation of ceremonies employed in the Catholic faith. We encountered some Indians, from whom we bought two horses. The banks of the river in this area are rather high, but the country to the interior is flat and unadorned.

On the twentieth we came to a spot at which the river drew

[3] Bibaud supplies a footnote that does not appear in the 1854 edition: "Landry died in the month of November from scrofula. Delaunay left Mr. Reed in the autumn and has not been seen since. He was a half-breed of crabbed bad humor, who married an Indian woman" (p. 216).

Quaife misread Bibaud's text, saying that it was Turcotte (Bibaud writes Turcot) who died of scrofula. The footnote clearly states that it was Landry. Quaife also says that the name of LaChapelle (Chapelle in Quaife) does not appear in the Manuscript (p. 209n.).

[4] Concerning this episode see also Alexander Ross, *First Settlers*, 230–35; and Ross Cox, *Columbia River*, 151–54.

[5] The remainder of the paragraph, says Quaife, is not in the Manuscript and was added by Bibaud (p. 209n.).

in sharply and we were forced to make a portage. Mr. Stuart and Mr. Ross left us, going on to the Spokane post to get provisions which would be needed for us to continue our journey.

On the twenty-first we lightened the load of three canoes. Those of us who were to cross the continent embarked in them in order to make greater speed. We passed several rapids and began to see some snow-covered mountains. On the twenty-second we also saw some pines on the rims of the neighboring hills, and in the evening we camped under trees, something that had not happened since the twelfth [of April].

At nine on the morning of the twenty-third we arrived at the post which Mr. D. Stuart had established at the mouth of the Okanogan. As compared to the country through which we had traveled for twelve days, this place seemed charming to us. The two rivers and the vast prairies covered with a beautiful greenness strike the observer's eye most agreeably; yet there is neither tree nor shrub to lend variety to the scene and make it a little less bare and monotonous. We found Mr. McGillivray and Mr. Ross at this trading post. Mr. Ovide Montigny, who had been employed by the North West Company, also stayed here, and asked me to carry a letter to his brother [in Canada].

We re-embarked about noon to continue our journey. After passing several dangerous rapids without accident—always through country diversified by steep rocks, hills, and verdant prairies—on the 29th we came to the portage at Kettle Falls. This is a falls where the water plunges over a rock of white marble veined with red and green, that crosses the river from northwest to southeast. We made the portage quickly and camped on the edge of a charming prairie.

At this spot we found some Indians who had been fasting, as they told us, for several days. They seemed to be effectively reduced to a most deplorable condition, little more than skin and bones, dragging themselves along with great difficulty.[6] This

6 Huntington varies the passage to read: ". . . so that not without difficulty could they even reach the margin of the river, to get a little water to wet their parched lips" (p. 279).

kind of thing often happens to these poor people when their hunting has not been successful. At such a time their chief food is only pine moss, which they boil, and which they reduce to a kind of paste, or black dough, thick enough to take the form of a loaf or of a biscuit. I had the curiosity to taste of this bread and I thought that I had put a piece of soap in my mouth! However, people who have eaten this paste tell me that when it is fresh it tastes rather good with meat.[7]

On the thirtieth, when we were still camped above Kettle Falls, Mr. Stuart and Mr. Clarke arrived from the Spokane post. The latter rode a horse of the finest stature and the most magnificent neck and shoulders that I have ever seen in these parts. Mr. Stuart had fallen from his mount while trying to spur him and had been severely hurt. They did not bring us the provisions that we awaited, because the hunters who had been sent to the Flatheads for this very purpose had not been able to get any. We agreed, therefore, that Messrs. McDonald, J. Stuart, and McKenzie should go on ahead, betaking themselves to the post situated east of the Rockies, so that they could send us both horses and provisions. These gentlemen left us on May 1. After their departure, we killed two horses and dried the meat, work that kept us busy the rest of that day and the day following. Toward evening, Mr. Alexander Stewart arrived at our camp. He was going to seek his family east of the mountains and bring them to the West Coast.[8]

We resumed our journey on the morning of the third and went on to camp that evening at the upper end of a rapid. From

[7] Huntington adds: "We partly relieved these wretched natives from our scanty store" (p. 280). And he puts in a footnote the following information: "The process of boiling employed by the Indians in this case, extracts from the moss its gelatine, which serves to supply the waste of those tissues into which that principle enters; but as the moss contains little or none of the proximates which constitute the bulk of living solids and fluids, it will not, of course, by itself, support life or strength" (p. 280).

[8] Huntington adds that Mr. A. Stuart had recovered from his wounds (p. 281). Again Huntington confused the names of Stuart and Stewart. Here Franchère printed Alexander Stewart in the 1820 edition. Quaife nowhere comments upon this confusion, and follows Huntington's rendering.

here we began to see mountains covered with forests, and the banks of the river were low and thinly strewn with trees.

On the fourth, after passing several large rapids, we reached the mouth of the Flathead River. This stream flows from the south and empties into the Columbia in the form of a cascade. At this junction it is perhaps 150 paces wide.

On the morning of the fifth we passed the confluence of the Kootenai River, which also flows from the south and is about as wide as the Flathead, or nearly so. Soon afterward we came to a lake, which we crossed in order to camp at its upper end. This lake may be about forty-five miles long and four or five miles wide at its broadest part. It is surrounded by high hills, which for the most part have their base at the water's edge, rising gradually in rows or terraces and offering a very pretty sight from the lake.

On the sixth, after we had run through a strait some twelve to fifteen miles long, we entered another lake, smaller than the one preceding. When we were nearly in the middle of this lake, an accident occurred—unusual but not serious. One of the men who had been sick for several days asked to be put ashore for a moment. Since we were not more than a mile from land, we granted his request. But when we were no more than three or four hundred feet from shore, our canoe struck sharply on the trunk of a tree that was rooted in the bottom of the lake but whose extremities rose between wind and water. It needed nothing more to break so frail a vessel; the canoe was pierced and filled, and despite all our efforts we could not free it from the tree trunk, which had penetrated inside about two or three feet. Perhaps that was a piece of good luck for us, for the rent was at least a yard long. We made a distress signal, and another canoe that was continuing its way in the middle of the lake came to our rescue.[9] They carried us to land, where it was necessary to make camp, both to dry ourselves and to repair the canoe.

On the seventh, Mr. A. Stewart, whom we had left at Kettle

[9] Huntington varies this story somewhat, but the substance remains unchanged.

Falls, rejoined us and we took up our journey together. In the evening, we came upon some Indians encamped on the banks of the river. They gave us a letter by which we learned that Mr. McDonald and his companions had passed there on the fourth.[10] Having bought several pieces of dried elk meat from these Indians, we went on our way. The countryside rose higher, the river ran very swiftly, and we made little progress on that day.

On the eighth we began to find snow on the sandy banks; the air became quite cold. The river banks presented only high hills whose crests were covered with dense forests. While the canoes were mounting a large rapids, I clambered up the hills with Mr. McGillis; and we walked along, following the course of the river for six or eight miles. The snow was very deep in the ravines and hollows that are found between the bases of these mountains. The most common trees are the Norway pine and the cedar. Here, as near the seashore, cedars are of prodigious size.

On the ninth and tenth the country presented the same aspect as on the eighth. Toward evening, we saw a chain of high mountains entirely covered with snow. The river was scarcely more than two hundred feet wide and was studded by banks composed of gravel and little pebbles.

CHAPTER 23

On the eleventh [of May]—exactly one month, that is, after we left The Dalles—we turned off the Columbia to enter a small stream that Mr. Thompson had, in 1811, named the Canoe River.[1] The course of the Columbia River, which above the Falls has (apart from some local meandering) a NNE direction, at this point makes a detour and appears to flow to the SE. Some travelers (particularly Mr. Regis Brugier) who have ascended this river to its source tell me that it rises from two little lakes

[10] Huntington adds: "The women at this camp were busy spinning the coarse wool of the mountain sheep: they had blankets or mantles, woven or platted of the same material, with a heavy fringe all round: I would gladly have purchased one of these, but as we were to carry all our baggage on our backs across the mountains, I was forced to relinquish the idea" (p. 284).

[1] Huntington explains: ". . . from the fact that it was on this fork that he constructed the canoes which carried him to the Pacific" (p. 286).

not far from the Rocky Mountain range, which at that place diverges considerably to the east.

According to Arrowsmith's map, from its mouth at the Pacific Ocean to its source in the Rockies the Columbia must be nearly twelve hundred miles long, or four hundred French leagues of twenty-five to the degree: that is, from about 250 miles, west to east, from its mouth to the first rapids; about 750 miles, SSW to NNE from the first rapids to the turn at the confluence of the Canoe River; and about 170 to 180 miles, NW to SE, from that point to its source.[2] We were not supplied with the instruments necessary to determine the latitude, much less the longitude, of our different stations. It must have taken us four or five days to get from Astoria to the Falls, and we could not have made less than sixty miles a day. As I have just said, we took a full month to get from the Falls to the mouth of the Canoe; and deducting four or five days when we did not travel, there remain twenty-five days on the way. It is not possible that we made less than thirty miles a day, one day following another.

We went up the Canoe River to the point where it ceases to be navigable, and camped at the same spot where Mr. Thompson had spent the winter of 1810–11. We began at once to make our canoes safe, and divided the baggage among the men, giving each fifty pounds to carry, including his provisions. A sack of pemmican, or pounded meat, that we discovered was a great relief to us, for our food supply was nearly exhausted.

On the twelfth we began to make our way toward the mountains, twenty-four strong. Mr. Alexander Stewart and his men remained at the portage to put into a safe place all the baggage that we could not carry, such as boxes, barrels, large kettles, and so forth. First we crossed some marshes, then a dense little woods, and finally, on the banks of the Canoe, we walked on gravel. Fatigue forced us to camp at an early hour.

On the thirteenth we went on our way and entered the mountain valleys where there were not less than four or five feet

2 Quaife states that this paragraph seems to be Bibaud's work. The narrative resumes in the Manuscript beginning with the following paragraph (p. 218n.).

of snow. We had to ford the river ten to a dozen times in the course of the day, sometimes in water up to our necks. These frequent crossings were necessitated by precipitous rocks, almost impossible to get around without plunging into the woods for a great distance. The river is very swift and dashes over a stony bed. One of our men fell, thereby losing a sack of salt pork that we had carefully preserved as a last resource. The circumstances in which we found ourselves caused us to regard this little incident as an unfortunate mishap. We camped at the foot of a steep mountain, and sent Mr. Pillet and our guide, McKay, ahead to get provisions for us.

On the morning of the fourteenth we began to scale the mountain that lay before us. We were obliged to stop often to catch our breath, the mountain was so steep. Happily, it had frozen solid the night before and the snow was hard enough to bear our weight. After two or three hours of difficulties and of unbelievable fatigue, we came to the summit and followed the tracks of those who had preceded us. This mountain is situated between two other much higher mountains, compared to which it is only a hill—that is to say, it is no more than a valley. Our progress soon became exhausting because of the depth of the snow which, melted by the sun's rays, would no longer support us as it had in the morning. We were forced to follow exactly in the tracks of those ahead of us and to plunge to our knees into the holes that they had made. It was as though we had put on and taken off, at each step, a large pair of boots.

Finally, we came to a good surface that our guide said was a little lake.[3] This lake, or rather these lakes—for there are two of them—are situated in the middle of the valley, or cup, of the mountains.[4] We had beside us a rocky slope, cut as perpendicularly as the walls of a fortress, which rose majestically some fifteen to eighteen hundred feet above the lakes and whose crest was covered with ice. Mr. J. Henry had given this extraordinary

[3] Quaife states that the Manuscript adds the following: ". . . which we could not perceive since it was covered with snow" (p. 222n.).

[4] Huntington adds a bit of color here, but it does not improve the text (p. 291).

139

rock the name of McGillivray's Rock.[5] The little lakes could not be more than two or three acres in size and not farther, one from another, than a few yards.

The Canoe River which, as we noted earlier, runs to the west and empties into the Columbia, has its source in one of these lakes.[6] The other gives birth to one of the branches of the Athabasca, which flows first to the east and then to the north, after its junction with the Unjighah, north of the Lake of the Mountains.[7] It takes the name of the Slave River as far as the lake of the same name, thence that of the Mackenzie as far as the Frozen Ocean.[8] After we had fetched water and lighted a fire, we made camp and spent a good night, although it was extremely cold. The most common wood was cedar and spruce.

On the fifteenth we got under way and soon began to descend the mountain. At the end of three hours we came to the banks of a brook that at first we found ice-covered, but that we soon found it necessary to ford. After a fatiguing march along an extremely arduous route through the middle of some woods, we camped at night under cypresses. I had struck my knee on the branch of a tree during the first day of our march, and I began to experience great pain.[9]

On the sixteenth we plunged through marshes and dense forests. We recrossed the little stream, after which our guide led us to the banks of the Athabasca River. We dried ourselves and continued our journey through a country far more pleasant than on the preceding days. We camped that evening on the

[5] No "J" Henry is to be found. In his Journal Franchère at first wrote the name Thompson, then crossed out all but the "T" and above wrote Henry. Bibaud misread the "T" thinking it to be a "J" and so printed J. Henry. See Quaife (p. 222n.).

[6] Quaife states that the information about the Canoe River, supplied by Bibaud, is not in the Manuscript (p. 223n.).

[7] Lake Athabasca.

[8] Huntington adds some descriptive detail in this passage, thereby interrupting the direct flow of the narrative; and he does little either to explain or to enhance its effectiveness.

[9] Huntington adds a sentence: "It was impossible, however, to flinch, as I must keep up with the party or be left to perish" (p. 293). Quaife says that this sentence is not in the Manuscript (p. 224n.). It does not appear in Bibaud.

border of a verdant plain which our guide told us was called Cow, or Buffalo [Coro], Prairie.[10] During the day we had seen the carcasses of several buffalo. Our supply of meat was almost exhausted, and our supper consisted only of a few handfuls of corn that we grilled in a pan.

We resumed our journey quite early on the morning of the seventeenth, and after we had passed a small woods of aspen, we returned to the banks of the river we had left the day before. Having come to a very high point of land, we were turned back by our guide, in order to pass this promontory at its lowest elevation. When we crossed it, we found some horse tracks so fresh that we presumed a horse was not far from us. When we left the woods, each man took the route he thought might lead us most quickly to some encampment. Soon we all came upon an old trading post that the North West Company had once built but had abandoned some four or five years previously. The site of this post is as charming as can be. Suffice it to say that it is built on one of the banks of the beautiful Athabasca River and is surrounded by smiling and lush prairies and superb groves. It is a pity that no one is there to enjoy these sylvan beauties and to praise, while admiring them, the Author of Nature.[11] We found Mr. Pillet there and one of Mr. McDonald's men, whose leg had been broken by the kick of a horse. After regaling ourselves with pemmican and fresh meat we set out, leaving two men to care for the lamed man, and made camp about eight miles from there.

On the eighteenth it rained. I took the lead, and when I had walked a distance of nine miles on the slope of a bald mountain I saw smoke [rising] from a valley bottom. I descended at once, and arrived at a little camp where I found two men who had come ahead of us with four horses. I made them fire some gunshots to warn the body of our men coming up in the rear.

[10] Quaife indicates that this name appears in the Manuscript as *La Prairie de la Vache* (p. 225n.). The same appears in Bibaud. "Coro" is Huntington's rendering.

[11] Quaife notes that this sentence was Bibaud's comment and that it is not to be found in the Manuscript (p. 226n.).

Soon we heard repeated from the river a signal that was not far from us. We went to that spot and found two men who had been left at the last portage and who, having a bark canoe, had descended the Athabasca River. Because my knee was causing me to suffer so much as to make further travel almost impossible, I asked one of the men to debark, and I took his place.

Meantime, the main body of our party arrived. They loaded the horses and went on their way. During the course of the day, my companion (who was an Iroquois) and I shot seven ducks. We doubled a promontory that is called Miette Rock. We sounded the river at the foot of this rock and found it fordable. Messrs. Clarke and Stuart, who were on horseback and who had not followed the usual route through the interior, descended the length of the promontory and passed at the fording, in this way avoiding the long and fatiguing route caused by the slopes which we had constantly to mount and descend. Seven of us camped at the edge of a little woods.[12] We made a good meal of our venison, but those who remained behind had nothing at all to eat.

CHAPTER 24

On the morning of the nineteenth [of May] we skirted a little lake on a sandy bank, having abandoned our canoe as much because it was nearly unserviceable as because we knew ourselves to be near the Rocky Mountain House. In fact, we had not gone far on our way before we saw smoke on the far side of the lake. We soon forded [the shallow water] and came to the post, where we found Messrs. McDonald, Stuart, and McKenzie, who had preceded us by only two days.

The post of the Rocky Mountain—in English, Rocky Mountain House—is situated on the edge of the little lake that I have mentioned, in the middle of a woods, and is almost entirely surrounded by steep rocks frequented only by the goat and white sheep. To the west can be seen the range of the Rockies whose

12 Huntington alters this to read: "We encamped, to the number of seven, at the entrance of what at high water might be a lake, but was then but a flat of blackish sand, with a narrow channel in the centre" (p. 296).

peaks are covered by perpetual snow. From the lake, Miette Rock, of which I spoke earlier and which is very high, looks like the portal of a church seen obliquely. This establishment [Rocky Mountain House] was in the charge of a Mr. Decoigne. He does not collect many furs for the company, which built the post only to facilitate the mountain crossings of those of its employees who are on their way to the Columbia River or returning from it.[1]

People so often talk about the Rocky Mountains and seem to know so little about them that the reader might naturally want me to say a word about them here. If one can credit travelers and the most recent maps, these mountains extend, almost in a straight line, from 35° or 36° of North Latitude to the mouth of the Unjighah, or Mackenzie River, into the Arctic Ocean, by 65° or 66°. This length of 30° of latitude, or about twenty-two hundred miles, is only the mean side of a right-angled triangle, of which the short side [or base] is 26° of longitude by 35° or 36° of latitude; that is, about sixteen hundred miles of which the mountain chain forms the hypotenuse. The southern extremity of this chain is about 114° and the northern extremity about 140° of West Longitude. Thus the real and diagonal length of this mountain range must be nearly twenty-seven hundred miles from southeast to northwest. In so great a length, the perpendicular height and the width of the base must necessarily be quite unequal. We took nearly four days to cross these mountains, a fact from which I conclude that, by the route we had to follow, they could at this point measure nearly 54° of latitude, or 120 miles in width.

The geographer, Pinkerton, is surely mistaken when he gives these mountains only a three-thousand-foot elevation above sea level. From my own observations, I should not hesitate to estimate six thousand. We very probably climbed fifteen hundred feet above the valley levels and we were not, perhaps, at half

[1] The next four paragraphs, according to Quaife, are "the work of Editor Bibaud, who, however, apparently drew, in part, upon data found elsewhere in the Manuscript" (p. 229n.). This statement makes it appear certain that either Mr. Quaife did not intend to make a collation of the complete Manuscript or was not permitted to utilize it in its entirety for the purposes of collation.

the total height; and the valleys must themselves be considerably above the level of the Pacific Ocean, in view of the prodigious number of rapids that we encountered in the Columbia from the Falls to the Canoe River. Be that as it may, if these mountains yield to the Andes in height and length, on both counts they surpass the Appalachians, regarded, until recently, as the principal mountains in North America. Moreover, they give birth to an infinite number of streams and to the greatest rivers of this continent.[2]

These mountains offer a vast and new field to natural history; neither botanist nor mineralogist has yet explored them. The first travelers called them the Shining Mountains because of an infinite number of rock crystals which, it is said, cover their surface and which, when they are not capped with snow, or in those spots where they are not covered, reflect afar the rays of the sun. The name of Rocky Mountains was probably given to them by people who crossed them later, because of the enormous rocks that they here and there present to view. Actually, Miette Rock and McGillivray's, above all, appeared to me almost as marvels of nature. Some people think that they contain metals and precious stones.

Except for the goat and sheep, the animals of the Rocky Mountains, if these mountains harbor any extraordinary species, are no better known than the mineral and vegetable productions. The [mountain] sheep usually keep to the precipitous rocks, where it is almost impossible for men, or even for wolves, to find them. We saw several of them on the rocks surrounding Rocky Mountain House. This animal has large, curled horns like those of the domestic ram. Its wool is long but coarse; that on the belly is finest and whitest. The Indians who live near the mountains make blankets of this wool, not unlike ours, which they exchange with the Indians along the Columbia for fish, glass beads, and so forth. The ibex is a species of goat that lives, like

2 Huntington footnotes as follows: "This is interesting, as the rough calculation of an unscientific traveller, unprovided with instruments, and at that date. The real height of the Rocky Mountains, as now ascertained, averages twelve thousand feet; the highest known peak is about sixteen thousand" (p. 300).

the sheep, on the summits and clefts of the rocks. It differs from the latter in that it has hair instead of wool, and does not have the curled horns but only those projecting backward. Its color is likewise different. The natives boil the horns of these animals and afterward make spoons, little dishes, and other items from them.

Mr. Decoigne found that he did not have sufficient supplies for all of us, for he had not expected to see everyone arriving at the same time. The hunters at the post were then going along the banks of the Smoke River.[3] In order to subsist, we killed a horse and a dog. We could not find enough birch bark to make more than two canoes, and we employed our men in constructing some of wood. For a want of something better they were forced to use poplar, a poor and unwieldy wood.

On the twenty-second the three men we had left at the old house arrived in a little canoe made of two elk hides sewn together and held by thongs, like a drum, on a frame of branches. On the twenty-fourth, with four canoes ready, we fastened them together, two by two, and embarked to descend the river as far as the old trading post called Hunter's Lodge. There Mr. Decoigne, who was to return with us to Canada, said that he had some bark canoes put in a cache for the use of people going downriver. The water was not deep and the current was rapid. We glided, so to speak, for a distance of thirty to thirty-five miles and camped, having lost sight of the mountains. As we advanced, the banks of the river became lower and the countryside more pleasant.

On the twenty-fifth, since we had only a little pemmican that we wanted to conserve, we sent a hunter on ahead in the small skin canoe to get some venison. About ten o'clock we found him waiting, with two moose that he had killed. He had hung the hearts of these animals on a tree branch as a signal. We landed some men to help him carry his game and continued to scud along without accident. But about two o'clock in the

[3] Bibaud adds the following footnote: "So called by the voyageurs who nearby saw a volcanic mountain vomiting dense smoke" (p. 238). Huntington inserts the note as a parenthetical comment in his text (p. 302).

afternoon, after doubling a point, we swept into a considerable rapid where by the ineptness of those who paddled the [two bound] canoes in which Messrs. Pillet, Wallace, McGillis, and I were seated, one struck a point of rock and was broken and the other capsized; and we all found ourselves in the water.[4] Two of our employees, Olivier Roy Lapensée and André Belanger, were drowned; and only by the greatest effort were we able to save Pillet and Wallace, along with a man named J. Hurteau.[5] The first had already gone down the rapids and was carried into another. He had lost all his strength and was able to do no more than to put up his hands and arms from time to time.

The employees lost all their supplies; the others recovered only a part of theirs. Toward evening, as I went upriver (I had gone downriver to find those articles that floated on the stream), I found the body of Lapensée. We buried him as decently as we could. We set in place a cross, on which I carved, with the point of my knife, his name and the manner and date of his death.[6] The body of Belanger was not recovered.

If anything could console the shades of the dead for an unhappy and premature end, it would, without doubt, be the knowledge that we gave their bodies the proper funeral rites and that they have given their names to the places where they perished. It was thus that the soul of Palinurus rejoiced in learning from the mouth of the Sibyl that the promontory near which he drowned would hereafter be called by his name, *gaudet cognomine terra*. The rapid and the point of land where the accident I have just described took place will bear, and probably already bear, the name of Lapensée.[7]

[4] Huntington varies this passage to explain in greater detail how the accident occurred (p. 304).

[5] Huntington says that attempts to resuscitate Hurteau were successful. Pillet and Wallace were saved before they were overcome (p. 305).

[6] According to Quaife, the Manuscript continues as follows: ". . . on which I carved with the point of my knife the unfortunate fate of those two young Canadians" (p. 234n.).

[7] This paragraph Quaife says is not in the Manuscript and was apparently supplied by Bibaud (p. 234n.).

Huntington adds a curious footnote: "Mr. Franchere, not having the fear of the *Abbe Gaume* before his eyes, so wrote in his Journal of 1814; finding con-

On the twenty-sixth, some of our men embarked in the three canoes that remained; the others followed the river banks on foot. In several places we saw veins of coal on the sides between the water's surface and the plain. We stopped toward evening near a little river where we built some rafts to carry all our men.

On the twenty-seventh I went on ahead with the hunters in a small skin canoe. We soon killed a moose that we skinned and whose hide we hung, still bloody, on the branch of a tree at the end of a point [of land], so that our men who followed would be aware of [the results of] our hunt. After refreshing ourselves with a bit of the meat, we continued on the river and made camp near a dense woods where the hunters had some hope of getting bears. This hope was not realized.

On the twenty-eighth, shortly after our departure, we killed a swan. While I was busy cooking it, the hunters went into the woods, and I heard a shot that seemed to come from a direction opposite to that which they had taken. They soon returned, and were very much surprised to learn that I had not fired the shot. Nevertheless, the canoes and rafts had caught up with us, and we went on our way down river. Soon we met two men and a woman who were in a bark canoe and who carried some letters and supplies to Rocky Mountain House. We learned from one of these letters addressed to Mr. Decoigne, several circumstances regarding the war and, among other things, of the defeat of Captain Barclay on Lake Erie.[8] That evening we came to Hunter's Lodge, where we found four birch-bark canoes. We loaded two of them and resumed our journey on the thirty-first. Mr. Pillet left very early in the morning with the hunters. They killed a moose, which they left on a point and which we picked up. The country through which we passed that day could not be more charming.

solation in a thought savoring, we confess, more of Virgil than of the catechism. It is a classic term that calls to our mind rough Captain *Thorn*'s sailor-like contempt for his literary passengers so comically described by Mr. *Irving*. Half the humor as well as of the real interest of Mr. Franchere's charming narrative, is lost by one who has never read 'Astoria' " (p. 306).

    [8] Quaife states that the manuscript supplies the date on one of the letters as October 14, 1813. Decoigne received it on May 28, 1814 (p. 236n.). The Battle of Lake Erie had been fought on September 10, 1813.

The river is wide, beautiful, and bordered by shallows covered with birch and poplar trees.

On the evening of June 1 we camped at the mouth of the Pembina River, which flows from the south. Ascending the Pembina for two days and afterward crossing a tongue of land about seventy-five miles wide, one comes to Fort Augustus on the Park, or Saskatchewan, River. Messrs. McDonald and McKenzie had taken this route and had left us a half-sack of pemmican at the mouth of the Pembina. After landing, Mr. Stuart and I amused ourselves by fishing with hooks, but we managed to catch only five or six little fish.

On the second we passed the mouth of the Little Slave Lake River. Toward eight in the morning we encountered a family of Indians who told us they had come to kill buffalo. We bought one from them for a small brass kettle. We could not have made a more opportune encounter, for our provisions were entirely exhausted.

On the third we reached the La Biche [Moose or Elk] River, which we began to ascend. This river is quite narrow and is filled with boulders. We were forced to debark and to skirt it, while some of the men towed the canoes.[9] This march was quite disagreeable, for it was necessary to cut across woodsy points which a fire had burned and which were filled with fallen trees, stumps, and brambles. When Mr. Wallace and I stopped to quench our thirst, the others got ahead of us; and since it was impossible to follow their trail, we got lost and wandered for three hours before finding our men, who had begun to fear that we had run into trouble.[10]

We continued our journey on the fourth, sometimes in our canoes, sometimes walking along the river, and camped at night, extremely tired.

[9] Huntington supplies description of the towing process, but it does not seem to improve the passage.

[10] Huntington adds: "and were firing signal-guns to direct us." He also adds that they found their hunters, "who had killed a moose and her two calves" (p. 310).

CHAPTER 25

On the fifth of June we crossed Lake La Biche, which is forty-five miles long and twenty-four to thirty miles wide. Here we met a small canoe paddled by two young women. They were looking for eggs on the islands in the lake—this was the season when the birds laid their eggs. The young women told us that their father was not far from the spot at which we met them. In fact, we soon saw him appear, rounding a little island. We joined him, and he told us that he was Antoine Desjarlais and that he had been employed by the North West Company but had left it in 1805.

When we told him of our need for food, he offered us a large quantity of eggs, and he made one of our men go with his daughters in his little canoe to look for some other provisions at his cabin on the other side of the lake. He himself accompanied us as far as a portage of about twenty-five yards, formed by a beaver dam. After making the portage and crossing a small pond, we camped to await the return of our man. He came back the next morning with Desjarlais, bringing us about fifty pounds of dried meat and ten or twelve pounds of tallow. We invited our host to breakfast with us—the least that we could do for him after the good offices he had rendered us. This man, with his family, lived by hunting and appeared quite content with his lot. No one disputed his possession of Lake La Biche, of which, it might be said, he was the master. He begged me to read to him two letters he had had for two years and of which he did not know the contents. They were from one of his sisters, and were dated from Vercheres [Varennes]. I even thought that I recognized the handwriting of Mr. L. G. Labadie, a teacher in that parish.[1]

Finally, after assuring this good man of our gratitude for the offices he had performed for us, we left him and went on our way. After we had made two portages we found ourselves on the banks of the Beaver River, which at this point was only a creek.

1 How Franchère could recognize the handwriting is difficult to understand unless, possibly, he had himself been a pupil of Labadie.

It is by this route that canoes descend the Athabasca, or the Little Slave Lake River, usually passing it to reach the Cumberland House on English River. We were forced to tow our canoes in the Beaver, walking on the sandy shoreline, where we were annoyed by mosquitoes. One of the hunters explored the woods, but without success. We came across a cabin in which we found an old trapper by the name of Nadeau. He was reduced to extreme weakness, having had nothing to eat for two days. However, a young man who had married one of his daughters arrived shortly afterward with the good news that he had killed a buffalo—and because of this we decided to camp.

We sent some of our men to get a part of the buffalo meat. Nadeau gave us half of it, and he told us that we would find, thirty miles farther downriver, some martin skins and a net which he begged us to take with us. We left this good man on the following morning and pursued our course. When we arrived at the place he had designated, we found his cache and took the net. Soon afterward we came to the Moose River, which we had to ascend to reach the lake of the same name. The water in this river was so low that we had to unload our canoes completely. We fastened them to poles so that those men who remained in them could carry them whenever they did not find enough water to float them. After dividing the baggage among the rest of the hands, we took our way through the woods, guided by Mr. Decoigne.

This gentleman, who had not traveled this route for nineteen years, soon lost his way, and we dispersed, one from another, during the afternoon. Nevertheless, since we had outdistanced the men who carried the baggage and the few provisions that old Nadeau had given us, Mr. Wallace and I thought it wise to turn back to the party bringing up the rear. We soon met Mr. Pillet and one of the hunters. The latter found, after a while, a fairly well-beaten path.[2] Then, the men who carried the baggage hav-

2 Huntington varies this passage: Pillet "soon gave a whoop, to signify that we should stop. Presently emerging from the underwood, he showed us a horse-whip which he had found, and from which and from other unmistakable signs,

ing joined us, we all followed the path single file and were led to the lake shores in a very short time. Night was falling. The canoes arrived before long—to our great satisfaction, for we were beginning to fear that they had passed ahead of our arrival.[3]

Early on the morning of the eighth, I left with a hunter to search for Messrs. Clarke, Stuart, and Decoigne, who had run ahead of us on the day before. The first one I soon found, camped on the lake shore. The canoes came up, shortly, to the same spot. Messrs. Stuart and Decoigne arrived, in turn, and told us that they had slept on the banks of Lake Puant [Stinking Lake], situated about twelve miles ENE from where we stood. Thus we were all reunited, and we crossed the lake, which is about eighteen miles in circumference and whose shoreline is very pretty. We camped early, to try our fishing net. I looked at it that evening, and brought back two carp and a duck. We set it for the night, and the next morning found twenty white fish in it.

We broke camp at an early hour and gained the mouth of a little river that flowed between some hills, and there we stopped for breakfast. I found the white fish quite as delicious as even the salmon. We again had to walk the banks of this little river— a painful enough task, since we had to break a path through dense brush during a rainstorm that lasted all day. Two men remained in each of the canoes and took them upriver for a distance of thirty miles—as far as Long Lake, on the borders of which we camped.

On the tenth we crossed the lake, made a portage of nearly a mile and a half,[4] and entered a small river which we had to skirt, as on other occasions, and which led us to Bridge Lake. This lake took its name from a kind of bridge or dam formed naturally

he was confident the trail would lead us either to the lake or a navigable part of the river" (pp. 315–16).

[3] Huntington adds further: "The splashing of their paddles was a welcome sound, and we who had been wise enough to keep behind, all encamped together" (p. 316).

[4] Quaife notes that the clause "made a portage of half a league" occurs at this point in the Manuscript. It is also in Bibaud, as I have translated it. Why Quaife did not note this fact and why Huntington did not translate it is inexplicable.

by trees blown down by the wind and covered over by earth and leaves piled up by high waters. At the borders of this lake we met a young man and two women who had the care of some horses belonging to the Hudson's Bay Company. We borrowed half a dozen from them and crossed the bridge [mounted on them]. After climbing a considerable hill, we saw a prairie that led us, in two hours, to an old trading post on the banks of the Saskatchewan River. Realizing that we were near an establishment, we made ourselves presentable before we came to it. Toward sunset we arrived at the post called Fort Vermillion. It is situated on the river banks, at the foot of a superb slope.[5]

We found about ninety people at this trading post—men, women, and children. To subsist, these people depend upon hunting and fishing—a precarious enough way to live. Mr. Hallet, the clerk in charge, was absent; and we were dismayed to learn that there were no provisions at the post—news disagreeable, indeed, for famished men such as we.[6] Mr. Hallet was not long in coming, however. He had two quarters of beef brought out that he had had put on ice, and had a supper prepared for us. This Mr. Hallet was polite, sociable, loving his ease passably, and wished to live in these wild areas as people do in civilized countries. We expressed our surprise to him upon seeing in the back of a large building a cariole, constructed in order to travel conveniently. But the workers had forgotten to take the measurements of the doors of the building before they started to build the carriage. Thus, when it was completed, it was found to be too large and could never be removed from the room in which it was standing. Apparently it was to remain there a long time, since Mr. Hallet was not inclined to destroy the house only for the pleasure of riding in a cariole.

Beside the North West Company establishment is another belonging to the Hudson's Bay Company. As a general rule, these trading posts are constructed in this way—one near the other,

5 That is, on the Saskatchewan River.
6 Huntington adds: "We had been led to suppose that if we could only reach the plains of the Saskatchewine, we should be in the land of plenty" (p. 319).

The Dalles, by John Mix Stanley. Franchère was the first to call this area on the Columbia "The Dalles." Mount Hood looms in the background. The present-day community named The Dalles is situated on the slopes south of the river.

"Chinook lodge," from a sketch by A. T. Agate. The lodge shown here is smaller than the one described by Franchère, but the general structure pattern is accurately represented.

Indian Canoe Tomb. Franchère's description of a Chinook Indian canoe burial indicates that often the canoe was hoisted upon rocks so that spring flood waters would not wash over it.

Cascades of the Columbia. This mid-nineteenth century litho-graph reveals the power of the mighty river and explains why both Indians and fur traders made portages rather than risk their lives in efforts to save time.

Kettle Falls. This spectacular rock formation, jutting precipitously across the Columbia, forced the Astorians to make another of their many portages. Usually, following the long transport of boats and suppplies, the fur traders encamped on the prairies in the distance.

The Palouse River, once called the Pavilion River by early fur traders. John Clarke took Astorians Pillet, Farnham, McLennan, and Cox up the Snake to this point; thence, by land, they rode horses purchased from the Nez Percé Indians northward to the Spokane near Lake Coeur d'Alene.

Jasper House, popularly known also as Rocky Mountain House. Franchère's party reached this tiny isolated post on May 19, 1814, on its way overland to Montreal. From Paul Kane, Wanderings of an Artist.

Fort William in 1805. Generally regarded as the "metropolitan post of the interior," Fort William became an oasis of luxury and good living for men who suffered the rigorous life of the fur hunter along the western trails.

surrounded by a common palisade and allowing one door of communication to the inside of the stronghold, thereby giving security in case of an attack by the Indians to the southwest. These savages, and particularly the Blackfeet, the Gros Ventres, the Gens de Sang, and those of the Yellow Rock [River] are very malicious. They live by hunting, but they bring few furs to the traders, and the companies maintain these posts chiefly to procure supplies.

On the eleventh, after breakfasting at Fort Vermillion, we resumed our journey, with six or seven pounds of tallow our entire foodstock. These provisions lasted only until the evening of the third day, when we had two ounces of tallow each for supper.

On the morning of the fourteenth, we killed a goose; and, about noon, we pulled up some *choux gras* which we boiled with our game. We did not forget to put into the pot a little of the tallow that was left, and we had a delicious meal. Toward the end of the day we had the good luck of killing a buffalo.

On the fifteenth Mr. Clarke and Mr. Decoigne, having left early to hunt, returned soon to tell us the happy news that they had killed three buffalo. We camped at once and sent most of our men to cut up the flesh of these animals and to cure it. This work kept us occupied until the following evening. We then got under way on the seventeenth with nearly six hundred pounds of half-cured meat. Toward evening we saw from our camp several herds of buffalo. But we did not hunt them, believing that we already had enough meat to last until we reached the next trading post.[7]

The Saskatchewan River flows over a bed of sand and clay, a fact contributing greatly to reducing the purity and clarity of its waters which, like the waters of the Missouri River, are muddy and whitish. But for that, it is one of the most beautiful rivers in the world. The banks of the Saskatchewan are altogether

---

[7] Quaife maintains that what follows, to the end of this chapter, is Bibaud's work and that Franchère supplied only a brief description of the river (p. 248n.). Certainly the style of the French in the 1820 text alters considerably at this point.

charming and offer, in several places, the fairest, the happiest, and the most diversified scenery that one can see or imagine: hills of varied formations, crowned with superb groves of poplar; valleys beautifully shaded, morning and evening, by the slopes and groves that adorn them; herds of light-footed antelope and of ponderous buffalo—the former bounding over the hill slopes, the latter trampling the grass under their heavy feet. All these rural beauties are reflected and doubled, as it were, by the waters of the river. The varied and melodious songs of a thousand different birds perched on the tree tops, the refreshing breath of the breezes, the serene sky, the pure and salubrious air—everything, in a word, brings contentment and joy into the soul of the enchanted spectator. Above all, it is in the morning when the sun rises, and in the evening as it sets, that the spectacle is truly ravishing. I could not take my eyes from this magnificent picture until the growing obscurity had darkened it a little. Then the sweet pleasure that I had relished gave way to a sadness, which is not to say a somber melancholy.

Why is it, I asked myself, that so beautiful a country is not inhabited by human beings? The songs, the hymns, the prayers of the laborer and the artisan, happy and peaceful—are they never to be heard in these lovely regions? Why, while in Europe and, above all, in England so many thousands do not own an inch of land, and cultivate their country's soil for proprietors who leave them scarcely enough to subsist on; why do so many millions of acres of land, in appearance rich and fertile, remain unplowed and absolutely useless? Or, at least, why do they nourish only the herds of wild animals? Will men always prefer rather to vegetate all their lives on an unyielding soil than to seek some fertile lands far away, to live out their last years in peace and abundance?

But I am deluding myself. It is less easy than one might think for a poor man to better his lot. He has not the means to travel to far-off lands, or he has no means of acquiring property there—for these lands, uncultivated, deserted, abandoned, are not for whoever wishes to settle them and cultivate them. They have owners, and it is necessary to buy from these persons the privilege of rendering them fertile and productive. One ought not, besides, to have illusions! These regions, at times so delightful, do not enjoy perpetual springtime. They have their winter, a rigorous winter. A piercing cold is spread through the air, a heavy snow covers the ground, the frozen rivers flow only for the fish, the trees lose their leaves and are covered with ice, the greenness has disappeared, and the hills and valleys display only a uniform whiteness. Nature loses all her beauty, and man has enough to do to build a shelter against the abuses of the weather.

CHAPTER 26

On the morning of June 18, we re-embarked and, as the wind was rising, we hoisted a sail—something that we had not done since leaving the Columbia River. We endured a storm accompanied by hail but of short duration. Toward evening we reached Fort de la Montée, so named because those who ascend the river leave their canoes there and take to horses.[1] We found, as at Fort Vermillion, two establishments joined together to make common cause against the Indians, one belonging to the Hudson's Bay Company, the other to the North West. The former was in the charge of a Mr. Prudent and the latter under Mr. McLean. Mr. de Rocheblave, who had wintered at this post, had departed and had been gone some time.[2]

There were some cultivated fields around the house. Barley and peas appeared to promise an abundant harvest. Mr. McLean received us as well as circumstances permitted; but he had no provisions to give us and, since our beef was beginning to spoil, we left on the following morning to go as quickly as possible to Fort Cumberland. In the course of the day we passed two old forts, one of which had been built by the French before the conquest of Canada. This was, according to our guide, the westernmost trading establishment that the French merchants had ever

[1] Huntington varies this passage slightly but in no way improves it.
[2] De Rocheblave was a partner in the North West Company. Huntington indicates that he had gone to Lake Superior to attend a meeting of his partners.

155

built in the *Haut Pays* [high country]. Toward nightfall we killed an elk. The perspective had altered considerably since [we had left] Fort de la Montée. The banks of the river were higher and the countryside was covered by forests.

On the twentieth we saw some elms, a species of tree that I had not seen since my departure from Canada. We reached Fort Cumberland a little before sunset. This fort, called Cumberland House by the English, is situated where the Saskatchewan River flows into English Lake, between 53° and 54° North Latitude. It is a depot for those who are going to Slave, or Athabasca, Lake, or who are on their way to Fort William.[3] The post was in the charge of Mr. J. D. Campbell who had gone to Fort William, leaving it in the hands of a Mr. Harrison. There are two establishments, as at Vermillion and Montée.[4] Mr. Clarke and Mr. Stuart, who had remained behind us, arrived on the twenty-second, and in the evening we had a dance.

They gave us four sacks of pemmican and we left about eight in the morning of the twenty-third. After we crossed a little bay in the lake, we sailed into a small river which flows through an extremely low terrain. We made sixty to eighty miles and camped on a low shore where the mosquitoes tormented us horribly the whole night long.

On the twenty-fourth we passed Muddy Lake and entered Bourbon Lake, where we met a Mr. Kennedy, a clerk with the Hudson's Bay Company. We gathered several dozen redwing eggs from the islands in the lake and in the evening, since we still had some flour, Mr. Decoigne and I amused ourselves by making some cakes, an occupation that took us nearly until daybreak, for the night lasts only a few hours in this season and at this latitude.

We got under way early on the morning of the twenty-fifth,

[3] Huntington adds: ". . . as well as for those destined for the Rocky Mountains" (p. 327).

[4] An interesting explanation appears in the Huntington text: "At this place the traders who resort every year to Fort William, leave their half-breed wives and families, as they can live here at little expense, the lake abounding in fish" (p. 327).

passing Cross Lake, descending several cascades, and arriving, toward noon, at the Great Rapid Winnipeg, which must be nearly five miles long. We debarked and the men took the canoes down [the rapid]. At the foot of this rapid we found an old Canadian who lived only by fishing and who called himself the King of the Lake. He could at least call himself king of the fish, which are abundant, since he fished alone. Afterward we set up a kettle and feasted on excellent sturgeon. Then we left the old man and soon entered into Lake Winnipeg, which appeared to me like a sea of fresh water. This lake is today too well known for it to be necessary for me to put down a particular description of it. I shall content myself by saying that it yields only to Lake Superior and Great Slave Lake in size. It is fed by several large rivers, among others, the Saskatchewan from the northwest, the Red River from the south, and the Winnipeg River from ENE; and it empties into Hudson's Bay by the Nelson River, NNE, and by the Severn, ENE. The shores that this lake bathes are generally quite low; it appears to be shallow and is sprinkled with a great number of islands near the shoreline.

We reached Egg Island, from which we had to cross to the south to reach the mainland, but the wind was so violent that it was not until the day's end that we could make the crossing. We profited from the calm by skirting along the shores all the day and part of the night of the twenty-sixth. But to make up for this, we rested in camp until the evening of the twenty-seventh. The wind would not allow us to go on our way, but it appeared to fall off a little at sunset, and we embarked. Soon, however, we were obliged to land.

On the twenty-eighth, we passed the entrances of several deep bays and the St. Martin Islands, and camped at the end of a little bay where the mosquitoes would not permit us to close our eyes. Dawn came at last and we felt nothing was more urgent than to embark in order to escape these annoying hosts. We had a calm that allowed us to make good time, and we camped [at nightfall] at Buffalo Strait. During that same day we saw two Indian wigwams.

On the thirtieth we began to ascend the Winnipeg River and we arrived about noon at Fort du Bas de la Rivière [Fort Alexander]. This establishment had more the air of a dairy farm than a trading post: a clean and elegant house situated on a fair-sized hill, surrounded by barns, stables, and sheds, by fields of barley, peas, oats, and potatoes, reminding us of the civilization that we had left so long ago. Mr. Crebassa and Mr. Kennedy, who had the care of this post, welcomed us with all possible hospitality and eagerly gave us all the political news that they had learned through the arrival of canoes from Canada.

They told us also that Messrs. McDonald and Rocheblave had passed by a few days before our arrival, having been obliged to go up the Red River in order to prevent the bloodshed that probably would have occurred but for their intervention in the colony founded on that river by the Earl of Selkirk. Mr. Miles McDonell, governor of this colony, or rather of the district of Assiniboyne, had issued a proclamation forbidding any person, whomsoever, from sending provisions out of the country. The Hudson's Bay traders had conformed to this proclamation. But the North West men had disregarded it, believing it illegal and, as was their custom, had sent their servants to get provisions up the river. Mr. McDonell had known that there were several hundred sacks of pemmican collected in a shed under the care of Mr. Pritchard and demanded that they be sent to him.[5] Pritchard refused to deliver them; whereupon, Mr. McDonell had them carried away by force. The men wintering on Little Slave Lake, English River, and the Athabasca learned about this; and since they knew that they would not, as usual, find provisions at Bas

[5] Bibaud adds this footnote: "Pemican, which has already been mentioned several times, is made in the following manner: having prepared a large vessel [perhaps a trough] made of a tree trunk, one throws in this a certain amount of pounded meat—50 pounds, for example; one melts an equal amount of tallow and pours it, boiling, on the meat; then one stirs the whole until the meat and tallow are thoroughly mixed, after which one puts it into sacks of undressed beef skin, the hair on the outside, so that one seals it hermetically. The meat thus mixed with tallow hardens and can be kept for years. Sometimes one adds some wild pears to improve the flavor" (p. 263).

Huntington varies this footnote in the 1854 edition, and Quaife reprinted the variation without referring to the original note in Bibaud.

de la Rivière, they were determined to recover [the supplies] by force if they were not surrendered with good will.

This was how things stood when Mr. Rocheblave and Mr. McDonald arrived. They found the Canadians armed and ready to give battle to the people in the colony, who obstinately refused to yield the sacks of pemmican. Mr. McDonald sought out Mr. McDonell and explained to him the situation in which traders of the North West Company found themselves; that they lacked the necessary provisions to transport their fur pelts to Fort William. He spoke of the anger of these men, who saw no other alternative but to recover their provisions or die of hunger, and he summoned Mr. McDonell to return them without delay. For his part, Mr. McDonell revealed the misery in which the colonials would find themselves without provisions. As a result of these mutual representations, the two men agreed that half the provisions would remain in the colony and half would be sent to the North West Company. Thus was compromised the first conflict between the two rival companies, the North West and the Hudson's Bay.

Since we had spent the first of July repairing our canoes, we re-embarked on the second and continued to ascend the Winnipeg River (also called the White River because of the great number of cascades which are very close to one another and present to view an almost continual foam and boiling).[6] During that day we made twenty-seven portages, all quite short.

On the third and fourth we made nine more, and on the fifth reached Lake of the Woods. This lake takes its name from the great number of heavily wooded islands that dot it. Our guide showed me one of the islands and told me that a Jesuit father had said mass there and that it was the most distant spot to which these missionaries had ever penetrated. We camped on one of the islands. The next day the wind did not permit us to make such progress, but on the seventh we paddled into Rainy

6 Bibaud spells the name "Ouenipic." In all cases I have supplied the English and modern spellings of place and river names. Thus "la rivière du Lac la Pluie" becomes Rainy Lake River in my text, etc.

Lake River. I do not recall ever having seen as many mosquitoes as were on the banks of this river. When we debarked near a small rapid to lighten our canoes, we had the misfortune, while walking, of dislodging these insects from beneath the leaves where rain the day before had forced them to take refuge. They attached themselves to us, followed us in our canoes, and tormented us all the rest of the day.

At sunset on the eighth we arrived at Fort Rainy Lake.[7] This fort is built about a mile from a great rapid. We saw nearby some cultivated fields and such domesticated animals as horses, oxen, and cows. The post serves as a depot for the men wintering on the Athabasca, and other remote parties who bring their pelts there and return with their stocks of merchandise. Mr. John Dease, to whose charge this post had been confided, welcomed us in the most amiable fashion possible. After an excellent dinner we danced for a part of the evening.

We took leave of Mr. Dease on the tenth, and after having crossed the rapid and Rainy Lake, which is about forty-two miles long, we camped at the mouth of a small river. On the following morning we continued our journey, now crossing a small lake, then a strait, where we found scarcely enough water to float our canoes.[8] On the thirteenth we camped near Dog Portage where, because of our failure to follow Mr. Dease's advice (which was that we carry a sack of pemmican along), we found ourselves utterly without food.

CHAPTER 27

On the fourteenth [of July, 1814], we got under way before daylight and reached Dog Portage, which is long and arduous.[1]

---

7 As Franchère apparently indicated to Huntington, many of these outposts housed both the large, though competitive, fur companies—the North West and the Hudson's Bay Companies. Fort Rainy Lake, however, was a North West post only, until it was taken over by the Hudson's Bay Company in 1821, the two companies then merging.

8 Huntington interpolates: ". . . now thridding streams impeded with wild rice, which rendered our progress difficult" (p. 336).

1 Huntington begins this chapter with an unusual, but effective, sentence: "Starving men are early risers" (p. 337). The matter-of-factness of the statement

At the foot of this portage we discovered a kind of cabaret, or inn, kept by a man named Boucher. We treated our men to a spot of brandy and ate some detestable sausages that were too heavily salted. After this wretched meal, we went on our way and, about noon, passed Mountain Portage. Here the Kaministikwia River flows over a high rock and forms a falls that is hardly less unusual to see than Niagara.[2] Finally, after we had made thirty-six more portages, at nine o'clock in the evening we reached Fort William.

Fort William is situated near the mouth of the Kaministikwia River on Lake Superior, about forty-five miles north of an old trading post called Grand Portage.[3] It was built in 1805, through a union of the two companies [Hudson's Bay and North West], and called Fort William in honor of Mr. (now the Honorable) William McGillivray, principal agent of the North West Company. The owners, perceiving that the fort of the Grand Portage was to be found on land claimed by the American government, decided to demolish it and build another on British territory. No spot appeared more favorable to their plan than the entrance of the Kaministikwia River, which offers a safe and deep harbor. True, they had to surmount all the difficulties that a low and marshy soil can present; but with great care and labor, they managed at last to drain the marsh and form a solid terrain.

Fort William actually has the appearance of a fort, with its fifteen-foot-high enclosure, and this makes a pretty village along with the number of buildings it surrounds. In the middle of a spacious square a large wooden structure rises in which the middle door is raised about five feet from the ground, and around which a long balcony extends. In the center of this building is a

is suggestive of the same kind of flatly presented irony that sometimes appears in Franchère's letters.

2 Huntington adds: "Below, the succession of falls and rapids is constant, so that we made no fewer than thirty-six portages in the course of the day. Nevertheless we pursued our laborious way with good cheer, and without a murmur from our Canadian boatmen, who kept their spirits up by singing their *voyageur* songs" (pp. 337–38).

3 For a complete story about this key post in the history of the fur trade, see Grace Lee Nute, *The Voyageurs Highway* (St. Paul, Minnesota Historical Society, 1941).

salon sixty feet long and thirty feet wide, decorated with several paintings and with pastel portraits of many of the partners. It is in this salon that the agents, clerks, and interpreters of the company eat their meals—at different tables. At each end of the salon are located two small rooms for the partners. The rear contains a kitchen and some bedrooms for the domestics.

On each side of this house there is another of the same size, but lower. These are divided lengthwise by a corridor, and each contains a dozen pretty bedrooms. One of these [houses] is assigned to the partners, the other to the clerks. To the east of the fort there is another building, constructed very much like the former two and used for the same purposes; and a huge warehouse where inspection of the pelts is made and in which they are baled by means of a press. In the rear, and still on the same side, are found the lodgings for the guides, another warehouse for furs, and a powder magazine. This last building is made of gray stone and is roofed over with tin plate. In a corner, or angle, is found a kind of bastion or observation post. To the west appears a row of buildings, of which some serve as stores, the others as shops. There is one for the equipment of the men, one for canoes, one in which they retail merchandise, another in which they sell hard liquor, bread, bacon, butter, and so forth, and there they treat the incoming *voyageurs*. This treat consists of a loaf of white bread, a half-pound of butter, and a half-pint of rum. The *voyageurs* have given this species of tavern the name *Cantine salop* [Trollop Canteen].

Farther to the rear is found another row of buildings, one of which serves as an office or countinghouse. This is a fine square and well-lighted building. Another serves as a store and a third as a prison. The *voyageurs* have named this last the *Pot-au-Beurre* [Butter Tub]. In the southwest corner is a stone warehouse roofed over with tin plate. Behind this are the workshops of carpenters, tinsmiths, blacksmiths, and so forth; then some spacious courts, and some sheds for the storage, repair, and construction of canoes. Near the entrance to the Fort, which opens to the south, are the quarters of the surgeon and of the resident clerk. Above the entrance they have built a kind of guardhouse.

Since the river is deep at its entrance, the company has had a quay constructed the length of the Fort for the landing of schooners that ply on Lake Superior, whether to transport furs from Fort William to Sault Ste Marie, or merchandise and provisions from Sault Ste Marie to Fort William. The land behind and on both sides of the Fort is cleared. We saw barley, peas, and oats there which had a very fine appearance. At the edge of the clearing is a cemetery. Moreover, there are, on the other side of the river, a certain number of houses all inhabited by old Canadian *voyageurs*, worn out in the service of the company without having become very rich in it. These men, married to women of the country and burdened by large families, prefer to cultivate a little Indian corn and potatoes and catch fish in order to subsist than to return to their native lands and give their relatives and old acquaintances definite evidence of their misconduct or their imprudence.

Fort William is the chief depot of the North West Company in the high country and the general rendezvous of the partners. The agents from Montreal and the wintering partners nearly all gather here each summer to receive their share of the profits, to prepare expeditions, and to discuss the interests of their business. Most of them were there when we arrived. The wintering parties who have come down [from the mountains] also spend a part of the summer at Fort William. They form a large camp to the west, outside the palisade. Those who engage themselves at Montreal to go only to Fort William or Rainy Lake, and who do not winter [further along the route], occupy another area to the east. The former give to the latter the name *mangeurs de lard,* or pork eaters. One can see between the two camps, which are made up of three or four hundred men each, an astonishing difference. That of the pork eaters is always very dirty, and that of the wintering men clean and neat.

In order to clear its land and improve its property, the company has taken care to obligate all those employed as canoemen each to give it a certain number of days of forced labor. In this way the company has cleared the land and made permanent the environs of Fort William. But when an employee has worked the stipulated number of days, he is thereafter always exempt, even when he remains twenty or thirty years in the wilderness and comes down to the Fort every summer.

They received us very well at Fort William, and I could see from the reception given to me, especially, that—thanks to the Chinook language, in which I was fairly proficient—they would have liked nothing better than to employ me at quite advantageous terms. But I was in a greater hurry to get to Montreal than to return to Astoria.

Shortly after our arrival at Fort William, Mr. Keith came in from Fort George [Astoria], bringing news of the appearance of the ship *Isaac Todd* in the river mouth. This vessel, which is a poor sailer, had been delayed a long time by contrary winds while doubling Cape Horn, and had not been able to rejoin the squadron of warships from which she had been separated. When she reached Juan Fernandez Island and found that the three warships had sailed, the captain and his passengers, seeing that they were short of provisions, decided to range the coast. They stopped at Monterey, on the coast of California, to take on supplies.[4] Here they learned that an English man-of-war was in distress at San Francisco.[5] They sailed there, only to discover, to their surprise, that it was the sloop *Racoon*. This ship, when leaving Astoria, had struck the bar with such force that a part of her false keel had been torn away; and she had had much difficulty making San Francisco with seven feet of water in her hold, even though the crew was constantly busy pumping her out. When Captain Black

[4] Bibaud adds a footnote: "Spanish Mission or *Presidio* at about 36° latitude." Huntington translated the term *Présidie* as "Presidency"; but it seems to me the Spanish word *presidio* is more nearly the meaning intended, and is in the proper context. It may be that the "o" at the end of the word was printed as an "e," and was originally a typesetter's error (p. 278).

[5] Bibaud adds a second footnote: "Another Spanish presidio at about 38° latitude, and the first European establishment one finds south of the Columbia River" (p. 278).

saw no possibility of repairing his ship, he had decided to abandon her and cross the continent to the Gulf of Mexico in order to reach the British islands [West Indies]. However, when the *Isaac Todd* arrived, a way was found of careening the *Racoon* to repair and make her watertight. The *Isaac Todd* then sailed away and into the mouth of the Columbia on April 17. It had been thirteen months since her departure from England.[6]

Later I learned of the arrival at a friendly port of the brig *Pedlar*. More fortunate than Mr. McKay, Mr. Hunt has received the fruits of his activity and his industry. This gentleman is now a member of the legislature in Missouri and enjoys the general esteem of his constituents.

CHAPTER 28

On the evening of the twentieth, Mr. D. Stuart informed me that he would leave the next day for Montreal, in a light canoe. I wrote at once to my parents; but on the following morning, Mr. Stuart told me that I myself would be the bearer of my letters by leaving with him. I got my effects packed, and in the evening we left Fort William in a large canoe manned by fourteen men, along with six passengers: to wit, Messrs. D. Stuart, D. McKenzie, J. McDonald, J. Clarke, and I, and a little girl eight or nine years old who came from Kildonan on the Red River. We paddled into Lake Superior and made camp near Thunder Island—so named because of the frequent thunderstorms that strike there in certain seasons.

On the twenty-second and twenty-third we continued to range the north shore.[1] Navigating this superb lake would be most agreeable but for the dense fogs that prevail during a part of the day, preventing any progress. On the twenty-fourth we dined at a small establishment called *Le Pic*. On the twenty-sixth

---

6 Huntington ends the chapter at this point. The following paragraph, however, appears in the Bibaud text. Neither Huntington nor Quaife followed the original 1820 edition.

1 An error occurs here in the Huntington text which reads: ". . . we continued to range the southern coast of Lake Superior" (p. 348). Bibaud clearly says *"septentrionale"* in the 1820 text. Quaife corrected the error in his reprinting of the 1854 edition.

we crossed Michipicoton [Bay], which is nine miles wide at its entrance. As we approached the eastern side of the bay, we encountered a small canoe occupied by Captain McCargo and the crew of one of the company schooners. Mr. McCargo told us that he had escaped from Sault Ste Marie, where the Americans had sent a detachment of 150 men; and that when he saw he would have to abandon his schooner, he set fire to her. As a consequence of this information, we decided that the canoe in which we were traveling should return to Fort William. I embarked with Mr. Stuart and two men in Captain McCargo's canoe, while the Captain took our place. In the haste and confusion of the exchange, which was made on the lake, they gave us a ham, a little tea and sugar, and a sack containing about twenty-five pounds of flour. But they completely forgot a kettle, knives, forks, and everything else that Mr. McCargo had not had time to put into his canoe. We lived miserably for two and a half days, as we progressed along the lakeshore, before arriving at a trading post. We moistened a little flour from the sack and, after kneading it, we made some small loaves that we baked on flat stones.

On the twenty-ninth we came to Batchawainon, where we found some women who prepared food for us and received us well. Batchawainon is a poor little post situated at the back of a sandy bay which offers nothing agreeable to the eye. Mr. Frederic Goedike, who resided at this post, had gone to see what had happened at Sault Ste Marie. He returned the next day and told us that the Americans had come, 150 strong, under the command of Major Holmes; that after they had pilfered whatever they considered to be of value that belonged to the North West Company and to Mr. Johnson, they had set fire to the houses and warehouses and left, without molesting any individual. In the evening our canoe returned from Fort William, along with Mr. McGillivray's. The following morning we went on to Sault Ste Marie, where we saw the havoc that the enemy had wrought. The Company's houses, sheds, sawmills, and so forth, were still smoking. The schooner was at the foot of the rapid; the Americans, wishing to go down the rapid, had run her aground and, as they could not get her free, burned her to the water's edge.

Sault Ste Marie is a rapid about five or six hundred yards wide and about three quarters of a mile long. Its base forms two bays on the shores of which are a number of houses. The north bank belongs to Great Britain, the south to the United States. It was on the latter side that Mr. Johnson had lived. He was, before the war, port collector for the American government. On the same side Mr. Nolin lived with his family of three boys and three very pretty girls. He had been a great trader and one can still see, in his house and furnishings, evidence of his former prosperity. On the north shore we found Mr. John Ermatinger, who owned a fine trading post. For the time being, he lived in a house owned by Mr. Nolin, but he was building a very elegant one of stone and had just completed a flour mill. Mr. Ermatinger believed that the mill would lead the inhabitants of the area to sow more grain than they did. They were, for the most part, *voyageurs* married to native women. Fish kept them alive for most of the year; and if they could gather up enough potatoes for the remaining part, they were content. It is to be regretted that these men are not more industrious and harder working, for the land could not be more fertile, particularly on the northern shores. Mr. Ermatinger showed us some wheat that was just ripening, the stems of which were three or four feet long. The other grains were equally beautiful.[2]

On the first of August, we sent an express to Michilimakinac [Mackinac], to inform the commandant of what had happened at Sault Ste Marie. While awaiting his return we took pains to put ourselves in a state of defense, in the event that the Americans should make more trouble. The thing was not improbable, for according to statements made by one of their number who could speak French, their plan was to seize the furs of the North

---

[2] These last two sentences are in Bibaud but do not appear in the 1854 edition. Quaife did not refer to the 1820 text and so followed Huntington's work verbatim at this point.

West Company. We invited some Indians who were encamped at Pine Point, some distance from the Sault, to help us in case we needed them, and they promised to do so.[3] The courier returned on the fourth without having carried out the object of his mission. He had found the island so completely blockaded by the enemy that it was impossible for him to reach it without running great risk of being taken prisoner.

On the twelfth we distinctly heard the discharge of artillery that our men were firing at Mackinac, although the distance was almost ninety miles.[4] We believed that this was an attempt by the enemy to retake the post, but soon afterward we learned that it was only a royal salute, honoring the birth of the Prince Regent. During our stay at Sault Ste Marie, however, we heard that the Americans had made an attack upon the island but were forced to retreat after having sustained a considerable loss.

On the nineteenth, Mr. McGillivray and Mr. McLeod arrived at Fort William, ahead of the canoes that were coming loaded with pelts. They sent Mr. Decoigne on, in a light canoe, with letters for Montreal. On the twenty-first the canoe in which I was a passenger was directed to go to the entrance of French River to observe the movements of the enemy.[5] On the twenty-fifth, forty-seven canoes arrived to enter this river. The value of the pelts carried by them was estimated at no less than £200,000 (British pounds)—an important prize for the Americans, had they been able to get their hands on it.[6] We numbered 325 men, all well armed, and we camped and kept a watch all night.

[3] Huntington adds: "Meanwhile we had no provisions, as everything had been carried off by the American forces, and were obliged to subsist on such brook trout as we could take with hook and line, and on wild raspberries" (p. 353).

[4] Quaife notes: "The distance from Saint Ignace to Sault Ste. Marie by U. S. Highway No. 2, substantially on air-line route, is 52 miles. Although the 1854 edition, which we reprint, says 'nearly sixty miles,' the Manuscript clearly says *pas de 30 lieues*" (p. 277n.). Curiously enough, Bibaud says *"bien que la distance fut d'à peu près 30 lieues,"* and I have translated the Bibaud version. A league is approximately three nautical or three statute miles.

[5] Huntington adds: "The route lay between a range of low islands, and a shelvy beach, very monotonous and dreary" (p. 354).

[6] Quaife indicates that the Manuscript shows 200,000 louis. Bibaud states the amount as 200,000 British pounds, while the 1854 edition says that "the furs which they carried could not be estimated at less than a million dollars" (p. 354).

The next morning we started up the French River, which flows from the northeast and empties into Lake Huron about 120 miles from Sault Ste Marie. At evening we camped on the shores of Lake Nipissing. Then on the twenty-seventh we crossed this lake and, after making several portages, camped not far from Mattawan. Early on the twenty-eighth we entered the Ottawa River and camped at evening time at the *portage des deux Joachims*.[7] On the twenty-ninth we passed Fort Coulange, where Mr. Goddin resided, and after we had made a number of portages occasioned by the rapids and falls obstructing navigation of this river, we came on the thirty-first to Chaudières portage (otherwise known as Hull).

The rock that stops the course of the Ottawa at this point slopes perpendicularly and is about fifty feet high, from one level of the water to the next. The river is held back at the summit of this rock, and at the spot where it plunges down, it passes through subterranean tubes [as it were] and comes out at the base, like boiling water, through seven or eight apertures. Mr. P. Wright made his home at this place, where he had a fine trading post and a large number of employees cultivating the land and cutting squared timber [probably scantlings—lumber commonly used for construction].[8]

We left the Chaudières a little before sunset and soon passed the entrance of the Curtain River. This river, which spills into the Ottawa over a rock twenty-five to thirty feet high, is separated in the middle of its falls by a little island, and resembles a curtain opened at the center and swept wide at the base. The scene is truly picturesque. The rays of the setting sun that struck the water obliquely when we passed greatly heightened the beauty and rendered it worthy of a brush more cunning than mine.

We paddled along until midnight, when we stopped to let the men have a little rest. But we paused only two hours, and at

7 Huntington makes slight variations of the 1820 text in this as well as in the following paragraph, but no changes in substance.

8 *Bois d'équarrissage*, meaning "squared timber." Bibaud used an older form of the noun *écarissage* (p. 282).

sunrise on September 1 we came to Long Sault. There, after procuring some guides, we swept through this dangerous rapid and put ashore near the home of Mr. McDonell, who sent us some milk and fruit for breakfast. Toward noon we passed the Lake of the Two Mountains, from which I could first glimpse the mountain of my native island. About two o'clock we drove past the St. Anne Rapids and soon came opposite Sault St. Louis. We passed this last rapid and debarked at Montreal shortly after sunset.

I hastened at once to my paternal roof, where the family were no less surprised than overjoyed to see me again. For my family, who had had no news of me since my departure from New York [in 1810], had believed the common report that I had been massacred by the Indians with Mr. McKay and the *Tonquin*'s crew. Surely it was by a stroke of good fortune or, more likely, the hand of Providence that I found myself once more, safe and sound, in the midst of family and friends, at the end of a journey fraught with perils in which so many of my companions had lost their lives.

Author's Preface to the 1854 Edition[1]

IN 1846, when the boundary question (that of the Oregon Territory in particular) was at its height, the Hon. Thomas H. Benton delivered in the United States Senate a decisive speech, of which the following is an extract:

> Now for the proof of all I have said. I happen to have in my possession the book of all others, which gives the fullest and most authentic details on all the points I have mentioned—a book written at a time, and under circumstances, when the author (himself a British subject and familiar on the Columbia) had no more idea that the British would lay claim to that river, than Mr. Harmon, the American writer whom I quoted, ever thought of our claiming New Caledonia. It is the work of Mr. Franchère, a gentleman of Montreal, with whom I have the pleasure to be personally acquainted, and one of those employed by Mr. Astor in founding his colony. He was at the founding of Astoria, at its sale to the Northwest Company, saw the place seized as a British conquest, and continued there after its seizure. He wrote in French: his work has not been done into English, though it well deserves it; and I read from the French text. He gives a brief and true account of the discovery of the Columbia.

I felt justly proud of this notice of my unpretending work, especially that the latter should have contributed, as it did, to

1 The following pages are not to be found in the Bibaud edition of 1820 but were added to the Huntington edition of 1854.—*Editor.*

171

the amicable settlement of the then pending difficulties. I have flattered myself ever since, that it belonged to the historical literature of the great country, which by adoption has become mine.

The reperusal of "Astoria" by Washington Irving (1836) inspired me with an additional motive for giving my book in an English dress. Without disparagement to Mr. Irving's literary fame, I may venture to say that I found in his work inaccuracies, misstatements (unintentional of course), and a want of chronological order, which struck forcibly one so familiar with the events themselves. I thought I could show—or rather that my simple narration, of itself, plainly discovered—that some of the young men embarked in that expedition (which founded our Pacific empire), did not merit the ridicule and contempt which Captain Thorn attempted to throw upon them, and which perhaps, through the genius of Mr. Irving, might otherwise remain as a lasting stigma on their characters.

But the consideration which, before all others, prompts me to offer this narrative to the American reading public, is my desire to place before them, therein, a simple and connected account (which at this time ought to be interesting), of the early settlement of the Oregon Territory by one of our adopted citizens, the enterprising merchant John Jacob Astor. The importance of a vast territory, which at no distant day may add two more bright stars to our national banner, is a guarantee that my humble effort will be appreciated.

Note by the Editor [J. V. Huntington]

It has been the editor's wish to let Mr. Franchere speak for himself. To preserve in the translation the Defoe-like simplicity of the original narrative of the young French Canadian, has been his chief care. Having read many narratives of travel and adventure in our northwestern wilderness, he may be permitted to say that he has met with none that gives a more vivid and picturesque description of it, or in which the personal adventures of the narrator, and the varying fortunes of a great enterprise, mingle more happily, and one may say, more dramatically, with the itinerary. The clerkly minuteness of the details is not without its charm either, and their fidelity speaks for itself. Take it altogether, it must be regarded as a fragment of our colonial history saved from oblivion; it fills up a vacuity which Mr. Irving's classic work does not quite supply; it is, in fact, the only account by an eye-witness and a participator in the enterprise, of the first attempt to form a settlement on the Pacific under the stars and stripes.

The editor has thought it would be interesting to add Mr. Franchere's Preface to the original French edition, which will be found on the next page.

Baltimore, February 6, 1854.

Author's Supplementary Chapter to the 1854 Edition

CHAPTER 29

Present State of the Countries Visited by the Author—Correction of Mr. Irving's Statements Respecting St. Louis.

THE LAST CHAPTER closes the original French narrative of my travels around and across the continent, as published thirty-three years ago. The translation follows that narrative as exactly as possible, varying from it only in the correction of a few not very important errors of fact. It speaks of places and persons as I spoke of them then. I would not willingly lose the verisimilitude of this natural and unadorned description, in order to indulge in any new turns of style or more philosophical reflections.

But since that period many changes have occurred in the scenes which I so long ago visited and described. Though they are well known, I may be pardoned for alluding to them.

The natives of the Sandwich Islands, who were in a state of paganism at that time, have since adopted a form of Christianity, have made considerable progress in imitating the civilization of Europe, and even, at this moment, begin to entertain the idea of annexation to the United States. It appears, however, that the real natives are rapidly dwindling away by the effects of their vices, which an exotic and ill-assimilated civilization has rather increased than diminished, and to which religion has not succeeded in applying a remedy.

At the mouth of the Columbia, whole tribes, and among them, the Clatsops, have been swept away by disease. Here again, licentious habits universally diffused, spread a fatal disorder through the whole nation, and undermining the constitutions of all, left them an easy prey to the first contagion or epidemic sickness. But missionaries of various Christian sects have labored among the Indians of the Columbia also; not to speak of the missions of the Catholic Church, so well known by the narrative of Father De Smet and others; and numbers have been taught to cultivate the soil, and thus to provide against the famines to which they were formerly exposed from their dependence on the precarious resources of the chase; while others have received, in the faith of Christ, the true principle of national permanence, and a living germ of civilization, which may afterward be developed among them.

Emigration has also carried to the Oregon the ax of the settler, as well as the canoe and pack of the fur trader. The fertile valley and prairies of the Willamette—once the resort of the deer, the elk, and the antelope—are now tilled by the industrious husbandman. Oregon City, so near old "Astoria," whose first log fort I saw and described, is now an Archiepiscopal see, and the capital of a territory, which must soon be a state of the Union.

Of the regions east of the mountains described in my itinerary, little can be said in respect to improvement: they remain in the same wild state. The interest of the Hudson's Bay Company, as an association of fur traders, is opposed to agricultural improvements, whose operation would be to drive off and extinguish the wild animals that furnish their commerce with its object. But on Lake Superior steamboats have supplanted the birch-bark canoe of the Indian and the fur trader, and at Sault Ste Marie, especially on the American side, there is now every sign of prosperity. How remote and wild was the region beyond, through which I passed, may be estimated by the fact that in thirty-eight years the onward-rolling wave of our population has but just reached its confines.

Canada, although it has not kept pace with the United States, has yet wonderfully advanced in forty years. The valley of the Ottawa, that great artery of the St. Lawrence, where I thought it worth-while to notice the residence of an enterprising farmer and lumber merchant, is now a populous district, well culti-vated, and sprinkled with villages, towns, and cities.

The reader, in perusing my first chapter, found a descrip-tion of the city of New York in 1810, and of the neighboring village of Brooklyn. It would be superfluous to establish a com-parison at this day. At that time, it will be observed, the mere breaking out of war between America and England was thought to involve the sacrifice of an American commercial establishment on the Pacific, on the ground of its supplies being necessarily cut off (it was supposed), and of the United States government being unable to protect it from hostile attack. At present it suffices to remark that while New York, then so inconsiderable a port, is now perhaps the third city in the world, the United States also, are, undoubtedly, a first-rate power, unassailable at home, and formidable abroad, to the greatest nations.

As in my Preface I alluded to Mr. Irving's "Astoria," as re-flecting, in my opinion, unjustly, upon the young men engaged in the first expedition to the mouth of the Columbia, it may suffice here to observe, without entering into particulars, that my narrative, which I think answers for its fidelity, clearly shows that some of them, at least, did not want courage, activity, zeal for the interests of the company, while it existed, and patient endurance of hardship. And although it forms no part of the narrative of my voyage, yet as subsequent visits to the West and an intimate knowledge of St. Louis, enable me to correct Mr. Irving's poetical rather than accurate description of that place, I may well do it here. St. Louis now bids fair to rival ere long the "Queen of the West"; Mr. Irving describes her as a small trading place, where trappers, half-breeds, gay, frivolous Cana-dian boatmen, &c., &c., congregated and reveled, with that light-ness and buoyancy of spirit inherited from their French fore-fathers; the indolent Creole of St. Louis caring for little more than the enjoyment of the present hour; a motley population, half-civilized, half-barbarous, thrown, on his canvas, into one general, confused (I allow highly *picturesque*) mass, without respect of persons: but it is fair to say, with due homage to the talent of the sketcher, who has verged slightly on caricature in the use of that humor-loving pencil admired by all the world, that St. Louis even then contained its noble, industrious, and I may say, princely merchants; it could boast of its *Chouteaus, Soulands, Céré, Chéniers, Vallées,* and *La Croix,* with other kindred spirits, whose descendants prove the worth of their sires by their own, and are now among the leading businessmen, as their fathers were the pioneers, of the flourishing St. Louis.

With these remarks, which I make simply as an act of justice in connection with the general subject of the founding of "Astoria," but in which I mean to convey no imputation on the international fairness of the accomplished author to whom I have alluded, I take a respectful leave of my readers.

▨▨▨

Author's Appendix Added to the 1854 Edition

APPENDIX*

In CHAPTER XVII. I promised the reader to give him an account of the fate of some of the persons who left Astoria before, and after its sale or transfer to the British. I will now redeem that pledge.

Messrs. Ramsay Crooks, R. M'Lelland [McClellan], and Robert Stuart, after enduring all sorts of fatigue, dangers and hair-breadth escapes with their lives—all which have been so graphically described by Washington Irving in his "Astoria," finally reached St. Louis and New York.

Mr. Clapp went to the Marquesas Islands, where he entered into the service of his country in the capacity of Midshipman under Commodore Porter—made his escape from there in company with Lieutenant Gamble of the Marine corps, by directions of the Commodore, was captured by the British, landed at Buenos Ayres, and finally reached New York.

D. M'Dougall, as a reward for betraying the trust reposed in him by Mr. Astor, was made a Partner of the Northwest Company, crossed the mountains, and died a miserable death at *Bas de la Rivière,* Winnipeg. Donald M'Kenzie, his co-adjutor, went back to the Columbia River, where he amassed a considerable

---

* We have thought it best to give this Appendix, excepting some abbreviations rendered necessary to avoid repetition of what has been stated before, in Mr. Franchere's own words, particularly as a specimen of his own English style may be justly interesting to the reader. [This footnote is from the 1854 Edition.]

178

fortune, with which he retired, and lived in Chautauqua County in this state, where he died a few years since unknown and neglected:—he was a very selfish man, who cared for no one but himself.

It remains only to speak of Messrs. J. C. Halsey, Russell Farnham, and Alfred Seton, who, it will be remembered, embarked with Mr. Hunt on the "Pedlar," in Feb. 1814.

Leaving the River about the 1st of April, they proceeded to the Russian establishment at Sitka, Norfolk Sound, where they fell in with two or three more American vessels, which had come to trade with the natives or to avoid the British cruisers. While there, a sail under British colors appeared, and Mr. Hunt sent Mr. Seton to ascertain who she was. She turned out to be the "Forester," Captain Pigott, a repeating signal ship and letter-of-marque, sent from England in company of a fleet intended for the South Seas. On further acquaintance with the captain, Mr. Seton (from whom I derive these particulars) learned a fact which has never before been published, and which will show the solicitude and perseverance of Mr. Astor. After despatching the "Lark" from New York, fearing that she might be intercepted by the British, he sent orders to his correspondent in England to purchase and fit out a British bottom, and despatch her to the Columbia to relieve the establishment.

When Mr. Hunt learned this fact, he determined to leave Mr. Halsey at Sitka, and proceeding himself northward, landed Mr. Farnham on the coast of *Kamskatka,* to go over land with despatches for Mr. Astor. Mr. Farnham accomplished the journey, reached Hamburg, whence he sailed for the West Indies, and finally arrived at New York, having made the entire circuit of the globe.

The "Pedlar" then sailed to the southeast, and soon reached the coast of California, which she approached to get a supply of provisions. Nearing one of the harbors, they descried a vessel at anchor inside, showing American colors. Hauling their wind, they soon came close to the stranger, which, to their surprise, turned out to be the Spanish corvette "Santa Barbara," which sent boats alongside the "Pedlar," and captured her, and kept possession of the prize for some two months, during which they dropped down to *San Blas*. Here Mr. Hunt proposed to Mr. Seton to cross the continent and reach the United States the best way he could. Mr. Seton, accordingly, went to the Isthmus of Darien, where he was detained several months by sickness, but finally reached Carthagena, where a British fleet was lying in the roads, to take off the English merchants, who in consequence of the revolutionary movements going on, sought shelter under their own flag. Here Mr. Seton, reduced to the last stage of destitution and squalor, boldly applied to Captain Bentham, the commander of the squadron, who, finding him to be a gentleman, offered him every needful assistance, gave him a berth in his own cabin, and finally landed him safely on the Island of Jamaica, whence he, too, found his way to New York.

Of all those engaged in the expedition there are now but four survivors—Ramsay Crooks, Esq. the last President of the American Fur Company; Alfred Seton, Esq., Vice-president of the Sun Mutual Insurance Company; both of New York city; Benjamin Pillet of Canada; and the author, living also in New York. All the rest have paid the debt of nature, but their names are recorded in the foregoing pages.

Notwithstanding the illiberal remarks made by Captain Thorn on the persons who were on board the ill-fated Tonquin, and reproduced by Mr. Irving in his "Astoria"—these young men who were represented as "Bar keepers or Billiard markers, most of whom had fled from Justice, &c."—I feel it a duty to say that they were for the most part, of good parentage, liberal education and every way were qualified to discharge the duties of their respective stations. The remarks on the general character of the voyageurs employed as boat-men and Mechanics, and the attempt to cast ridicule on their "Braggart and swaggering manners" come with a bad grace from the author of "Astoria," when we consider that in that very work Mr. Irving is compelled to admit their indomitable energy, their fidelity to their employers, and their cheerfulness under the most trying circumstances in which men can be placed.

With respect to Captain Thorn, I must confess that though a stern commander and an irritable man, he paid the strictest attention to the health of his crew. His complaints of the squalid appearance of the Canadians and mechanics who were on board, can be abated of their force by giving a description of the accommodation of these people. The Tonquin was a small ship; its forecastle was destined for the crew performing duty before the mast. The room allotted for the accommodation of the twenty men destined for the establishment, was abaft the forecastle; a bulk-head had been let across, and a door led from the forecastle into a dark, unventilated, unwholesome place, where they were all heaped together, without means of locomotion, and consequently deprived of that exercise of the body so necessary to health. Add to that, we had no physician on board. In view of these facts, can the complaints of the gallant Captain be sustained? Of course Mr. Irving was ignorant of these circumstances, as well as of many others which he might have known, had some one suggested to him to ask a few questions of persons who were within his reach at the time of his publication. I have (I need scarcely say) no personal animosity against the unfortunate Captain; he always treated me, individually, as well as I could expect; and if, in the course of my narrative, I have been severe on his actions, I was impelled by a sense of justice to my friends on board, as well as by the circumstances that such explanations of his general deportment were requisite to convey the historical truth to my readers.

The idea of a conspiracy against him is so absurd that it really does not deserve notice. The threat, or rather the proposal made to him by Mr. M'Kay, in the following words—"if you say fight, fight it is"—originated in a case where one of the sailors had maltreated a Canadian lad, who came to complain to Mr. M'Kay. The captain would not interpose his authority, and said in my presence, "Let them fight out their own battles:"

—it was upon that answer that Mr. M'Kay gave vent to the expression quoted above. I might go on with a long list of inaccuracies, more or less grave or trivial, in the beautifully written work of Mr. Irving, but it would be tedious to go through the whole of them. The few remarks to which I have given place above, will suffice to prove that the assertion made in the preface was not unwarranted. It is far from my intention to enter the lists with a man of the literary merit and reputation of Mr. Irving, but as a narrator of events of which I was an EYEWITNESS, I felt bound to tell the truth, although that truth might impugn the historical accuracy of a work which ranks as a classic in the language. At the same time I entirely exonerate Mr. Irving from any intention of prejudicing the minds of his readers, as he doubtless had only in view to support the character of his friend: that sentiment is worthy of a generous heart, but it should not be gratified, nor would he wish to gratify it, I am sure, at the expense of the character of others.

Note by the Editor of the 1854 Edition, J. V. Huntington

Perhaps even contrary to the wish of Mr. Franchere, I have left the above almost word for word as he wrote it. It is a part of the history of the affairs related as well in Mr. Irving's *Astoria* as in the present volume, that the reclamations of one of the clerks on that famous and unfortunate voyage of the Tonquin, against the disparaging description of himself and his colleagues given in the former work, should be fairly recorded. At the same time, I can not help stating my own impression that a natural susceptibility, roused by those slighting remarks from Captain Thorn's correspondence, to which Mr. Irving as an historian gives currency, has somewhat blinded my excellent friend to the tone of banter, so characteristic of the chronicler of the Knickerbockers, in which all these particulars are given, more as traits of the character of the stern old sea-captain, with hearty contempt for land-lubbers and literary clerks, than as a dependable account of the persons on board his ship, some of whom might have been, and as we see by the present work, were, in fact, very meritorious characters, for whose literary turn, and faithful journalizing (which seems to have especially provoked the captain's wrath), now at the end of more than forty years, we have so much reason to be thankful. Certainly Mr. Irving himself, who has drawn frequently on Mr. Franchere's narrative, could not, from his well-known taste in such matters, be insensible to the Defoe-like simplicity therof, nor to the picturesque descriptions, worthy of a professional pen, with which it is sprinkled.

Index

189

The text for *Adventure at Astoria, 1810–1814* has been set in 11-point Linotype Baskerville, a faithful weight-for-weight, curve-for-curve copy of John Baskerville's celebrated printing type. The paper on which the book is printed bears the watermark of the University of Oklahoma Press and has an effective life of at least three hundred years.